PROOF ANIMALS HAVE SOULS
Animal Souls Serialization

JACKIE JONES-HUNT PHD

House of Light Publishers Ltd

WHAT PEOPLE ARE SAYING ABOUT
PROOF ANIMALS HAVE SOULS

This engrossing serialized volume is a "must read" for all those who consider themselves religiously or spiritually inclined as it stimulates readers to reflect on our true relationship to the rest of sentient creation. I fully and sincerely recommend this outstanding book.

Professor Judith Barad PhD
(Indiana, USA)
Author of Aquinas on the Nature &
Treatment of Animals.

Pure Gold Again! I am delighted to wholeheartedly endorse Dr. Jackie Jones-Hunt's captivating research. Everyone should read it. It is important to continue to disseminate the 'light' on a global level - to balance the materialistic negative energy one comes across every day. I too, am concerned about animal welfare - the public has to be educated to the horrific animal cruelty which goes on in so many ways.

Victor James Zammit
Psychical Researcher & Retired Attorney of the Supreme Court of New South Wales & the High Court of Australia
Author of A Lawyer Presents the Case for the Afterlife, Irrefutable Objective Evidence. www.victorzammit.com

I thoroughly endorse and recommend this insightful serialized research.

Rev. Dr. Elizabeth W. Fenske

There have been a number of credible stories of people on their deathbed seeing their deceased pet companions waiting to greet them. This serialized research suggests an affinity with our pets that transcends physical death. In this intriguing work, Jackie Jones-Hunt PhD helps us incorporate the animal kingdom into our overall spiritual awareness.

Michael E. Tymn
Vice-President of the Academy of Spirituality &
Paranormal Studies, USA
Author of The Articulate Dead & The Afterlife Revealed.

This gripping and excellently researched volume split into a series will change lives. This thought-provoking research awakens us to the fact that many of the founders of religions and spiritual philosophies taught us to show compassion and to commit no harm to our animal relatives.

These pages note in view of the modern-day mass slaughter of animals, present-day 'humanity' has lost contact with such spiritual teachings, many of which have become lost, forgotten or distorted.

Raising awareness of the authentic, ancient, global spiritual teachings commanding us to show respect and compassion to all animals is enormously important in view of the modern-day plight of animals. Certainly, readers' understanding of Jesus will be profoundly and irrevocably deepened.

Crawford Knox PhD
(Oxford, UK)
Author of Changing Christian Paradigms &
Their Implications for Modern Thought, Brill.

"What is religion? Compassion for all things which have life." (Hinduism, Upanishads.) Readers will be unable to put this life-changing series down, alerting us to the fact that all religions command us not to harm animals but to show them compassion. All animals are welcomed and cared for at my ashram in India.

Dr. Niranjan Rajyaguru
Author of 20 books, Spiritual Guru (Teacher) &
Managing Trustee of the Animal Welfare Sanctuary,
Anand Ashram, Gujurat, India.
www.anand-ashram.com

"Ahimsa-paramo-dharmah" – "Non-injury to living beings is the highest religion (Jainism): Because he has pity on every living creature, therefore is a man called 'holy.'" (Buddhism, Dhammapada). I am pleased to thoroughly recommend this truly inspired life-changing series of books.

Professor Nathalal Gohil
Author of 25 books on Spiritual Philosophy &
Mysticism, Gujurat, India.

This serialized research should be read and inwardly digested by all human beings who adhere to the various world religious belief-systems – and who also feel at liberty to still ignore the suffering of animal-kind in their own communities and further afield.

Rev. Lyn Guest de Swarte
Former Editor of Psychic News,
Hydesville Magazine & Spiritual News
President of the New Spiritualists' Society
Internationally renowned teaching medium and healer
Author of More Principles of Spiritualism.
www.lynguestdeswartepsychicnews.com

Being compassionate to animals should be a fundamental principle from which to order our lives. The Animals Souls series shows us how the most spiritual strands of many of the world's spiritual teachings can bring this about.

Clarissa Baldwin OBE
Dogs' Trust Chief Executive.
Dogs' Trust: A Dog is For Life
www.dogstrust.org.uk   (Registered Charity.)

One Kind welcomes this new serialized book which will help people to re-connect with the other animals with whom we share this planet. They are like us, sentient creatures with thoughts and feelings that matter. What's good for them is ultimately good for us too. After all, humankind, animalkind, we are all One Kind.

Ross Minett
'One Kind' Science & Research Manager.
www.onekind.org (Registered Charity)

We welcome any book that promotes compassion and respect for animals and shows people how to incorporate a philosophy of animal rights into their everyday lives.

Sandra Smiley
Press Officer **PETA**, UK.
(People for the Ethical Treatment of Animals)
www.peta.org

Dr. Jackie Jones-Hunt's latest excellent and highly informative Animal Souls serialization, is a "must read."

I am Sonia Rinaldi, author of 8 books on Instrumental Transcommunication (ITC): the use of audios/voices and photography and videos proving that life continues after death for all animals, human and non-human.

Presently, in my laboratory, fascinating trans-contacts with dogs are occurring. The photographic and audio experiment results are currently evidencing trans-contacts with dogs proving beyond doubt that dogs (animals) do indeed have post death consciousness and intriguingly, they are able to communicate!

The non-human animal communications and photographs received through our apparatus, continues to astonish our dedicated research team.

Prior to these miraculous communications from dogs which also reveal their great sensitivity it was obvious to us that all animals deserve our love and support.

After these expcriment results - after receiving these on-going after death communications from dogs- myself and my team are emphatic that we should respect all animals even more because these after death communications demonstrate that they have a soul, alternatively known as consciousness.

Dr. Jackie Jones-Hunt's fascinating present serialized research is a notable contribution awakening us to the fact that we humans, as their elder brothers and sisters, should demonstrate the utmost compassion and respect to them all!

Sonia Rinaldi, Brazil
Author of 8 books on ITC
(Research results clearly & irrefutably demonstrate visual and audible contact & communications with both human and non-human animals after death)
Winner of 3 European Awards for Research.
http://www.ipati.org

As a psychic, psychical researcher with 38 years intense involvement with physical mediumship and its phenomena, I know personally that life continues after physical death for all sentient beings (human and non-human animals).

Near death experiencers discuss their life reviews during which they felt the pains of another as if they were their own - these pains were inflicted on others as a result of their neglect or misdeeds during their earlier physical lifetime. Such knowledge should impinge on a person's ever evolving spiritual unfoldment. Consequently, I support this interesting serialized research by Jackie Jones-Hunt PhD. which reminds us that we should demonstrate empathy and compassion to all animals during our own lifetimes.

Dr. Robin Foy
Author of Witnessing the Impossible –
The only true & complete report of every sitting of The Scole Experimental Group, 1993-1998.
For Mediumship Advice See:
http://physicalmediumship4u.ning.com

This fascinating research split into a series uncovers long forgotten teachings found in many world religions about humanities relationship with nature.

I have run a very busy practice as a Psychic & Medium now for over 10 years, and in all of the thousands of readings I have done, I have been bewildered and often times warmed in my heart to see that animals do in fact survive physical death and carry on in the Afterlife.

The sum of all of my experiences as a 'medium' so far, has led me to the conclusion that life is not defined by physicality. In fact, 'life' is defined by spirit. Whether that be their personality shining through or the brightness of consciousness; I know that my beloved pets are just as "alive" and as real as I am.

I love that Jackie Jones-Hunt PhD has yet again used her research to shine a spotlight on the long forgotten truths that our 'animals' are more than just background scenery in our world - they are our Divine Heritage. And as precious gifts we must cherish them and see to it that they have all of the rights to freedom and peace that we do.

Brough Perkins (USA)
International Televised Medium & Radio Host.
www.broughperkins.ca

Fifteen years ago I lived on a small farm. We rented our land for farmers to fatten their animals and then to be slaughtered. It was then, after seeing my animal friends herded off for the kill I could no longer partake in the eating of those who roam the earth alongside us.

As a Medium I have been gifted an insight in the 'lives' of our Animal Kingdom on the 'other side.' Communicating with them on this level has taught me so much about their purpose in the Universe - and it is not to eat them!

My faithful companion, Tao, before his death, communicated to me the reason for his coming passing. I cried so much listening to him, on a telepathic level, why it was time for him to leave me. He gave me a completely new understanding to the meaning of 'a dog is a man's/woman's best friend.' He has come to me since his passing often, guiding me, still as my beloved friend-healthy again and happy.

If only we all took some time to understand our animal friends are not just for our food source, or to kill for the thrill of murder, then our very existence on earth would be much richer for remembering who they really are! Allow Dr. Jackie Jones-Hunt's series of books named Animals Souls to enter your heart with a deeper understanding of our non-human beings-it will change your thinking forever!

Jen-Irishu
Medium & Author of: Messages of Love -
My Spiritual Awakening ~ The Angel in My Dreams
& The Adventures of Angels & Eli.
www.jen-irishu.com

Everybody loves their pets, and many people see their pets on the other side. This research is important and I believe it will be popular among NDER's and researchers. Thank you for this excellent contribution to the journey of our soul's literature.

Diane Corcoran PhD
President of the International Association for
Near Death Studies Inc., USA (IANDS).

This research represents an insightful look into the truth that animals deserve our compassion and respect at the same level as we give to our fellow human animals. Jackie Jones-Hunt PhD has put to paper so many wonderful descriptions of the complex emotions and interactions we have with all animals. I highly recommend this serialization and hope it is read far and wide as we could use so much more of the wisdom it contains!

Elizabeth Jane Farians PhD., Ohio, USA
Elizabeth Farians is listed in the Directory of American Scholars & Who's Who of American Women. Actively involved in organizations including: People for the Ethical Treatment of Animals (PETA), Vegan & Vegetarian Resource Groups, In Defense of Animals, Animals, People & Environment (APE).

As a medium of many years' experience I have received and given proof of the fact that all animals human and non-human survive to the world of spirit. It is refreshing to see that Dr. Jackie Jones-Hunt has written the (serialized) volume Animals souls clarifying this point and advocating compassion for ALL Animals.

Rev. Gary Cooke
(Minister of Scottish Spiritualist Churches, UK).

I endorse books that remind and encourage us to show compassion to animals.
Gordon Smith
International Televised Medium and Author.
This timely serialized research explores the most spiritually elevated strands of ancient global spiritual teachings (world religions) which teach us not to kill animals instead to

show them all the utmost compassion and respect. I confirm that the most elevated Spiritualist teachings endorse these most spiritually elevated world religious teachings which implore and command humankind not to kill animals and show them all love and kindness.

Eric Hatton
Honorary President of the Spiritualists' National Union, Minister of the SNU & Chairman of the JV Trust.

The world badly needs a book about the fact that – like human animals - non-human animals have souls. I admire the courage of Jackie Jones-Hunt PhD in starting the change of paradigm, reversing the damage done to animals through ignorance and arrogance.

Sarah, webmaster for www.spiritualistresources.com

This fascinating serialized research not only raises awareness of the plight of our animals in the world today but also illustrates, through ancient spiritual and religious teachings, that animals have always held a reverend place within cultures throughout the world, throughout time.

Sadly, somewhere along the road we have lost sight of the fact that our animals are living sentient beings just like us, capable of feeling love, joy, pain, anxiety and fear.

This insightful book beautifully demonstrates that the idea of sharing a world respectfully with love and compassion for all living creatures isn't anything new – but is a belief that is intrinsically embedded within many spiritual and religious traditions.

Sarah-Jane Le Blanc
Author of Pet Whisperer
www.soul2therapy.co.uk

Dr. Jackie Jones-Hunt's understanding of the animal kingdom will make us all sit up and listen the animals need us all to find the truth within our hearts. This series is an essential read. Well done Jackie.

Joanne Hull
Author of The Pet Psychic & Puppy Tales.
www.joannehull.com

This interesting serialization brings a new, well-researched spiritual and religious dimension to animal welfare and environmental matters. I believe it is important to raise awareness of these vital concerns.

Gill Russell
Anti-Vivisectionist & Animal Welfarist, UK.

This is a very worthwhile serialized volume which should be read in order to understand how important it is to show kindness, mercy and respect to animals and to remind people to be more compassionate to them. The human race seems to have neglected to show compassion to the Animal Kingdom for far too long, but now is the time to rectify this.

Melody Macdonald (Pemberton)
Author of Caught in the Act: (The Feldberg Expose, 1990)
melodypemberton@mac.com

It took me a year to walk from Britain to the Far East to study spiritual philosophy and martial arts for health and protection with the vegetarian Buddhist monks in their shaolin temple who kindly welcomed me.

I learned many things including that all animals live in harmony with nature, with the exception of the human animal who has divorced itself from its animal relatives and is speedily destroying our shared home, planet earth, which does not belong to us alone!

Spiritual philosophy teaches, when you take you must give back and the only species who takes and gives nothing back is the human animal which will have devastating consequences for all.

Dr. Jackie Jones-Hunt's enthralling, entrancing, highly informed and perceptive research is in harmony with such soul-touching, profoundly elevated compassionate spiritual teachings.

I cannot recommend Jackie's extremely vital, insightful and powerful series of animal books more highly. The results of her captivating, fascinating and compelling research will change your life forever.

Mike Gavaghan
Wildlife Consultancy: Specializing in All Protected Species
& Badgers.

As a dog specialist for various breeds for over 40 years, championship show-breed specialist judge for the world famous Crufts (founded in 1891) and top UK breeder 2008-2011, I am extremely enthusiastic to thoroughly recommend Dr. Jackie Jones-Hunt's fascinating, thought-provoking serialized research.

Her investigations are both absorbing and enlightening, raising awareness of the ancient, typically vegetarian, compassionate, spiritual teachings regarding animals which lay at the foundations of world religions.

Jackie's research reminds all of us human animals to treat all of our fellow, emotional, sentient, feeling, flesh and blood animals with the respect and compassion every one of these individuals rightly deserve.

Gordon Rattray
Championship Show-Breed Specialist
Judge for the world famous Crufts
& Top UK Breeder, 2008-2011.

Two Worlds as a monthly Spiritualist Magazine endorses compassion to animals and so wholeheartedly endorses this well-written serialized research.

Tony Ortzen
Editor of the Two Worlds Magazine (founded by the famous medium Emma Hardinge Britten in 1887)
& Former Editor Psychic News
www.twoworldsmag.co.uk

Dr. Jackie Jones-Hunt has excelled herself in this remarkable and generously sized serialized publication...Indeed, this writer is one who really knows her subject matter due to having academically specialized in other world Faiths and not just that of Western Christendom.

Yes, indeed, Jesus said:

"Other sheep I have which are not of this fold and them also I must bring!" Well, such is the concept of the writer of this most helpful volume which conveys a love for all creation and also a most necessary emphasis on ourselves; our relationship with animals; and – most of all – our terrific responsibility to be caring guardians over them:

Yes, factors which 'so called' Christianity has failed to address for far too long! The gifted writer of this serialized research knows that our Good Shepherd 'has the whole world in His hands' and that His love embraces all animals and not just a group of self-interested humans concerned about their own salvation!

God grant all power to the pen of Dr. Jackie Jones-hunt whose books should be 'top priority' reading for Semenarians, Bible students, and animal loving folk of all Faiths!

Finally, one thing is sure: once you start reading this author's books, you'll have difficulty in putting them down. The fact is she not only appeals to the head but to the heart as well.

The Animal Padre, Rev James Thompson

www.animalpadre.org

I am a Spiritualist and one of our guide's teachings is: It is wrong to extinguish another's life in order to sustain your own. In other words —

Don't kill animals and eat them!

As A Spiritualist I also know that like us animals live on in the next world and can communicate with masters and mistresses still on the earth. I have always believed that when God said:

"Thou shalt not kill"

He was not just referring to humans but to all living creatures and I have always believed that Jesus himself would have been a vegetarian. I hope this well researched serialized volume will cause others to re-think and change their life and eating habits.

Ada A. McKay Author, Aberdeen, Scotland, UK

This serialized research will prove to be a valuable asset to our work, with its painstakingly researched information.

Through its contents, we now know that not only Jesus' vegetarian teachings regarding animals were suppressed, but also those of Confucius, Pythagoras and other ancient, spiritual philosophers who brought a message so unambiguous that it is infuriating to recall no mention made of it in lessons on the subject during our school years.

Much more than a book, it appears to have been brought, at this time, as part of the Divine Plan.

A captivating and thought-provoking, work. Jackie Jones-Hunt PhD also provides, through her heart rendering account of her beloved dog, Edward's life and death, remarkable evidence to skeptics that our animals not only communicate with us from the Spirit World but do so with the same love, understanding and intelligence as their human families.

Elissa Rattigan
Animal Rights in Spiritualism
www.arisgroup.org

It comes as no surprise to me to read in this astonishing ground-breaking serialized volume by Jackie Jones-Hunt PhD that all animals have souls. Every time I look into their eyes I see their souls. They may even have more advanced souls than us.

David Dane
Vegan Landscape Artist, Norfolk, UK
www.dfdaneoilpaintings.co.uk

Fascinating, well-written and inspiring, one of the best books we have read. Having spent our entire lives working with dogs, Parson Russell Terriers in particular, we are pleased to say we thoroughly recommend this fascinating and thought-provoking serialized book.

Jimmy and Louise Scott,
Dog Specialists. Cambridge, England, UK.

I wholeheartedly recommend this serialized volume to everyone who loves animals.

Steve Hutchins
The originator & healing breeder of the famous Ratpack Terriers of the International Breeding & Kennel Club Show Kennels ~ Nurturing Happy, Healthy & Contented Parson Russell Terriers in mind, body & spirit with 100% Temperament.

PROOF ANIMALS HAVE SOULS

Copyright © 2014 Jackie Jones-Hunt
ISBN PRINT 978-0-9928661-1-2
ISBN EBOOK 978-0-9928661-2-9

HOUSE OF LIGHT PUBLISHERS LTD, UK

Author & Owner
of House of Light Publishers Ltd: Jackie Jones-Hunt PhD
First published by House of Light Publishers Ltd, April 2014

www.jackiejones-hunt.com
Email: jackiejones-hunt@btconnect.com
Tel: 00-44-(0)779-158-8005
Text copyright: Jackie Jones-Hunt PhD 2014

House of Light Publishers Ltd seek to utilize an ethical publishing philosophy seeking to disseminate fiction and non-fiction books around the world with an informative, thought-provoking or spiritual message. Our authors keep their own royalties.

DEDICATION

This book is dedicated to my husband Tony and dogs Jac, Sioux, Edward, Lizzie and Eric. Most significantly it is dedicated to Edward, our incredible, Parson Russell Terrier, who tragically, unexpectedly and suddenly became severely ill at the young age of 10 and returned to the heavenly spirit realms over a traumatic ten days. Parson and Jack Russells typically live to the age of 16-20.

Extremely handsome, Edward possessed the kindest and deepest loving eyes and face. He had a wiry, short haired, white, tan and black face with a white body, none of which had begun to go grey. My dearest, devoted companion sat with me daily whilst I carried out this research and heartbreakingly passed to spirit whilst I was nearing completion.

As part of our family forever, due to his untimely and premature passing, Edward now lives with my two-legged and four-legged family members in the spirit realms, who have communicated to me, promising to lovingly look after Edward on my behalf during my absence.

I know that on countless occasions throughout the course of my remaining physical life I will glimpse and hear Edward and spend time with him during my sleep state because love is eternal and indestructible, creating the all-powerful, tangible, love link responsible for these reunions and love will ultimately reunite each of us with our loved ones in the end.

Words cannot describe the fathomless depths of each of our dogs' love nor express our immense love for them. It is clear to see why so many companion animals return to the spirit spheres long before us, as they are such innocent, trusting, vulnerable, big-hearted, emotional babes. These fun-loving souls who offer limitless, unconditional, often tragically unrequited love are often spiritually superior to some people who adopt them; they have little to learn and oceans to teach fellow human animals.

As the physical years pass many who share their lives with our four-legged family members become tenderly aware that it is a privilege and a gift to share our lives with them and that they are indeed forgiving, peace-loving spiritual teachers who deserve to be given long, happy, healthy, fun-packed lives with outings and holidays and an abundance of contented dreams. Sharing my life, typically 24/7, with each of my dogs, adopting and living with two at a time, has caused me long ago to discover that it is a most meaningful, momentous, unforgettable, joyous honor to share precious, tender and memorable years with them and to incorporate our dogs into our physical and spirit family forever.

Each of them has proved and still proves him/herself to be an intelligent, sensitive, well-rounded individual with a unique personality however they each possess boundless dignity, bravery and devotion. All are funny, mischievous, character dogs, giving endless love and ever faithful loyalty. Unreservedly and unconditionally, our dogs give my husband and me, fathomless depths of love, steadfast, constant commitment, happiness, healing, comfort and companionship.

I thank Tony, my husband who, at our first meeting 22 years ago, instantly adored and admired Jac my first Jack Russell. Jac was followed many years later by Sioux who in her later years shared our home with Edward our first Parson Russell. Edward went on to share our home with the new addition, Lizzie a further

Jack Russell. It then became Lizzie with Eric, our second Parson Russell and the two of them have been more recently joined by Eric's three sons Charlie Brown, Jack and Bob making a family of five Russell terriers!!

I thank all of our Russell family members for their steadfast devotion and companionship and the vast amount of fun and love they bring into my life. I am grateful to my mother Eileen and each of my family in spirit: father Eric, grandparents Elizabeth-Eileen and Bob, Aunt Lucy, Uncle Bert and our spirit twins, my husband's father Charles, his uncle Ron and his grandmother Helen, each of whom is kindly committed to caring for our doggie family in the spirit realms.

I also thank our wonderful Jack Russells, Jac and Sioux who continue to survive in the realm of spirit and of course Edward, for the privilege of sharing our lives together and the honor of being inseparable throughout eternity, forever connected by our love-links. My dogs' photographs are on the back covers of this serialization. I also thank the renowned, Glasgow-based medium Gary Cooke who recently gave me astonishingly detailed information proving beyond a doubt that Edward is now with my spirit family, human, Jack Russell and Parson Russell.

It is my aim if funding became available to open an Animal Sanctuary in the name of the benefactor where all animals needing love, food, water, medical attention and a home for life would be welcomed.

It is my deepest hope that the reader will find the serialized Animal Souls research, of substantially sized books, deeply thought-provoking, life-changing and health-enhancing, spiritually and physically. If this is the case then Animal Souls has done its part to help alleviate the suffering of all animals, human and non-human.

TABLE OF CONTENTS

Animals share with us the privilege of having a soul.

Pythagoras

Although we seem to be separate individuals, in reality we are all expressions of one primal imagination. We assume we are many, but in fact we are one. And what we do to each other we do to ourselves.

Timothy Freke

Differences in religious beliefs, politics, social status, and position are all secondary. When we look at [any being] with compassion, we are able to see beyond these secondary differences and connect to the primary essence that binds all…together as one.

The Dalai Lama

Life is an endless series of choices illustrating the depth, level and all-inclusiveness of our compassion and respect for all animals, human and non-human. The simple, easiest and most elevated choice can only be expressed through vegetarianism.

Jackie Jones-Hunt PhD

Life is not discovery of fate; it is continuous creation of future, through choices of thoughts and actions in the present.

Sanjay Sahay

OLD NATIVE AMERICAN INDIAN PROPHECY

When the earth is ravaged and the animals are dying
A new tribe of people shall come unto the earth
From many colors, classes, creeds, and who by their
actions and deeds
Shall make the earth green again
They will be known as the
'Warriors of the Rainbow.'

Foreword I

By Professor Judy Barad, Ph.D. Author of Aquinas on the Nature and Treatment of Animals, professor at Indiana State University, Indiana, USA.

Spirituality and religion should help us to be better, more ethical people. An ethical person is one who, at the very least, avoids creating unnecessary suffering for others. Of course, since human beings can suffer, an ethical person does not engage in activities that involves the unnecessary suffering of human beings.

Do other animals suffer? The overwhelming majority of people, who have lived with an animal companion, know that indeed other animals can and do suffer. Now no ethical person would seek benefit for himself if it means that other feeling beings will be forced to suffer, especially if the suffering is disproportionate to the benefit. Given the suffering of animals, how should a spiritual and/or religious person respond?

Dr. Jones-Hunt helps to give some direction to this response throughout her intriguing, well-written serialization. This fascinating serialized research delves into many important and often overlooked topics regarding animals. The issue of how we view animals is crucial, given the horrendous treatment most animals receive each day. This involves billions of animals worldwide. Are animals mere things to do with as we please?

Do their lives only have the value that we assign to them? If we forget that animals have a beating heart just like we do, if we ignore that they feel pain, pleasure, anger, affection, and fear, then we may treat them in ways that result in tremendous suffering. By thinking of an animal as an "it" rather than "he" or "she," by thinking of an animal as "something" rather than "someone," we make it easy for ourselves to treat animals as if they were inanimate objects. After all, it doesn't matter how we treat inanimate objects.

One way that animals are treated as inanimate objects is on the factory farm. In this setting, they are crammed into tiny spaces so that farmers can maximize their profits. Five chickens, for instance, are forced to "live" in cages the size of a record

1

album cover. Their upper beaks are cut off with hot irons. Calves raised for veal are chained in wooden crates only 22 inches wide. Due to the lack of space, they cannot walk or turn around. Cattle are dehorned, branded and castrated without anesthetics. Pigs are held in metal stalls no larger than their bodies. Their tails are severed. Many of these animals become insane due to their horrific stress.

Further, many companies still use the Draize eye irritancy test in which substances such as laundry detergent and oven cleaner are dripped into the eyes of rabbits. Many millions of animals are shocked, poisoned, burned and otherwise tortured in product testing and experiments that are often repetitious and unnecessary. Cats dissected in classrooms are embalmed while still alive.

They have been observed to clench their jaws when injected with embalming fluid, which is a clear reaction to pain. This happens even though alternatives exist, such as cell and tissue cultures as well as computer models. Some other issues involving excruciating suffering for animals are hunting, trapping, puppy mills, rodeos, circuses, and dog fighting. Often companion animals, such as cats and dogs, are neglected and abused.

Given such atrocities, it is important to understand our kinship with other animals. Dr. Jones-Hunt explains this important fact early in the book. By taking the broader view, she shows us that what we do to other animals, we do to our nearest relatives on the evolutionary scale. Yet the book is not all gloom and doom for Dr. Jones-Hunt explains what we can do as individuals to bring about change. Society is an abstraction. In reality, it is composed of individuals, like you and me, who change society by our choices and actions.

One argument that has been used to justify our vile treatment of animals appeals to the teachings of seventeenth-century Renee Descartes, a French philosopher. Arguing that animals are essentially machines, lacking feelings and awareness, his theory became very popular. Scientists used his theory to justify cutting live dogs open without any anesthetic, while nailing their paws to a table. They explained that their screams didn't

2

signify pain, but meant no more than the mechanical sounds of a clock. In current dog labs, dogs' vocal cords are removed so that their "mechanical" screams won't disturb the students or researchers who cut them open. Descartes theory is still very influential. This series contains further discussion about this matter.

Not only did Descartes propagate the notion that animals are unfeeling machines, but he also popularized the new idea that animals do not have souls. In Western Europe, the recognition of animals having souls was common before the time of Socrates and throughout the middle ages. Descartes changes this view in order to consistently claim that animals are no better than machines. His view was so widely accepted that today many people find the notion of animal souls astonishing. Yet we find claims about animal souls in other cultures as well as throughout Western European history. The book tells us just how pervasive the claim is.

Yet another historical excuse for our disturbing attitude toward animals comes from a misunderstanding of religion. Many people appeal to the Old Testament account, which says that God gave humans dominion over other animals. They interpret this passage to mean that God gave us animals to do whatever we want with. Yet the early books of the Old Testament have often been interpreted in the wrong way. For instance, most theologians acknowledge that the seven day account of creation should not be taken literally. For one thing, it conflicts with a great deal of empirical evidence.

Even Pope Benedict XVI has acknowledged that evolution does not conflict with religion. Scholars have long recognized that the Old Testament developed over time, reflecting a people who became more religiously sophisticated. It is also clear that Jesus came, in part, to correct the misunderstanding of religion that people have clung to. A Christian is, by definition, a follower of Jesus. Christians, then, should seek to imitate Jesus, especially as they claim to be his

3

followers. But when we look in the Gospels to see Jesus' actions and teachings regarding animals, we see him as a teacher of compassion and love. As Dr. Jones-Hunt points out, Judaism also counsels that we treat animals respectfully and justly.

Eastern religions are very insistent that we should extend compassion to all sentient beings. The person who practices compassion can feel the same depth of love, the same intimacy for all sentient beings that he or she feels toward family and friends. Hinduism, Confucianism, and Buddhism, which are treated in this series, counsel that compassion can make us feel connected to all sentient individuals in a way that transforms us into better people.

Writing about what animals can do for us, Dr. Jones-Hunt describes the experiences we have with animals. Those of us who have lived with animals and learned to appreciate their humor, their intelligence, and their affection will find their views reinforced by reading this chapter. For many of us, our animal companions are family members, whose lives can't be measured in monetary terms.

Yet Dr. Jones-Hunt doesn't hide the darker side of our treatment of our non-human friends. She details the many animal cruelty issues, including the genocide perpetrated against animals that takes place in industrial settings. Here she also explains why we have nothing to fear from a vegetarian diet. In fact, we have a lot to gain -- our health! In tough economic times, it also helps to be a vegetarian. Once a person becomes a vegetarian, he or she rarely regards this practice as a sacrifice.

There are so many vegetarian cookbooks and delicious, mouth-watering recipes that there is no reason to miss eating someone's flesh. There is even vegetarian fast food for those of us with a busy lifestyle! Yet aside from health and economic concerns, the most compelling reasons to become a vegetarian is both the fact that we should not be willing to participate in taking someone's life, merely to satisfy our taste preferences and the egregious treatment animals suffer on factory farms. Dr. Jones-Hunt opens our eyes to really look at practices most people take for granted.

The series closes on a positive note. People who care about animals want to make a difference. Dr. Jones-Hunt shows us how we can do so by our individual choices. Addressing spiritually inclined people, she includes quotes from famous vegetarians in her books. This gives the reader a sense that vegetarianism is not some weird practice, engaged in by eccentric people. Rather it is the case that people who are deeply involved in public life, those who are committed to making the world a better place to inhabit, are frequently among those who live a vegetarian lifestyle.

The series closes on a positive note. People who care about animals want to make a difference. Dr. Jones-Hunt shows us how we can do so by our individual choices. Addressing spiritually inclined people, she includes quotes from famous vegetarians in her books. This gives the reader a sense that vegetarianism is not some weird practice, engaged in by eccentric people. Rather it is the case that people who are deeply involved in public life, those who are committed to making the world a better place to inhabit, are frequently among those who live a vegetarian lifestyle.

Foreword II

Reverend James Thompson: The Animals' Padre
Christians Against all Animal Abuse.
www.all-creatures.org

In an age of what I consider to be "Blinkered Ecumenicalism" the works of Jackie Jones-Hunt PhD come to us as a true breath of fresh air! Here is a lady who, to my mind, very much sees the difference between major churches compromising on doctrine so as to accommodate each other for services of 'united church witness:' and of that far greater need to include, and learn from, a whole host of God's faithful of other philosophies and persuasions. Yes and not forgetting brands of Christianity which, for far too long, have been moved by traditionalists, at the most: to the very fringe of their circumference!

Well, what a contrast with Jackie Jones-Hunt's valuable insights! Her writings reveal a wealth of knowledge and experience from movements sometimes, paradoxically, quite as diverse and yet complementary to each other as – shall we say? – a Swedenborg's 'Church of the New Jerusalem' with that of branches of the Spiritualist National Union! (See also her book: Moses and Jesus the Shamans).

To my mind, congregations of 'true Christians' who have an understanding of our unbroken relationship with the animal creation – and whose 'fruits' may range from assurances given of Pet presences in the hereafter; to Vegetarian Camphill creations in the here and now! – put traditional Ecumenism (with its rejection of animal souls – and the horrendous fruits ensuing from it) to utter shame.

As one often addressed by the media as 'the animals padre' I look towards a far more embracing 'coming together' of 'the people of God' than that envisaged by today's Ecumenicals! Consequently, for a Christendom that has shamelessly shrunk the image and compassion of its God, I unreservedly commend the timely works of Jackie as 'top priority' reading. Yes, and in contrast with so many within the academic field, her style is truly

6

a bright and vivacious one. It is something that many of our theological foundations could learn from! Indeed, I sense her writings will become a true blessing to animal loving Christians worldwide.

Foreword III

Dr. Anabela Cardoso, Author of Electronic Voices, Contact with Another Dimension? Editor of the ITC Journal (Instrumental Trans-communication), Spain, & Founder of Abrigo Animal Sanctuary, Portugal. www.abrigo.me.

Jackie's serialized research about the ordeal inflicted on animals on our planet and the teachings we have received from high spiritual entities, throughout time, to do just the opposite, could not be timelier.

In this time of technological barbarism and loss of even the basic values, maybe non-human animals can help us escape from the horror we are creating for ourselves and for all life on planet earth. We need only to look into their eyes with humility and innocence and learn from them.

Jackie Jones-Hunt PhD does just that – a compassionate, enlightened person who understands that we, humans, are on the wrong path and need to reverse our ways, she has done us all a big favor by showing us the way. We should read and ponder this serialized research with an open mind and a clear soul.

Let us learn also from St. Francis of Assisi who received the gift of divine illumination: All animals are our brothers and sisters, let us honor and respect them as one of us, because that is what they are.

Foreword IV

Sonia Rinaldi, Author of 8 books on ITC, (Research results clearly demonstrate contact with human and non-human animals after death): Winner of 3 European Awards for Research. http://www.ipati.org > Bulletins

A New Look at Animals through Instrumental Trans-communication Phenomena.

Since the dawn of time, humanity has showed by its actions that its greatest fear in life is death everyone knows it will come, but the fear of the unknown unbalances us- not so much by his or her disappearance, but perhaps by an unconscious fear of the settlement of scores, as preached by all religions.

How might the afterlife experience be, if it does exist? Will they measure individual mistakes and those mistakes we have collectively made together? Collective errors would be, for example, the mistreatment of animals. Helpless at they are they remain in the hands of a cruel and insensitive majority. Although we consider ourselves superior beings, we can't even manage to open the range of our intelligence – expanding our vision and audition to frequencies that human's cannot reach.

This is where Instrumental Trans-communication comes in. It is through it that we can overcome our disability – it's possible to hear through devices what our ears can't capture. Could animals communicate through this feature?

A trans-communicator from Portugal, the diplomat Anabela Cardoso, has already disclosed that she had made recordings with her dead dogs. As absurd as this sounds; it would be a non-scientific attitude not to test it. So I did. A friend and protector of animals, Fatima, came to me wanting news of her beloved deceased dogs. To our surprise! We recorded several communications!

Fatima was amazed with the answers we received to the questions, for as a good skeptic, she never thought a contact of this nature was even possible. She admitted being wrong, and testified to the fact that she observed details that surprised her. Among them, she reported that she had never before had any

9

contact with me, revealing that I knew nothing about her deceased companion animals. So she was surprised when, in the recording, she asked the question of her late dog, "which was the game he most loved to play with her?" and he replied in the recording: "the toy car!" Yes, it was true. She used to play with him with a toy car and he loved it.

How is this possible? How can an animal retain memory? How is it that each animal manifests? So, Dr. Anabela Cardoso was right. Animals can and do communicate.

From this first contact via trans-communication, getting news from animals, I immediately thought that there might be a way for Electronic Voice Phenomena to become a vehicle that could change the relationship between humanity and the various species of the planet.

Still, with Fatima we have had another very significant experience: She coordinates a project castrating the stray cats in a cemetery here in Brazil. Her daughter Rachel is in charge of catching the cats and taking them to the vet for castration. One day Rachel, at the cemetery, used her cell phone to communicate with Fatima, and Rachel perceived interference on the telephone line. Rachel thought at first that it was simply a problem in the unit, so they both hung up and called again.

At this point, Rachel realized that a male voice was addressing her, and shortly other voices were speaking though the cell phone. The girl came to discover that this voice was from a former gravedigger, whose dog remained living in the cemetery after his human parent's death. The voice of the deceased man asked Rachel not to take Tico, (his dog's name) away from the cemetery.

Fatima and Rachel researched data from former employees and in fact, they found the data regarding the former owner of Tico, they heard from witnesses that he was a former grave digger who had passed to spirit and that he loved his dog, Tico, very much, taking care of him as his child.

From this moment on, I made several recordings by phone with Rachel – and we have compiled valuable data about the "life of the dead" in a cemetery. The full case is on our site.

Many reports of clairvoyance and clairaudience towards animals have been published worldwide. But with technology advancing every day, I believe that Electronic Voice Phenomena is the most obvious and necessary way to demonstrate that we know very little about animals' minds, live or so-called "dead."

I have faith that one day instrumental trans-communication will be accepted and recognized by all, this important science will enhance human evolution, revealing, recording and observing that we are not alone and that every individual's thought, action, movement and gesture is recorded and questioned by those surviving death on the other side of life. Only then, can we expect that in the future humanity will have more humility, respect and compassion for all living species on this planet.

I would like a greater spread of ITC, especially in the mass media, since the vast majority of human beings know nothing about the survival evidence gained through ITC and mediumship. They think that they will go unpunished for both their actively deliberate and passively thoughtless evil acts, including their supportive role condoning animal suffering because they mistakenly believe that in a material sense everything begins and ends with their physical earthly life here. Transcommunication shows with irrefutable proof that life continues after physical death and we are answerable for all the mistakes we make, including each individual's active and passive role in the mistreatment of animals.

CHAPTER 1 - PROOF OF OUR DOGS' POST-DEATH SURVIVAL: JAC, SIOUX & EDWARD

"The thinking man must oppose all cruel customs no matter how deeply rooted in tradition and surrounded by a halo. When we have a choice, we must avoid bringing torment and injury into the life of another, even the lowliest creature; to do so is to renounce our manhood and shoulder a guilt which nothing justifies."

Rev. Dr. Albert Schweitzer, (1875-1965).

The introduction which follows summarizes the contents of this serialized research split into a short series of generously sized books.

At the outset here, I would like to say a few words about our dear dog Teddy Edward who passed to spirit as my first installment was ready for print. Due to his transition to the spirit realm this manuscript lay untouched on my desk for many months. The evidence for my dog Edward's transition to the alternate coexistent dimension of spirit and his continued survival has been overwhelming. Offering a brief summary of the verification for Edward's continued survival here is in total harmony with the theme of my research.

Below, I provide my brief account of Edward including an extract taken from the large amount of proof given to myself and my husband, Tony, by the distinguished Scottish medium Gary Cooke. The evidence of Edward's continued survival after death continues to this day to be confirmed by mediums who know nothing about me and are unknown to each other.

The continued post death survival of our two earlier dogs, who passed to the spirit realms some years before, named Jac and Sioux, has also been proven and verified by other mediums, at differing intervals over many years. Evidence of their continued lives has been given to me by mediums providing spiritualist church demonstrations and in one to one conversations with mediums, independently of each other and unknown to each other.

Evidence of our dogs' survival has come from many sources including mediums such as Keith Noble, Jean Hole, Caroline Wilson, Ricky Martin, Jean Brown, Aileen Wallace, Billy McFadzean, Virginia Swann, Kay Cook and Anne McCutcheon.

Returning to the medium Gary Cooke, the accurate and detailed communications Gary received through his mediumship have further fuelled my existing concrete conviction that Edward has survived physical death, and is alive and well. Gary's evidential proof has given me and my husband great comfort as has the kindness of Gary's wife Maureen.

After carrying out decades of psychical research observing and listening to a wide range of physical mediumistic phenomena, including communications from spirit manifestations and entranced mediums and a broad spectrum of mediumistic demonstrations together with my own personal spiritually transformative mediumistic and psychic experiences, of seeing and hearing human and animal spirits, I am convinced beyond a shadow of a doubt that all animals, human and non-human make an inevitable and natural transition to the spirit realm at physical death as a fact of nature.

Each sentient two-legged and four legged animal shares the same flesh and blood and nerve endings which transmit pain to the brain. It is my conviction that each soul, alternatively known as 'spirit' or 'consciousness/personality' survives in an indestructible pure energy form, (as energy cannot be destroyed), continuing to live in a recognizable, dynamically alive state intact for eternity and has the choice to reincarnate periodically. The ancient wise sages referred to this as the transmigration of the soul from one species to another for the purposes of soul growth.

The following brief summary account explains the events leading up to Edward's transition to spirit and the verification of Edward's continued survival after his physical death. This initially tragic yet uplifting account should help all those who love their adopted innocent, trusting, emotional animal babes and grieve for them after they pass to the spirit realms.

Those who adopt pets are well aware that they exude endless unconditional love, loyalty and companionship from the moment of their arrival to the moment of their death. The following account should prove that our pets' devotion, friendship and loyalty continue without end after their physical deaths. All pet owners would agree that their typically four-legged pet-emotional-babe soon becomes an additional family member and his/her physical passing fractures their soul with grief as deeply as the loss of a two-legged child.

Returning to the events that led to Edward's transition to spirit, one evening I lay on our settee to watch TV, putting a cushion under my head, when our gentle and loving Jack Russell, Edward, came over and stood on the floor beside me. As I leaned over to scoop him up to cuddle him, as I had done an infinite number of times before, our faces converged and shockingly at that moment he had a wild enraged fit.

Suddenly, wildly and uncontrollably enraged, Edward sitting on my chest, lashed out and bit off part of my top lip, fractionally lifting his face he returned to take another bite which included my nose and just beneath my eye. Thankfully this second bite was stopped by Tony, my husband.

Moments later, as Edward's glazed eyes cleared, recognition returned and he reverted back to his usual quiet, loving, placid, sensitive self. Now sitting on the kitchen floor, kind and calm again, Edward raised his paw to shake my hand. Peace-loving Edward used to offer his paw to shake hands with any vet after they had given him an injection, clearly asking each vet to be his friend instead of hurting him!

At this juncture, obviously both Edward and I were traumatized with blood and disbelief. Immediately afterwards

14

Tony took me to the hospital, I thought I was there to receive a tetanus injection only but was kept in for three days and underwent an operation to stitch up my lip. I watched the hospital clock throughout the first night and did not sleep a wink - I could not believe or understand what had happened.

When I came out of the anesthetic I could not breathe which was extremely frightening. The day after I returned from hospital I had the vet check Edward out with blood tests and a liver scan. She discovered Edward had a urine infection and initially I wondered if that had been severe enough to make him hallucinate as had been the case with my granddad. This did not seem to be the case.

During the following days we noticed on more than one occasion he lost his balance and strangely in the car his whole body shook with terrified anxiety. Edward also chased Lizzie our younger smaller female Jack Russell away on two occasions, she is our extremely feminine, two year old Jack Russell and we, like Edward himself, became afraid he might one day hurt her. Edward and Lizzie have always adored each other. From the outset Edward took on the paternal role, regularly washing and protecting her and conducting himself like the perfect gentleman he was/is.

I know after the event with me our shocked Edward realized what he had done to me, due to the fact he instantly returned to his usual calm, loving self, wanting to shake hands. Some days after the event, I asked my tarot cards was Edward aware of what he had done, as his actions shocked both himself and me. Astonishingly, after shuffling the cards I picked out the Strength card which shows the lady calming the lion, clearly telling me he did know he had become uncontrollable like the lion. Indeed, he was aware that he had acted totally out of character and that this new uncontrollable periodic instability may cause him to hurt Lizzie when he was not himself.

After the event, he frightened her on two occasions. He made it clear to me that he wanted to sleep besides me in my office at home as usual but to no longer be in the same room as playful, unpredictable, young Lizzie. For instant rage and aggression to come on that fast and then disappear, the crisis had

15

to stem from a deep-seated, neurological problem. Obviously Edward's usual loving personality was being intermittently adversely affected through the manifestation of intense aggression brought on by pressure and pain. However, soon after the event, we had him on medication to avoid further pain.

Everything pointed to Edward having a brain tumor or an intra-cerebral aneurysm caused earlier in his life by violence towards him, such as being kicked in the head or thrown against an object or a wall. An aneurysm in the brain is a progressive swelling of the blood vessel secondary to head trauma, growing larger with age, behaving much the same way as a tumor.

Five days later we visited the hospital to have my stitches out those inside my mouth were left to dissolve naturally. Due to the intricacy of the procedure the pain added to the emotional pain and in tears I told the nurse the sad situation about Edward. I could no longer trust our loving dog due to his illness causing his fit of uncontrollable rage.

The nurse offered me a mirror from which I flinched. I did not want to see the mess my lip was in and the damaged nerves that prevented me from being able to smile as I could no longer hide my wound behind the stitches and plasters. I did not want to see the new 'me' whose life with Edward my loving, devoted doggie son and funny swimming companion had tragically been turned upside down!

En route to the train station to return home, we stopped in a shopping mall for something to eat before which I visited the bathroom to wash my hands. Still not wanting to see my wounded lip, inadvertently, as I entered the room, I glimpsed myself in the mirror. At that exact same moment, fluted music rang out the words: "So take a good look at my face, you'll see my smile looks out of place, if you look closer it's easy to trace the tracks of my tears….I tell a joke or two…deep inside I am blue…." Some months later I have learned that the song was sung by Smokey Robinson.

As I exited, the words of the next song rang out: "It's hard to say goodbye to the one you love." I was astonished by the precise, exact and unique relevance of the above words for the situation Edward and I had found our self in. My deepest intuition

16

told me that these songs were indeed specific messages for me, though I was still shocked and traumatized by the whole situation.

At home again, increasingly we knew our wee Edward was ill, he lacked energy, he wanted to sleep most of the time and his eyes showed he was not always himself. I frequently told him he was a good boy to reassure him but was frightened to pick him up and cuddle him as I had done thousands of times before. I bought a Rottweiler cage and placed it by the radiator in our bedroom, in Edward's spot, and put his usual bed and purple blanket inside it, the only difference now was that he would be sleeping in the large cage at night to protect Lizzie and prevent her from bothering him in the night as she slept besides him in her dog-bed.

Nearly two weeks after Edward had bitten my face, on the Friday night I asked the angels to guide me. A few hours later Edward woke me in the middle of the night for the toilet. I awoke knowing what I had to do. Shockingly, painfully, I knew I had to let Edward go. I have never had my prayers answered so quickly and sadly the answer fractured my soul. I awoke now clearly knowing that we could not heal Edward that the answer was not antibiotics, pain killers, an unused muzzle or a cage. I could no longer let him play with Lizzie or trust him in this condition.

I had to protect Edward from himself and I had to protect small, young Lizzie. Tony my husband was to go away shortly so I would not have help in keeping them separated or to get Edward off me or Lizzie if his obvious illness caused him to be enraged again.

The real Edward would have given his life for Tony, me and Lizzie, who still wanted to play with him. If ever a loving soul such as Teddy Edward deserved 'a forever home' Edward did, now illness was taking him away – my heart broke as I wondered how much of his illness was the legacy of his cruel persecutor, the drug addict who kicked him in the head and body and threw him about since he was a defenseless puppy. What a terrible, unfair, heartbreaking and tragic hand of cards Edward had been given for this incarnation?

I awoke knowing that we had to say goodbye and send the physical Edward to the spirit realm to be healed and cared for. I

17

sent my prayers out to God, the angels and members of my family in spirit, particularly to my father, Eric, my nana, Eileen-Elizabeth, my granddad Bob and our twins asking them to look after Edward for me.

I took some comfort in the fact that Sioux our sixteen year old matriarchal Jack Russell who had passed to spirit two years and two months earlier who had mothered Edward, taking him under her wing, would do so again. Sensing he had been through a rough time, Sioux washed and cared for Edward, I knew she would look out for him again as a familiar and loving maternal companion. It was tragic he should follow her at the age of ten so soon after her passing.

I remembered how it took Edward a full year before he would use one of the many dog beds around our house. I believe he did not want to offend Sioux as he thought they all belonged to Sioux as they were all in the house before he arrived. Sitting at my computer some years ago now, I put Sioux in a dog-bed that I had placed on my immediate left hand-side and similarly I placed Edward in a dog-bed I had put on my right hand-side, immediately Edward jumped out of it and to support him Sioux jumped out of hers. I had a Jack Russell rebellion on my hands. This happened on a number of occasions until Edward learned he was not offending Sioux by sitting in a comfy dog-bed!

Both Sioux and Jac, our female Jack Russells had each woken me days after they had passed to the spirit realm, thirteen years apart. A few days after her passing, Jac woke me in the night licking my face pressing me with one paw just below my neck. Two months later when I hemorrhaged, losing approximately six units of blood, verifying my earlier predictive sleep state experience of an impending life and death situation, Jac returned to me and lay across my right calf.

I could feel not only the weight and warmth of my female dog Jac's body but also her silky fur. Days later at that time, I was diagnosed with a deep vein thrombosis (DVT) in the calf Jac had deliberately chosen to lay across. When the DVT healed quickly I knew this was the result of the healing Jac had transmitted to me.

Many years later, some days after my female dog Sioux passed to the spirit realms she woke me sitting at my side on the bed in the middle of the night. Wide awake I watched her progressively and astonishingly shrink smaller and smaller apparently disappearing into the wooden skirting board at the foot of the bedroom walls, presumably changing dimension again.

I believe her reduction in size and ultimate disappearance occurred as she returned to the non-physical spirit dimension from which she had come. Incredibly, for some weeks after Sioux's passing I saw a distinct pink haze of energy hovering over her white bed located in front of the fireside in the living room. I am sure she wanted to stay with us and stubbornly refused to leave during this time.

On the Saturday, a few days before Sioux past to the spirit realms on the Tuesday, she walked weakly into the garden bushes which lined our back wall. Partly obscured by the foliage I knelt in front of her, she stared at me with the saddest, knowing eyes, telepathically communicating that this was the end of our journey together. In this heartbreaking and poignant exchange, Sioux's emotionally expressive eyes told me that she and I had fought our hardest with medicines and liquid foods but it was time for me to stop and it was time for her to leave us for the spirit world. This silent conversation was so clear and heartrending. Flooded by tears, I gently picked her up and carried her indoors, placing her in her bed besides the fireside.

Sioux's body virtually collapsed, shutting down during the early hours of Tuesday morning and Sioux passed to spirit in August 2010 around her birthday. A few days later, standing alone in our local park, I suddenly caught sight of a miraculous spectacle in the sky. I was amazed to see each of the fluffy white clouds as far as I could see had become entire, flawless distinct sketches of a multitude of different breeds of dogs, every feature was perfectly defined.

This was not sky gazing in the sense of imagining or searching for something these picture-perfect portraits which manifested simultaneously and ranged across the sky were strikingly evident, unmistakably clear and certainly unmissable. They had caught my attention, not the reverse!

After Jac, Sioux and Edward had passed away I sent each of them my thoughts and prayers asking them to visit me whenever they want and if I don't see them in the awakened state for them to visit me in the sleep state. I have always known that Jac and Sioux and now Edward would be with Alice, the lovely corgi sized Alsatian, I had rescued, named and rehomed who knew Jac and Sioux well.

Returning to Edward, after awaking with the knowledge that Edward was no longer his usual self I got up and telephoned the vet who had suggested we put Edward to sleep almost two weeks ago. On this rainy Saturday, 13 October 2012, Edward was given an injection which made him go into a deep and comfortable sleep then after ten minutes he had another injection which caused him to pass to spirit.

I tried to gently close Edward's eyes and sent my thoughts out to the angels, spirit guides and helpers asking them to care for and accompany Edward. At home, broken hearted I telephoned Gary Cook a highly respected Glasgow medium and his wife Maureen who both kindly said they would come to our house the next day, Sunday.

That Sunday morning I woke up remembering an incident that occurred when on holiday in Cancun, Mexico over four years earlier. Our dogs did not come with us on this particular holiday due to the exceptional distance from Scotland instead they stayed in our home with kindly, professional dog-sitters. Staring into the large pond, crowded with large character fish, situated in our hotel foyer, I had pointed to a fish with a large growth on the side of his head, saying: "I am feeding Edward, I miss him very much." Daily I had fed the many sizeable eccentric looking fish swimming there. Immediately afterwards, I puzzled saying, I should not have called that fish Edward, it should not have reminded me of Edward.

I had long forgotten this event until the day after Edward passed to spirit, realizing that this long disregarded incident was indeed a predictive event offering us further confirmation that Edward like that fish had suffered with a brain tumor. Edward had suffered an enraged fit which was decidedly not in keeping with his typically mellow, quiet and gentlemanly character. I had cuddled him, face to face, thousands of times like a teddy bear for five years and five months. Edward had always been my gentle, loving, obedient boy, who, as a member of our family gave Tony, me, Sioux before her death and Lizzie limitless depths of love. In the days following he had chased and frightened Lizzie, this was definitely not Edward's usual loving nature.

I had collected Edward from the rescue center on Saturday 5 May 2007, the date of my 'dead' Taurean father's birthday. I am honored to have shared my life with him almost 24/7 for five years and five months. The name Teddy Edward spontaneously came to me when I saw him in his cage in the rescue center however, after seeing him I had to wait one week before he could be released to come home with me. For the first couple of weeks I repeatedly found myself calling Edward by my father's name, Eric, my father had passed to spirit some years before.

This fact left me wondering if my father had guided this loving lost soul to us and us to him. Over time I realized his name Teddy Edward fitted him perfectly as whenever I picked Edward up without fail he used to put his arm around my shoulder as countless photographs verify! Thankfully I have many photographs of Edward and my other dogs as these pictures practically immortalize physical events in our lives during our physical time here.

Over the years I believed Edward was most definitely a Pisces, due to his deep emotions his highly sensitive and gentle nature and his immense love of water. He was overjoyed to go swimming and surfing the waves back to shore using his paws alone without a surfboard! In France on various holidays I would stand waist deep in the sea, holding his extending lead attached to his harness whilst his surfing antics brought hilarity and entertainment to a highly amused ever-growing audience on the beach. We swam together in the swimming pool and it was a job to get him out of the water!

Edward had taught me his goally game which we played endlessly in our back garden. He would repeatedly choose to place the tennis ball in a spot and I would kick it. He would act as a hilarious goal-keeper studying which foot I would use and what angle I would choose, yet over and over his clever and agile goal keeping skills stopped the ball! One day, by accident, he ran into the small apple tree, it split in half I planted the broken shoot and

21

it grew, Edward had given us an apple tree! Loyally, at home, my devoted Edward dutifully sat with me whilst I wrote my books. I knew he had been drawn to me, a psychic, psychical researcher and writer of poetry and books on animals and religions, and to my husband, a medical doctor, as each of these are very Piscean attributes.

On the afternoon of Sunday 14th October, the highly reputable Glasgow based medium Gary Cooke with his wife Maureen came to our home. We were extremely fortunate as Gary gave us the most wonderful evidence of Edward having made his transition to spirit. On arrival Gary asked for something of Edwards,' I handed him the last T-shirt Edward had worn, sky blue with a light green edging. It still has tiny splashes of mud on it from Edward's last walk on the wet grass before going into the vets.

Holding Edward's T-shirt, Gary became aware of Edward in spirit barking and sitting on the settee next to me and him. Within a second or two, Lizzie ran over to the spot Edward was occupying, which Tony, my husband, a published scientist, found particularly astonishing and evidential as Lizzie had already excitedly greeted Gary and Maureen and had settled down and gone to sleep next to Tony on the second sofa in the same room several feet away.

Detailed evidence began to pour out of Gary, firstly he told me that Edward now plays with Jake, and that they are now good friends. About five years earlier I had looked after Jake, soon after we had adopted Edward, sadly Jake had attacked Edward and after that I kept Jake separate from Edward for the most part of three weeks. Gary had no way of knowing any of this and Gary was definitely not reading my mind as I did not know that Jake had passed away! It was certainly relevant that Gary told me that they are friends now! Weeks later I had it confirmed Jake had been knocked down by a car and had passed away some months before Edward had made his own transition! This was incredible proof of Edward's continued survival!

Gary told me that he could see my father in the spirit realm taking special care, cuddling and comforting Edward because I had asked him to. Gary told me that my father is accompanied by my father-in-law who had an Alsatian dog. The fact my father was described as cuddling Edward was highly relevant to me as I could not cuddle him during his last couple of weeks due to my fear that he might have another sudden and unexpected enraged fit.

Instead, I regularly told Edward that he was a good boy and stroked and patted him from time to time. I knew over time Edward would be upset about not being cuddled as usual and this state of affairs would mess with his emotions.

At the vets sadly I was too afraid to cuddle Edward instead I fed him some treats and later laid him down on one of our cushions for his injections, in fear if I held him intermittent excruciating pain from his brain tumor might cause him to suffer an aggressive biting fit again. Significantly, I had never met my father-in-law who had long since passed to spirit and he did indeed have an Alsatian dog!

Gary's guide told him that Edward desperately wanted to say: "I am terribly sorry I hurt you, I did not know you at the time, I lashed out as a reaction to pain: I will always be around you and protect you: thank you for loving me: thank you for giving me back my dignity: you will have a second operation which will help you smile again and I will be with you: wear a scarf as I know the cold weather hurts your lip: thank you for giving me so much happiness and fun."

Significantly, my husband and I, and obviously Edward, were the only ones who knew I would be having a second operation next year! Gary told me that Edward made him aware of the pain he suffered around the back of his head, neck and eyes. Telepathically with the help of Gary's spirit guide Edward told Gary that there was a room in our house he did not like and rarely entered because it was darkish like the room his first owner used when he hurt Edward.

Edward continued to communicate, telling us about the bullying drug addict who persecuted Edward. He beat him, kicked his head and body and bounced him off the walls, put drugs in him and teased him with food whilst starving him. Edward communicated that in the past he was paralyzed with fear, terrified that if he ran away and was caught, he may not be able to survive the beating he would be given. However, one day the door was left open and Edward ran and ran, literally for his life, he did not stop running. Gary was correct Edward did have a terrible time before coming to us as an emaciated frightened, sick victim and there was a darkish room in our house he rarely entered!

The suspected aneurysm in Edward's brain could certainly have been the result of damage to Edward's head, caused and set in motion by a kick to the head or throwing him off a wall when he was a puppy when he would have had thinner and more fragile arterial walls within his brain. He may also have been an adult when this terrible, unthinkable, unforgiveable violence occurred to him.

If this was the case then Edward's tyrannical drug addict persecutor, oppressor and jailer had not only traumatized Edward in his formative years but the long, cruel arm of this disgusting bully had reached into Edward's long awaited and long yearned for, happy future with us in his forever home and taken it away by cutting it tragically short! The dye would have been set sealing Edward's cruel fate long before we adopted Edward. It was if this drug addict had acted like a tragic poison that had taken some years to kill Edward, leaving Edward and myself initially clueless and shocked as this was something we least expected in this otherwise happy and healthy dog!

Edward wanted to prove to me that it was Edward communicating and that he is alive and well, consequently Edward offered further proof that it was him. With the help of Gary's spirit guide Edward told Gary my first words to him when we met for the first time when he was newly standing in his cage at the dog rescue center. Edward told Gary, reminding me, that when I looked at Edward's kindly, friendly face and wagging tail I had repeated the words of a song saying: "How much is that doggie in the window?" Gary's accuracy offered further extremely valuable proof that Edward was indeed here communicating with us.

Gary told us he was also hearing; "Give a dog a bone this old man came rolling home." This had great relevance too as Edward certainly loved the vegetarian pig ears and veggie bones I had given him, and by arriving in the heavenly spirit realms, Edward had indeed returned home.

Gary told me Edward wanted to convey to us the words of the song named Amazing Grace. I later looked at a hymn book and noted the words below. This magnificent hymn is most fitting for a wonderful dog who suffered years of fear, cruelty and physical and emotional torture!

AMAZING GRACE

By John Newton English poet and clergyman.

"Amazing Grace! How sweet the sound
That saved a wretch like me!
I once was lost, but now am found;
Was blind, but now, I see.
'Twas grace that taught my heart to fear,
And grace my fears relieved;
How precious did that grace appear?"

Since he was an extremely young, weak and vulnerable puppy, Edward was terrorized, alone, suffering and lost in a cruel world, trapped and imprisoned in a world of fear, violence and hostility by his aggressive, deeply cruel drug addict jailer in this sad house.

Edward and I are indeed thankful that 'Grace/God/guardian angels/spirit guides and helpers' heard the cries and pleas from Edward's heart and soul as he longed to escape to something better, 'grace' led him half-starved, frightened and ill to us, so his view of life would no longer be 'blinded' by the viciousness this drug addict inflicted on him. Edward was indeed 'found' and able to 'see' that the world can be a happy place as he progressively became a precious, cheerful and contented member of our family.

We gave him a new life of joy the happiest and best years of his life yet tragically in his 'forever home' his tender life was prematurely cut short at the youthful age of 10. Once 'found' by us, Edward has again been 'found' by our shared spirit family, who are indeed his family in the realms of spirit, never to be lost, sad, afraid and alone again.

Gary told me Edward wished to thank me for adding a poem to my book for Edward, only I knew that I had done this and obviously Edward did too! Gary added that Edward informed him that I was having a new coat made for Edward and that he had tried it on recently but not received it yet and that he is going to get that new coat in the spirit realms! I was indeed having two new coats made out of strong Kevlar material to protect both him and Lizzie from potential attacks from aggressive dogs! Again this was wonderful evidence that Edward was indeed talking to me telepathically through Gary.

I became aware that drugs and drink are indeed the negative, destructive side of Pisces, disastrously encountered by Edward in his earliest years of his most recent incarnation. This was all because someone was utterly careless with Edward's life! They gave this tiny, trusting, vulnerable, cute, playful and very handsome puppy to a violent drug addict who gave him starvation, sadness, pain, misery, suffering, abuse, torture and incarceration.

Gary reminded us that we were granted the gift of soothing, comforting and saying goodbye to Edward when he made his transition to the spirit realms and not everyone has this physical opportunity to say goodbye. Gary told us that poor brave Edward had concealed his pain for some time and his poor little body could not take any more and that he would have soon entered a stage of rapid decline and suffering, from which we had spared him.

Gary told me that Lizzie and another dog who would join our family in the future would both regularly see Edward's spirit body and that Lizzie is indeed grieving along with us, as she misses Edward so much she needs to be kept close, supported and reassured and that the new addition to the family would comfort her greatly.

I was reminded of a medium in Paignton Spiritualist Church in Devon, UK, who I saw more than two decades ago, a woman I have never seen before or since who told me she could see a brown and white Jack Russell sitting at my feet and every time I cried my dog cried and that I thought it was disloyal to get another dog yet it is my duty to because I can give another dog a loving home- she informed me that she was being told that my dog had an unusual name yet she could hear the popular name of Jack- I explained to her later that she my dog was a girl called Jac because my name is Jackie which is an unusual name!

Ever since that day I have accepted that it is indeed my duty, everyone's duty to offer a safe, healthy and loving home to another dog or pet whenever I and they have the space, time and money to do so. When animals, these emotional innocent trusting babes arrive in this physical world they are so alone making them incredibly and dangerously vulnerable to all manner of harm. Our love for each additional animal family member is a separate, concrete and permanent thing and does not detract from the love of any other pet.

Gary told me he could hear a name sounding like 'JES' - I wondered if he was spelling the names of my dogs in spirit Jac, Edward and Sioux or Jazza, Tony's father's Alsatian, who I never met. Gary added that Edward is also with a dog I hand fed. Wonderfully this would be Sioux, I nursed with a pipette, regularly squirting drops of liquid food, electrolytes and water onto her tongue for some weeks due to the return of her cancer before her legs were too weak to walk and I took her to the vet where she passed peacefully to the spirit realms.

Gary told me we would see and hear Edward and even smell Edward's scent. I told him I had already glimpsed Edward in the kitchen and heard his bark in the house that very Sunday morning. Gary told me Edward again wished to confirm it was him communicating with me by informing Gary that he, Edward, had travelled on a long train journey with us. Indeed, again this evidence was correct, Edward and Lizzie had travelled with Tony and I overnight in a sleeper cabin from Nice to Paris, whilst our car was simultaneously transported on another train, wearily we were all returning home from Italy!

At this point Gary said Edward had moved to sit by our fireside. Gary told me both our two-year old Lizzie and our next dog will grow old naturally. He said the newcomer will have a lot of black in his coat, will be sweet, crafty, cute and clever and that he will be a chewer with lovely eyes who will sense the love in the home and settle in well as that is his nature. Gary said he will have a purple colored blanket and he said he will be very protective and will certainly see Edward perhaps even more so than Lizzie. All of this has proved to be accurate.

Gary told me Edward will be on our bed many a night but we will not always be aware of him. Gary also told me that Edward was aware that I was planning to and would put a photograph of Edward on my computer screen saver and that my father tells me to stop looking at Edward's photographs on the wall as they make me sad and that Edward is a little angel who will always be there for us and my father will always take special care of him for me.

I have sensed Edward in the bedroom however I believe my strong pain killers induced in me a deep, drugged sleep which would have dulled my awareness of Edward's presence. Some weeks after Edward passed to spirit, whilst alone, awake but still in bed, with Lizzie our dog at the side of me in bed the bedside touch lamp lit up of its own accord. This was the morning of Thursday 8 November, the day before I travelled to collect a parson's puppy who would soon join our family. I touched the lamp and it went off. Repeatedly six or seven times the lamp came on of its own accord and I touched it to put it off.

Speaking with Gary on the telephone, he informed me my father, accompanied by Edward, put the light on offering me 100% proof that he and Edward are alive, well and very pleased I am now getting on with my life by giving a new dog a home. They both wanted to show me they are frequently around me. Gary added you took Lizzie a walk today and you had something of Edward's with you and Edward came with you!

He was correct my husband had taken Edward's extending lead instead of Lizzie's by accident! On my birthday on Saturday 15th December 2012 the same thing happened however this time my husband was in the bedroom and I pointed to it saying did you see this I am glad I have a witness this time!

When Gary and Maureen heard my account of my experience with the fish with the brain tumor in Mexico they agreed it was indeed a predictive event. Maureen found it most significant that Edward had been symbolized by a fish in view of the fact that I believed Edward to be a Pisces, an astrological sign symbolized by a fish.

At the age of eight I had dreamt I was the only person at my father's funeral, forty years later the event played out exactly as it did in my childhood dream. I have had many predictive, psychic and mediumistic experiences throughout my life.

Interestingly, a lady named Isobel came to visit me, she had never met Edward nor had she ever visited our home before, she told me she had mentioned to a neighbor, a medium I do not know, (who keeps her mediumship private amongst a few of her friends only), that she was visiting a friend, myself, whose dear dog had passed to the spirit realms.

Incredibly, her neighbor instantly replied to Isobel saying he has a black, tan and white face and white body, he has a lovely nature, he worshipped her and never meant to hurt her and he tried to say sorry when he was here! Isobel added this medium was emphatic that when I picked Edward up he was floored by an absolutely shattering and unbearable piercing noise which overtook his whole being and caused him to lash out biting in agony.

This medium added Edward is happy now and out of the increasing pain he has been enduring for some time and that she will have personal experiences of him. Significantly, this mediumistic woman spontaneously gave further conclusive proof of Edward's brain tumor and continued survival. Edward's handshake after his fit was indeed Edward's way of saying sorry!

Edward came into our lives in one week and left within two weeks, he came in the spring and left in the winter, he came on my father's birthday and left on my sister's birthday, he passed to the spirit realm in October the same month as my father who passed some years ago. He brought endless love and laughter and taught me so much about his intelligence, emotions, sensitivities, thought-processes and feelings, this little soul possessed gigantic limitless love.

Gary said that our adoption of Edward was no coincidence. Personally I feel the pleas and cries from Edward's heart and soul were felt by those compassionate angels and spirits in the non-physical dimension and step by step this abandoned soul was guided home to us.

However, I will go to heaven asking why our dearest Edward could not stay with us in his 'loving forever home' for more than five years and five months, naturally we wanted to share our physical lives with him for many more years, especially when Jack Russells usually live to 16-18-20 years old. I would have nursed him when he became a senior citizen, my little old man, as I had done with Jac and Sioux. However, I do know that the love we bear for him and his for us is eternal. As mentioned before, for me and many others, losing an adopted animal soul is the same as losing a child, thankfully there is so much proof that all beings make their transitions to the spirit realm at physical death.

Entering the many levels of Heaven I would ask: Is Edward to reincarnate soon? Throughout my life with Edward I frequently clearly saw an ancient Egyptian pharaonic headdress around Edward's most regal, handsome, princely dignified face, was he therefore a very old soul and what was the purpose of his most recent incarnation?

Edward has now taught me to have a deep love for the poignancy of the song Amazing Grace, which, since Edward's communications through Gary, will forever have a profound meaning for me now. Edward was/is humorously called "Teddy Edward" as he loved cuddling always putting his arm across my shoulder: "Edward Long-Shanks" because as a parsons Russell he possessed longer legs than Jack Russells: "Edward the Couch Potato" who loved to stretch out laying on the sofa watching TV: "Edward Scissor-Hands" as he pawed my leg asking to go to the toilet or gently licked our ears to wake us up and "Edward McSquirter" when he emptied his 'water-pistol' in the garden.

Isobel kindly uttered the following words for Edward, so relevant for all those who inevitably physically lose their adopted pet children:

A little flower,
Lent not given,
To bud on earth,
And bloom in heaven.

I know we gave Edward the happiest years of his life - he was as large as life, he loved playing football and his own invented goalie game which he taught us - he was ill for only one day in five years five months after walking amongst swan excrement, he was typically full of energy and never ill. He walked with such regal dignity around hotels in Italy, France and Spain and hilariously entertained everyone when he swam in the warm seas and swimming pools in Europe and most of all he was given lots of love which helped to heal the unforgiveable earlier emotional and physical wounds he endured in his first physical years in this earthly incarnation.

Many people say that time heals but for me I believe that time buries grief like a bandage over a gaping, spliced and fractured wound, a puncture as deep as any beings soul. For me, true healing is having evidence that Edward including my other dogs Jac and Sioux and other family members are alive and well that he and they continue to live and survive each day as I do, that he and they are happy and you and I can look forward to countless happy reunions when it is our time to make our transitions to the non-physical spirit realms.

I know that throughout my physical life I will see glimpses of them around me and I will meet and communicate with them during my sleep state proving they visit frequently and I will be aware of thoughts being dropped into my mind – for me such experiences are jewels far better than a lottery win – all of this will be crowned with reunions with all of my dogs including Edward, Sioux and Jac and other beloved relatives when I, like them, return home to the spirit realms.

In my opinion time buries grief including the fractured emotions beneath it – I believe the best healing and comfort is through personal evidence gained ourselves from personal mediumistic experiences and the evidence gained from other mediums proving that they have merely emigrated to other shores. Surely this alone gives true sustenance, nourishment and healing for the heart and soul helping each of us to carry on each day in the knowledge that they are too!

I have a feeling that Edward will be asked if he would like to meet in the spirit realms the inexcusable drug addict who viciously wounded him on all levels as inevitably that is where this angry sadist's addiction will lead him. Knowing generous-hearted Edward as I do, he would forgive him and have nothing more to do with him, which is something I cannot do.

It breaks my heart pondering whether it was this man's violent legacy that stretched out reaching into Edward's happy 'forever home' prematurely ending Edward's newly found happiness as our family member by drastically shortening his life. I asked the mediumistic friends who telephoned as a matter of course after Edward's passing, what they felt?

They each live miles away from us and had not been told of his heart-breaking transition. Each confirmed, unknown to each other, if Edward had physically stayed with us, he would have had an attack of pain again causing him to lash out and his health was about to deteriorate badly. Thankfully we saved him this pain and prevented him doing anything to Lizzie which he would have regretted, though could not be blamed for as the enraged Edward was certainly not him but the result of his illness.

The following two poems are dedicated to Edward and our dogs and all beloved pets. These are followed by the introduction to this serialized research.

WILL YOU BE THE VOICE FOR THE VOICELESS:
THEY ASK 'HOW CAN I MAKE YOU LOVE ME?'

By Jackie Jones-Hunt PhD

Dedicated to our Jack Russell & Parson Russell family honoring our eternal, steadfast reciprocal devotion: Jac, Sioux, Edward, Lizzie, Eric, Charlie Brown, Jack and Bob.

Will you be the voice for the voiceless?
Whose innocent cries go unheard.
Human hearts are sealed up shut,
Bolted, cold and uncaring;
Callous indifference reigns over animals' blood stained sorrow.
How is it, human animals don't see their suffering?
How is it, we don't hear their cries, and goodbyes to each other?
Cos money has them hidden away in countryside slaughterhouses and laboratories,
Hidden away from prying eyes!

These vulnerables live in entirety,
In pitch dark, noisy, overcrowded hell-houses,
They die in slaughterhouses, knee deep in blood and guts,
In laboratories, monkeys pale and thin, with bolted skulls,
Their crippled bodies, tortured eyes and tormented faces have much to tell,
But no-one listens,
Cos there are no windows,
And doors and cages are locked shut,
That is why no-one can look!
What have we become?

Defenseless animals knowingly go to their deaths,
Death quenches their desperate thirst for their suffering to stop like welcome water,
Helpless, they ask for little, they can take no more,
All these tragic victims reach death slowly, piece by piece,
Until they grasp him like a welcome friend,
Born beautiful as all are God's children,
Mutilated by 'humanity,' their bodies and souls are broken,
Conveyor belts of murder, machines don't stop,
When terrorized screams and agonized cries for MERCY
Saturate the blood drenched air,
As parts of their loved ones leak out onto the floor,

Oblivious human animals dress their relatives' once desperate and helpless, butchered bodies,
And traumatized souls on their dinner plates,
With fancy sauces and recipe names,
EATING THEIR SUFFERING,
Dying themselves of cancers, and cholesterol induced strokes and heart disease,
Karmically caused by eating animal flesh?
Therefore, what change will you make?
WILL YOU BE THE VOICE FOR THE VOICELESS?
There, but for the grace of God, go I.

IF TOMORROW STARTS WITHOUT ME

If tomorrow should start without me and I'm not there to see,
If the sun should rise and find your eyes all filled with tears for me;
I wish so much you wouldn't cry the way you did today,
While thinking of the many things we didn't get to say.
I know how much you care for me, and how much I care for you,
And each time that you think of me, and how much I care for you,
And each time that you think of me I know you'll miss me too;
But when tomorrow starts without me, please try to understand,
That an angel came and called my name and took me (by the hand),
And said my place was ready in heaven far above,
And that I'd have to leave behind all those I dearly love.
But as I turned to walk away, a tear fell from my eye,
For all my life, I'd always thought I didn't want to die.
I had so much to live for and so much yet to do.
It almost seemed impossible that I was leaving you.
I thought of all the love we shared and all the fun we had.
Of all the times I spent with you, whether good or bad
If I could relive yesterday, I thought just for a while,
I'd say goodbye and cuddle into you and maybe see you smile.
But then I fully realized that this could never be,
For emptiness and memories would take the place of me.
And when I thought of worldly things that I'd miss come tomorrow.
I thought of you, and when I did, my heart was filled with sorrow.
But when I walked through Heaven's gates, I felt so much at home.
When God looked down and smiled at me, from God's great golden throne,
God said, "This is eternity and all I've promised you,
Today your life on earth is past but here it starts anew.
I promise no tomorrow, but today will always last.
And since each day's the same, there's no longing for the past.
But you have been so faithful, so trusting and so true.

Though there were times you did some things you knew you
shouldn't do.
And you have been forgiven and now at last you're free.
So won't you come and take my hand and share my life with me?"
So if tomorrow starts without me, don't think we're far apart,
For every time you think of me please know I'm in your heart.

ANONYMOUS

Quoted as a Sonnet to ALL animals and pets who have
passed to spirit and especially for my forever loved, constant,
trusty companion, "TEDDY EDWARD," our loving, gentle
Parson Russell hero who passed to spirit on Saturday 13th October
2012.

Giving so much faithful love and devotion and endless
laughter, dutifully as my companion, he sat with me during the
long hours of writing this volume.

Edward's first years of immense horror and suffering at
the hands of an evil, angry, Renfrew drug addict who starved, beat
and regularly kicked him like a football, tragically curtailed his
life-span, impacting and limiting his years with us in his 'forever
home.'

I thank God the angels helped our terrorized, lost, wee
hero to run away from his violent imprisonment, bringing him to
us, to join our family forever.

CHAPTER TWO – INTRODUCING THE ANIMAL SOULS RESEARCH

I am the good shepherd. The good shepherd lays down his life for his sheep. (Jesus' statement quoted in the Gospel of John 10:11)

Are not five sparrows sold for two pennies? And not one of them is forgotten before God. (Luke 12:6)

For that which befalleth the sons of men befallest beasts … As one dieth, so dieth the other. Yet they have all one breath… a man hath no pre-eminence over a beast. (Ecclesiastes 3:19)

A righteous man has regard for the life of his beast. (Proverbs 12.10)

He that killeth an ox is as if he slew a man; He that sacrificeth a lamb, as if he broke a dog's neck. (Isaiah 66:3)

The facts of Jesus' Vegetarianism

Jesus did not eat animal flesh yet ironically many people today would consider this revelation an astonishing discovery. This is a catastrophic and heartrending indictment on a large proportion of humanity through no fault of its own, many of whom erroneously believed they followed Jesus' authentic example.

Throughout incalculable generations most Christians have unquestionably believed the flawed information that they were indoctrinated with as children. This misrepresentation of Jesus' teachings which occurred at an early date in Christian history has been passed on almost endlessly to countless children's children; a calamitous error being redressed today.

Knowledge regarding the facts of Jesus' vegetarianism has long since been lost, unsurprisingly due to the opposition Jesus himself regularly experienced and contested. On-going after his death, Jesus' disciples, now known as the apostles, endured the same hostility, persecution and misrepresentation. Finally, the leadership of the first followers of Jesus, the first converts to the Jerusalem church, namely the Jewish–Christians, was wrested from the apostles, ultimately resulting in the original version of Jesus' ethically advanced spiritual teachings, expressed through and embodied in, vegetarianism, being silenced and progressively lost for posterity.

The fundamental and central principle, the very foundation stone of Jesus' all-inclusive, loving ministry as the Good Shepherd, excluded no socially rejected, denigrated, depreciated, devalued, neglected or exploited animal, human or non-human. Jesus' all-inclusive, limitless compassion was extended to the disparaged prostitute, to the hated tax collectors and despised Samaritans and was most clearly demonstrated by Jesus' specifically chosen, public liberation of the innocent, defenseless, frail animals in the temple.

Terrorized, these harmless, child-like, emotional babes awaited the start of the forthcoming, relentless sacrificial bloodbath and butchery in the temple, after which these helpless, sentient, aware, flesh and blood infants would be eaten.

Jesus' Liberation of the Animals

Notably, scholars are universally agreed that it was Jesus' deliberate, prearranged, rebellious and compassionate public animal liberation spectacle in the temple that provoked the temple authorities to demand his crucifixion. Jesus' empathetic and revolutionary statement, freeing the naive, powerless, inoffensive animals, clearly denounced, opposed and countered the temple authorities, who encouraged, sanctioned and profited from the temple slaughterhouse.

Notably, Jesus predicted his own forthcoming death obviously the Good-Shepherd was well aware that his premeditated, outrageously rebellious, passionately brave and kind-hearted demonstration would not be tolerated by the temple authorities, and their outrage would inevitably lead to Jesus' execution.

The wide-ranging research of Animal Souls has been split into a series of sizeable books which will cumulatively evidence and elaborate on all the points raised in this introduction. Later pages will also discuss the opposition, suppression and destruction of original scriptural writings, some by means of repeated deliberate mistranslations of ancient texts which originally told humankind that all animals, human and non-human are 'living souls.'

During this latter part of this series, research is set out evidencing the true and original vegetarian teachings of Jesus, graphically illustrating his all-embracing love for all animals. Significantly, each reader will then be in a position to mentally contrast Jesus' authentic vegetarian doctrines with the regulated, systematized, dogmatic and censored teachings of the institutionalized church.

Jesus courageously and dutifully fulfilled his all-encompassing, compassionate earthly mission, never more clearly demonstrated than by his very public liberation of the animals; an act he knew would lead to his own death. Mathew 26:39b records Jesus as praying: "My Father, if it is possible, may this cup be taken from me. Yet not as I will, but as you will." Aware that God wished him to accomplish his "mission," wholeheartedly accepting this "cup," dedicating himself to the implementation of God's will, as the only way forward.

The cruelly misled populace bought animals to be sacrificially murdered extensively and indiscriminately in the temple with the incongruous and bizarre belief that these evil, murderous acts, killing trusting, emotional infants, would absolve them of their sins!

The temple authorities propagated this murderous money-spinning myth, potentially profiting three-fold from this extra income. They were closely associated with the receipt of abundant and highly profitable payments for selling animals to be killed and they profited by their consumption of the animal flesh as free food afterwards.

Notably, animal sacrifice inevitably led to the consumption of the animals' flesh afterwards. Consequently, callously, many used the abhorrent and condemned practice of animal sacrifice as an excuse to eat animals. Thus, the sacrificial killing of animals, followed by the consumption of their burnt flesh was fundamentally and irrevocably an intertwined process.

Significantly, the cruel and murderous sacrificial animal atrocity interlaced with eating animal flesh was vehemently and relentlessly denounced by the 7th and 8th century BC prophets who will be discussed in detail later. Notably, Mathew 5:17, records Jesus teaching in the Sermon on the Mount, that he had not come to abolish the law and the teachings of the prophets but to fulfill them.

Indeed, this would include his revivification, breathing life back into the ignored and forgotten condemnations of animal cruelty of his prophetic predecessors, thereby 'fulfilling' the commands transmitted to them from God, ending animal sacrifice, a practice interwoven with the consumption of the animals' flesh afterwards. Notably, Jesus also fulfilled God's first and foremost priority commands to humanity, charging them to live a vegetarian lifestyle, set out in Genesis, the first book of the bible, including Genesis 1:29-31, 2:16 and 3:18.

The Lucrative Temple Slaughter-House

For many centuries the temple had increasingly fallen under the control of the greedy religio-political authorities, reducing these domains to little more than an enormous profit-making slaughterhouse regularly awash with the blood of traumatized emotional babes, the animals. They smelt death and worse still horrified they watched and stood in each other's blood and guts.

Importantly, rescuing and freeing the vulnerable, abandoned and panic-stricken animals, Jesus taught his followers to respect and copy his all-encompassing, compassionate example, opening their hearts to inevitably include all fellow sentient beings. All of whom are made of flesh and blood, they are emotional, aware, demonstrating thought processes and memory, they are responsive and breathing, and importantly they feel anxiety and fear pain, homicide and massacre.

It is important to become sensitive to the fact that whatever any beings intelligence level in the case of lower life forms each would certainly feel discomfort, pain, suffering and murder. As stated, scholars universally accept that Jesus' deliberate staging of this very public liberation spectacle, rebuking the cruel and avaricious, money-making temple authorities, affronted and infuriated them, triggering their determination, to have Jesus' challenging animal emancipation silenced through crucifixion.

It will be proven in later pages in this series that the distortion and later suppression of Jesus' authentic and accurate, all-embracing, compassionate vegetarian spiritual teachings occurred when Christianity was in its infancy, progressively becoming lost to future generations of Christians, reflected in the ignorance and utter obliviousness of countless Christians throughout the ages, until today.

It is an endless, heartbreaking tragedy for the animals and Jesus alike that Jesus' lifelong, boundless, loving mission, perpetuating the most ethically elevated spirituality embodied in vegetarianism became a little known truth to countless future followers who each considered himself/herself to be devout and dedicated Christians, both historically and in the world in which we live today. It is tragic for Jesus who died demonstrating his all-embracing lofty vegetarian spiritual mission to his followers, yet his compassionate vegetarianism subsequently became suppressed, distorted, lost and ignored.

Hidden Ancient Texts Prove our Ignorance

Significantly, Muhammad, the prophetic founder of Islam in the 7th century AD was emphatic that as Christianity spread throughout the Roman Empire in its formative state in the early years, those populations enticed to convert to Christianity were misinformed and thereby manipulated by religio-political authorities, through the suppression and distortion of some of Jesus' less popular, genuine and fundamental teachings. This was certainly the case with the silencing, censorship and negation of Jesus' vegetarianism.

This truth is further substantiated by the precious 20th century archaeological discoveries spotlighting Christianity's troubled past. These revolutionary excavations unearthed many original, ancient, hitherto unknown and lost scriptures, hidden to safeguard them for future generations by spiritual communities, who sought to protect them from destruction by the increasingly powerful Orthodox Church. These deliberately concealed ancient spiritual writings and gospels are known as the Dead Sea Scrolls and the ancient library of Nag Hammadi.

Due to the increasingly controlling influence of the leaders of the organized church, many invaluable writings were destroyed, suppressed and prohibited from entering the biblical canon where they would have been preserved, enlightening successive generations of Christians for all time. Other ancient writings were edited and distorted prior to inclusion in the biblical canon. This historic fact is graphically evidenced by the discoveries made at the two above named archaeological sites at which hitherto missing and wholly unknown ancient writings have been excavated.

Archaeologists Unearth Ancient Dead Sea Scrolls

Clarifying the importance of the Dead Sea Scrolls (dated to 250 BC - 100 AD), discovered 1947-1956, in eleven caves in the Khirbet Qumran area of the Judean desert I write in my earlier book, Moses and Jesus: the Shamans:

"These invaluable documents have been dated to the intertestamental period (250 BC -100 AD). The textual formation of the Old Testament had been carried out by this time. However, Christianity and rabbinical Judaism had not yet been standardized…The scrolls, written by the hands of hundreds of scribes reveal the heated debates between competing Jewish-Christian sects.

These diverse ancient religious Hebrew scrolls express differing perspectives and interpretations, each of which competed to monopolize the opinions of future generations. Importantly, they provide us with a window into the past when Christianity was enduring its gestation period. The scrolls also enrich our understanding of early Christian debates regarding the decisions to establish Jesus as both 'the Messiah' and 'the Divine.'

They take us to a time which clearly reveals the human element in the interpretation of religion and the human choices of what was acceptable regarding the teachings of long dead prophets. The debates and decisions taken…crystallized the form that Christianity would take for posterity. The future generations who were not privy to these discussions might not have accepted the dogmas systematized by religio-political church leaders at that time [and later, and] may not have adhered to the unquestioning [dogmas] that [were] subsequently born." *1*

Archaeologists Discover Ancient Nag Hammadi Library

The Nag Hammadi library (200-300 AD) represents a second unique and irreplaceable, archaeological discovery, which yet again vividly illustrates the increasingly powerful Orthodox

Churches' historic attempts to destroy ancient religious texts. Fortunately, its desperate custodians successfully concealed this ancient archive, avoiding its utter obliteration.

Unearthed in 1945 by a Bedouin, this matchless collection consists of thirteen brown, leather-bound volumes or codices. These texts, written on papyrus and sealed for posterity in a red, earthenware jar were found beside an ancient grave in the Egyptian village named Nag Hammadi.

It is believed that in 390 AD, monks from the historic, nearby monastery named St. Pachomius, buried these manuscripts, preserving their contents from destruction for the edification of future generations. These 55 ancient volumes consist of lost and unseen early sacred Christian scriptures including gospels penned by early Gnostic Christians.

In Moses and Jesus: the Shamans, I underline the incredible importance of these recently unveiled ancient religious texts, explaining that some of these hunted down writings actually provided the original source material for the books accepted for inclusion into the bible at a later date, however to gain this favor they were reworked, edited and distorted in accordance with the decisions and articles of faith decreed by dominating religio-political leadership:

"The Coptic Gospel of Thomas was found among these concealed manuscripts. This Gospel is considered to be older than the four canonical Gospels of Mathew, Mark, Luke and John (those included in the Bible). Importantly, it is thought that the Gospel of Thomas actually provided the source material for the Gospels of Mathew and Luke. Despite this fact the Gospel of Thomas was obviously condemned and sought after by the greater church, with the intention of destroying it." *2*

Thomas, the Twin Brother of Jesus

Astonishingly, spotlighting huge gaps in modern day knowledge, an ancient writer discovered at Nag Hammadi introduces his accounts by casually informing us that he is Thomas the twin brother of Jesus. This dispassionate, nonchalant, unconcerned passing statement was obviously of secondary importance to Thomas whose main concern is to document his record of some of Jesus' teachings for posterity.

Significantly, Thomas, heralded as the twin brother of Jesus, in the ancient writings unearthed at Nag Hammadi, provides us with 114 hitherto unknown 'secret' sayings of Jesus regarding life after death. Incredibly, there is a remarkably important sense of truth about it, whilst we should remember twins are rarely identical.

Thomas himself tells us that Jesus schooled his growing numbers of devoted followers to learn by his example and to therefore strive daily to become like him. Historically, the leaders of the increasingly formidable institutionalized church would have sought to quash and destroy all texts referring to the twin brother of Jesus, his other brothers and sisters, his parents, probable spouse and inevitable children and Jesus' plea that his pious converts copy his example in all that they do, increasingly becoming like him.

The ever more powerful, daunting, intimidating and controlling orthodox leadership believed that all texts that made reference to topics that they had decreed as prohibited, unmentionable and taboo would undermine their premeditated, consciously invented status and diluted mission of Jesus.

Orthodoxy had dogmatically bequeathed Jesus to have a unique and preeminent status as the son of God, born of a virgin birth including the perpetual virginity of Mary. Creating and emphasizing Jesus' primacy they dramatically distanced Jesus from his followers and the public alike, doing Jesus and his spiritual mission a tragic disservice. Increasingly no-one believed they could be like Jesus and over time many Christians stopped trying, the corollary of which they paid ever less interest in Jesus' authentic and entire message!

Having intransigently attributed to Jesus, preeminence, a practically divine status, the greater church feared Jesus' divinity would be undermined if his later followers learned that he was a physical man with a physical family including of all things, a twin brother, no matter how fundamentally spiritually elevated and devout both Jesus and his supportive family were, clearly and further illustrated and expressed through their compassionate vegetarianism, all of which will be evidenced in later pages.

Powerful, religio-political, decision-making individuals cumulatively created orthodox opinion, consisting of unquestioned dogmas and rigid decrees set as articles of faith, including that Jesus was born of a virgin mother. Due to its tragically flawed interpretation of Jesus, orthodoxy was bent on suppressing multitudes of religious texts detailing Jesus' authentic and entire teachings because they inadvertently illustrated Jesus' humanity and referred in passing to his familial status in contrast to his divinity, attributed to him by orthodoxy.

Tragically, orthodoxy chose to have Jesus worshipped, instead of adhering to Jesus' message in its totality. Jesus' entire message was often unpopular and inconvenient for less spiritually orientated individuals, epitomized by obeying Jesus' all-inclusive, non-violent, peace-loving, all-embracing, compassionate vegetarian doctrines as Jesus had commanded. To worship Jesus, naive followers were forced to turn to orthodoxy to be tutored in orthodox dogmas.

In turn, this raised the status, authority and power of the religio-political orthodox leaders. By worshipping Jesus as the figure head orthodoxy had created, in turn, Jesus' vulnerable followers came to worship human decision makers, interpreters of Jesus' teachings, in Jesus' stead. Increasingly, over the years, these ever more wealthy, powerful leaders replaced and in effect stood in for Jesus who, in sharp contrast taught his followers not to be materialistic and to live the simple, compassionate, vegetarian life!

Disastrously, spiritually inferior, self-appointed human articles of faith were to be increasingly and dogmatically upheld. Tragically, orthodoxy destroyed ancient religious texts and had others edited and re-worked to reflect their own approved dogmas of belief. It was these alone that they included in the biblical canon. Later pages will clearly set out the all-pervading evidence for Jesus' vegetarianism.

Orthodoxy Discarded Jesus' Vegetarian Family

Orthodoxy paid henchmen to stalk, track down and destroy many ancient and original religious texts pertaining to Jesus and his authentic teachings as briefly clarified above. Silencing and deleting inconvenient, unpopular, unprofitable aspects of Jesus' original, genuine, spiritually elevated, all-embracing, compassionate vegetarian doctrine will be shown to have become a notable and tragic casualty of this censorship.

Notably, by deleting Jesus' family from history, orthodoxy also erased the fact of their lifelong vegetarianism from history. Deliberately and relentlessly, they concealed information about Jesus' vegetarian family, including the fact that this eminent spiritual teacher asked his highly respected brother James, a known vegetarian since birth, to lead, after his crucifixion, the infant Jewish-Christian church, from James' long term home in Jerusalem.

Jesus' brother, known as James the Just, as research proves was a former disciple and as such an apostle. James led the early church from Jerusalem for thirty years until his own death which was the result of the machinations of a high priest related to the high priest who sought Jesus' execution! This fact alone graphically illustrates the on-going oppression and hostility faced by the apostles attempting to faithfully transmit Jesus' entire and genuine ministry after Jesus' death.

By wielding Jesus as orthodoxy's exalted and divine banner, they in turn, gained recognition, influence and power, increasingly utilizing their religio-political leadership of the growing Orthodox Church for their own ends. Knowledge about Jesus' brothers, sisters and remaining family members obviously challenged the dogmas orthodoxy ascribed to both Mary and Jesus, including their dictatorial doctrine of the 'perpetual' virginity of Mary and practical divinity of Jesus.

Hopefully, it is becoming increasingly clear why ancient, sacred writings containing historically accurate details about Jesus' brother, James' thirty year vegetarian leadership of the early church were condemned, destroyed and excluded from most biblical records by the hands of orthodoxy. Notably, James, a

47

vegetarian since birth, faithfully perpetuated the vegetarian teachings of his brother, Jesus. Such historical truths regarding Jesus' spiritually elevated vegetarian doctrines continued by Jesus' brother, corroborated by highly reputable, early and contemporaneous writers were unwelcome, rejected and discarded by the increasingly Orthodox Church.

Continued Persecution of Jesus' Disciples/Apostles

After Jesus' crucifixion, from the outset of their apostleship, the first followers of Jesus continued to live in persecuted, oppressed and highly troubled times. Consequently, ancient scrolls containing the vegetarian truths of Jesus' ministry and familial details would have been destroyed whilst others were hidden by their custodians attempting to safeguard them for posterity, to educate future generations of less-indoctrinated, less-shackled individuals, some of which have now been excavated.

Due to the fact that Jesus' and James' vegetarianism has been calculatingly cut out of history and hidden from us for the most part of two thousand years, arguably people throughout the ages have not lived in informed, religiously liberated epochs, however, this censorship is currently being changed.

Bizarrely, even today we have people believing themselves to be Christians, yet incompatibly, they are not following Jesus' authentic command of vegetarianism. Vegetarianism was of paramount importance, being central to Jesus' all-inclusive, compassionate mission, perpetuated by Jesus' brother James, chosen by Jesus to lead the first Christians, the Jewish-Christians of Jerusalem.

With reference to Thomas' writings unearthed at Nag Hammadi, which combined statements about 'the man,' Jesus and his family life with accounts of some of Jesus' previously unknown original teachings, all writings such as these once discovered were condemned as heretical as they challenged the Orthodox Church's dogmas regarding Jesus' preeminence and divinity.

48

Similarly, as the result of orthodoxy's machinations, cruel fate branded the first generations of faithful vegetarian followers of Jesus as heretics as they followed the vegetarian man Jesus and his vegetarian family, daily complementing Jesus, the esteemed spiritual teacher, by striving to be like him and by following his example in all matters! It has been shown that Jesus' authentic teachings, including the fact he was part of a human family, fatefully undermined the greater churches' above man-made dogmatic creeds, consequently many original texts were destroyed, reworked, edited, distorted, lost and hidden.

Paul Branded Jesus a Sacrificial Victim

Generated by Paul's man-made, personally crafted brand of Christianity, Paul who had never met the man Jesus, let alone study under his tutelage, declared Jesus to be a necessary sacrificial victim whose murder enabled others to receive the keys to Heaven.

Significantly, as a result of Paul's sacrificial doctrine every time an animal was killed and eaten it was equated with a necessary sacrificial victim, powerfully legitimizing the eating of animal flesh, in total contravention of Jesus' reliably accurate vegetarian teachings. The vegetarian apostles' aversion and hatred of Paul for overturning and distorting Jesus' vegetarianism will be discussed in later pages.

Orthodoxy sanctioned for posterity popular and enticing Pauline theology which differed at times dramatically to the original teachings of Jesus, most notably in Paul's dilution, quashing and suppression of Jesus' vegetarianism. Significantly, orthodoxy endorsed, thereby perpetuating for posterity, Paul's doctrine describing Jesus as the sacrificial Lamb of God. This concept alone contravened the teachings of the 7th and 8th century prophets supported and fulfilled by Jesus who, likewise condemned animal sacrifice and the eating of their flesh afterwards, re-affirmed by Jesus in his Sermon on the Mount.

Jesus did not die to enable others to go to the labyrinthine hierarchical realms of heaven, all beings undertake a natural transition at death to the non-physical realms as energy cannot be destroyed it merely transmutes in form, a fact of life for all beings.

Furthermore, it will be shown that Jesus did not die as a sacrificial victim, Paul was a highly educated man, who subtly altered, distorted and reinterpreted Jesus' heroic, defiant, compassionate, animal liberation message, turning it on its head, using his own version and interpretation of this event Paul sanctioned animal sacrifice rather than the reverse!

Instead, Jesus bravely, courageously and knowingly, laid down his life for the animals, demonstrating the highest virtue one soul, human animal or non-human animal, can give to another. Jesus was aware that the temple authorities who endorsed this most profitable animal slaughter and the eating of their flesh afterwards would not rest until he had been executed for challenging them in the same vein as his 7th and 8th century prophetic predecessors.

Indeed, Jesus fulfilled his compassionate convictions regarding animals recorded in the Gospel of John 10:11: I am the good shepherd. The good shepherd lays down his life for his sheep. Through this act of freeing the animals bound for slaughter in the temple, Jesus made a most dramatic and revolutionary statement. Giving his life for the animals, Jesus' all-consuming, all-inclusive compassion for these representatives of all vulnerable animals provided a role model for Jesus' followers for all-time, teaching his dedicated and sincere followers to do likewise.

Certainly, appointed by Jesus himself, James, based in Jerusalem, led for thirty years, the infant vegetarian church Jesus' first vegetarian followers. Soon after Jesus' crucifixion, the apostles and early Jewish-Christians faced Paul's violent onslaught, seeking to utterly quash the movement.

Later Paul, an educated man, changed tactics, mounting enormous on-going conflict with the apostles enticing and charming increasing numbers of gentile converts overseas to be non-vegetarian Christians.

Astonishingly, not wishing to be schooled in Jesus' original teachings by the apostles, he rarely saw them and there was a great deal of tension when he did. However, as Paul's power grew abroad he challenged and competed with James'

50

authority and his and the apostles' perpetuation of Jesus teachings!

Most significantly orthodoxy popularized Paul's teachings for posterity whilst they had James, Jesus' brother and vegetarian leader of the first followers of Jesus for thirty years practically expunged from orthodoxy's historical records! Luckily other records exist informing us about Jesus' and James' vegetarian leadership which will be brought to the light of day in later pages.

In view of Pauline Christian assertions, perhaps Paul also consciously intended his sacrificial doctrine to calm hatred of Roman rule, as they carried out the demands of those Jews instrumental in Jesus' execution. Crucially, Pauline theology was upheld by the increasingly fierce Orthodox Church, despite many facets of it being in open conflict with Jesus' original vegetarian teachings, perpetuated by his faithful vegetarian disciples.

Consequently, Paul's sacrificial doctrine progressively opened the flood-gates of Christianity to highly indulgent animal flesh eating cultures, including that of the Romans, each of which cumulatively converted to Christianity, bringing their carnivorous, spiritually inferior, flesh eating customs with them.

Jesus ~ No Sacrificial Victim Facilitates Heaven

Evidencing Jesus' far-sightedness, prior to his own transition to the non-physical after-death realms, Jesus proved beyond doubt to his disciples that life continues after physical death, clearly revealing that no sacrificial victim is needed in order for any being to enter the after-death realms of spirit consisting of many levels or as Jesus described it to be many mansions.

This remarkable demonstration occurred during the event known as the Transfiguration on the Mount. Notably, Jesus took several disciples to watch and witness him in conversation with the physical manifestations – the recognizable communicating spirit bodies - of the long dead Moses and Elijah. Through this wonderful demonstration Jesus proved that all beings, as a fact of nature, make their transitions at physical death to the nonphysical, eternal spheres of spirit.

Indeed, Jesus irrefutably proved during his own lifetime that no sacrificial victim is ever needed to enable any being to enter the after-death state of existence, demonstrated by the materialization of Moses and Elijah who had made their transitions, having physically died, many centuries before. Obviously Jesus demonstrated to his disciples for the benefit of their future converts that in keeping with the laws of nature, Moses and Elijah and all other living souls at death, inevitably gain eternal life in the co-existent, non-physical, after-death dimension.

Importantly, that recognizable, dynamic, personality component of all animals, human and non-human, that survives physical death, having passed to the spirit realms, is historically called 'the spirit' or 'the soul.' Today many psychical researchers and scientists describe the spirit or soul as 'the consciousness.'

Societies for psychical, out of body and near death experience research, including global expert teams of scientists who record spirit voices and video spirit manifestations of deceased animals, human and non-human, known as instrumental trans-communication and electronic voice phenomena, have each amassed irrefutable evidence that life habitually continues for all animals, human and non-human alike, as an irrefutable, recurring fact of nature.

Voices, conversations, communications, dialogues and responses have been recorded and most particularly those of dogs barking responses. Certainly there is no sacrificial victim needed to fulfill this most natural, persistent and all-inclusive law of nature.

Chay Nephesh ~ All Animals are Living Souls

Significantly, the earliest, authentic scriptures, found in the Book of Genesis 1:21, of particular relevance to Jews and Christians, teach us that animals are "chay nephesh." Translated,

52

this extremely ancient, original and accurate Hebrew, phrase tells us that "animals are living souls."

Notably exactly the same ancient Hebrew phrase is used in Genesis 2:7 to describe humans; similarly "humans are also living souls." Significantly, God's clarifying and edifying announcement that all animals, human and non-human, possess souls, is intricately inter-connected with God's first and foremost commands to humankind directing them to eat a vegetarian diet.

Deliberate Mistranslations Attempt to Negate Animal Souls

Tragically, it is a fact that bygone human translators including those who developed the NRSV bible, either chose or most likely obeyed orders and wrongly translated "chay nephash," as "living creatures" when referring to animals, instead of the correct translation of "animals are living souls!" This calculating, deliberate and premeditated mistranslation has had enormously tragic implications for animals and has deceived duped, unaware, ill-advised, uninformed religious devotees alike.

Fostering the lowly position attributed to our fellow animals, creating callous indifference to their wretched lives wracked with pain and suffering, treating them as an inanimate product rather than an emotional, aware, flesh and blood being has tragically facilitated among religious devotees the almost total rejection of spiritual commands to eat a vegetarian diet.

As stated, when referring to humans, these same translators used the correct translation of "chay nephash," differentiating and describing humans alone as "living souls." By this shrewd, calculating, scheming, manipulative, conniving and contemptuous act, using a powerful mistranslation of the ancient scriptures, to segregate the human animal from the rest of their animal kin, the public, most particularly Jews and Christians have been lied to.

They have been graphically misinformed that humans are 'living souls' and fellow animals made of the same flesh and blood, nerve endings and nervous systems which feel pain are but soulless creatures!'

At this juncture, in view of these deliberate mistranslations, it is useful to recall my earlier reference to Muhammad, the founding prophet of Islam, who, in the 7th century AD, warned that on a number of issues from the earliest times Christians have been misled. Muhammad believed he transmitted many direct communications from God, including that all animals, human and non-human have souls, each of whom return to God at death.

It is important to remember that although the millions of historic and contemporary bibles do not say it, all animals, human and non-human were originally described in sacred, authentic, ancient Hebrew, notably in Jewish and Christian scriptures, as 'living souls,' each of whom inevitably survive physical death and return to God in the non-physical, after-death landscapes.

Those treacherous and cunning mis-translators and their overlords, translated humans as 'living souls,' yet tragically denied the status of 'living souls' to our fellow, related, aware, breathing animals. Falsely categorizing sentient flesh and blood animals as 'creatures' for all time, has made it easier, both historically and today, for the masses to act in a blindfolded, gagged and totally unfeeling manner when it comes to animal abuse and exploitation.

Surprisingly, many individuals who consider themselves religious, spiritual or humanitarian eat animals, an act that endorses the merciless genocidal cruelty that animals face, murdered by the billion every year.

The wise proverb is correct 'bad things happen when good people do nothing,' likewise, educated, intelligent, seemingly kind, 'good' people, similarly allowed the evil and sadistic, profitable slave trade to continue for decades too. These mistranslations have led the masses, throughout history, to wrongly believe that the whole range of animals who share with us mental, physical, emotional and indeed spiritual characteristics, including 'souls,' belong to some sort of absurd, half-way house, of 'creatures.'

Shunned into this limbo state, they are not given human rights instead they are perceived as practically inanimate, like a tin of peas. Our fellow animals share the same ancestor they like us, have evolved over millions of years. Sharing this planet with the human animal, their animating souls are housed in flesh and blood. They are feeling and aware, conscious, perceptive, responsive and thinking beings who have dreams during their sleep and happy or tormented memories!

The appalling, incorrect, illogical categorization of 'creatures' is indeed a halfway house limbo state, imposing an endless, merciless prison sentence on fellow animals who, as a consequence have few rights if any. It is an inconsistent contradiction that prevails in many people's thinking or lack of it to this day.

Notably, this deeply flawed and deliberate false classification, shaping attitudes and severely limiting human compassion, allows for the highly profitable ruthless treatment of animals. Routinely and daily, they endure untold suffering, incarceration and a heartless mechanized butchered, piece by piece slaughter.

Despite the repeated pleas and protests of countless global animal charities governments will not allow the installation of cameras to film the treatment of animals in factory farms and who are gradually slaughtered in hell-houses. Charities hoped that by raising public awareness some degree of compassion and mercy may enter these infernal places or close them down all together.

These catastrophic mistranslations in the bible have paved the way for the development of a global trade, not to create anything, but with the sole intention of slaughter, carnage, massacre, murder and butchery by the billion! If a person can call global bloodbath and mass-murder, an industry, the world currently and appallingly possesses an annual multibillion dollar bloodshed and slaughter industry.

Knowledge of mistranslations along with invaluable archaeological discoveries, of reliable, ancient, hidden scriptures and documents offer an invaluable spotlight on a mere fraction of the suppressions and falsifications of original scriptures including those concerned with Jesus' authentic vegetarian ministry.

Deliberate mistranslations, the destruction and concealment of ancient, original, religious texts and the religo-political usurpation of religious leadership are responsible for the increasingly ingrained ignorance of Jesus' vegetarianism that has been transmitted throughout the millennia to us today; all will be clarified in later pages in this serialized volume.

The Human Influence on Gnosticism

This serialized volume, will cumulatively evidence that the Christianity we have today is not wholly pure and undiluted but instead has been corrupted and contaminated by many passionate, ambitious, religio-political characters who dominated the spiritual landscape after Jesus' physical death. This historical fact is further illustrated when considering the sad fate of the Christian Gnostics which impacted both historic and today's brand of Christianity, further revealing that Christianity as practiced today is entirely the product of religio-political vicissitudes.

We know of the activities of the Christian Gnostics in particular, around 100-150 AD. The following brief summary offers an additional example of the religio-political usurpation of leadership, control and censorship of the early Christian Church. Gnosis is a Greek term meaning, 'the act of knowing,' relating to direct, personal, interior experiencing and is in sharp contrast to wholly rational, logical knowledge. The Gnostics, therefore, were diametrically opposed to blindly obeying the decrees and dogmatic systems of belief introduced by the increasingly aggressive, and domineering, institutionalized church.

Orthodoxy Extinguishes Gnostic Christians

The Christian Gnostics claimed that they dutifully followed many of the uncorrupted teachings and practices of Jesus, their loyalty rewarded they were the custodians of sacred esoteric Christian gospels, traditions and rituals. In these early days, around 100-150 AD, embryonic, nascent, emerging Christianity continued to experience oppressive, regulatory and filtering influences.

Despite this, Christianity had not yet become standardized and fossilized into a single set of unquestioned dogmas and articles of faith, which, once set in stone, were fiercely protected by the formidable, controlling institutionalized church. Once decreed, orthodoxy expected their dictates to remain unquestioned for all time.

In my book called Moses and Jesus: the Shamans, I point out that:

"During this period there were diverse struggling Christian groups declaring their own individual expression of Christianity. For some of these groups, to varying degrees, Christianity was absorbed and blended with previously held religious convictions. Records indicate that the highly educated and respected Gnostic teacher Valentius, from Alexandria, was nearly made Bishop of Rome around 150 AD.

The results of this decision represented a pivotal turning point for the future destiny of Christianity. Amazingly, if Valentius had become Bishop of Rome this experiential 'lost Christianity' might have survived and been practiced by Christians today....Some of Valentius' core beliefs differed from those of the other ambitious church leaders who were fast monopolizing power. Inevitably, members of the greater church would have been challenged by the fact that, as a Gnostic, Valentius could regularly access new scriptures containing a continuous stream of elevated spiritual truths that differed from the orthodox fossilized version." *3*

The Inferior 'Human Version' of Christianity

Importantly, this enlightening serialized research will show that worldly, politico-religious leaders namely, the human element, has impacted and shaped the version of Christianity with which we are familiar today. This inferior human version of Christianity has lost sight of Jesus' spiritually advanced quest advocating peace, harmony and love for all animals, human and non-human, embodied by the highly developed spirituality of non-violence and compassion inherent in vegetarianism.

Jesus' spiritually elevated compassion for animals has been covertly and overtly rejected by the powers that be, throughout the passage of the centuries. Many businessmen throughout the millennia have something in common, since ancient times the murder of animals has been a most profitable, money making commerce, culminating in todays' largely unquestioned, obscene, global, multibillion dollar animal carnage business.

Tragically as the eyes of the terrorized animals wracked with pain prove, industrialized killing machines know no mercy, nor do they hear animals' agonized frenzied pleas as these emotional flesh and blood victims scream with horror, torture and grief as they are slowly, piece by piece, conveyor belted to their tormented murder often knee deep in blood and guts. Jesus' superior and celebrated spirituality actively demonstrated in his exalted vegetarian 'works' revere the sanctity of all life, condemning the murder of our related animal brothers and sisters. Jesus and his apostles taught the importance of 'works,' spiritual actions, not blind faith alone.

Jesus' Brother: James' Vegetarianism since Birth

Progressively, this serialized research reveals that Christians for more than twenty centuries, including today, who eat animal flesh have been wrongly led to believe they were following Jesus' unadulterated role-model. It will be shown that the fact of Jesus' vegetarianism is also clearly substantiated by the vegetarianism of Jesus' brother, James, who is factually known to have been a vegetarian since birth.

Prior to his own personally predicted and anticipated execution in retaliation for his planned prime time public liberation of the temple animals destined for slaughter, Jesus inevitably made plans for James' leadership of his followers and his infant movement.

58

Importantly, James led Jesus' early Jewish-Christian converts, Jesus' first followers from his long term home in Jerusalem for a lengthy three decades. James was highly respected and admired by his fellow disciples due to his like-mindedness to his brother, Jesus. James was known as James the Just, for his devotion, vegetarianism and piousness he was highly regarded in all contemporaneous circles, far and wide.

Yet, astonishingly, this famous vegetarian Christian leader, living in vegetarian harmony with his brother Jesus, has historically been silenced to the state of non-existence by the later machinations, editing and suppressions of the institutionalized church which opposed the existence of Jesus' earthly family and their vegetarianism.

Irrefutably, Jesus' parents, Mary and Joseph, belonged to a Jewish sect, of which there were many, who did not eat animal flesh. Fortunately, all will be evidenced in detail in later pages, as this vitally important figure, James, is unearthed from the ancient archaeological ruins of history!

Human Opposition to Vegetarianism

Soon after Jesus passed away, making his own transition to the non-physical realms of spirit, the disciples, now the apostles had Paul's execution of Jesus' first followers, the Jewish-Christians with which to contend. Paul's early brutality towards Christians was replaced with his later opposition to vegetarianism and the leadership of James supported by the remaining apostles.

James, together with the other apostles made their detestation of Paul apparent, their euphemistic code name for Paul, long after Paul had stopped having Christians tortured and killed was 'the enemy.' The ancient authentic records documenting Jesus' and the apostles' vegetarianism and biblical texts describing the rows concerning Paul's dilution of vegetarianism will be discussed in detail later in this serialized volume.

Research proves that James, the brother of Jesus had indeed been a disciple of Jesus. Relentlessly, these apostles were threatened by Paul, who after ending his reign of terror, annihilating the early Jewish-Christians, proclaimed himself as an apostle. From this self-appointed position, Paul instigating his own Pauline, non-vegetarian theology, competed with the ministry of James and the apostles in a constant bid to usurp authority from them impacting and changing the face of Jesus' original Christianity with Pauline doctrines whilst Christianity was in its infancy. Indeed, this was an extremely early, vitally vulnerable, emergent phase of Christianity.

Paul purported to transmit his own - Paul's version - of the newly flourishing Christianity to the increasingly foreign converts who, like Paul, imported and overlaid Jesus' original, spiritually elevated teachings with their own 'human,' non-vegetarian preferences and traditions. Rejection and outright omission resulted in the misrepresentation of Jesus' ethically advanced vegetarian ministry at an exceedingly early juncture. The heart and soul, the very kernel and life blood of Jesus' spiritual philosophy, which taught truth-seekers to demonstrate all-embracing compassion and mercy to all animals, human and non-human, epitomized by vegetarianism, became dispossessed.

The deeply rooted all-embracing, compassionate vegetarian foundation stone, the founding principle, the fundamental soul, core, kernel, crux and essence of Jesus' most spiritually lofty, non-violent vegetarian teachings became diluted, distorted, opposed, suppressed and ultimately lost to countless future generations of Christians, impacting Christians today. Vulnerable, unsuspecting Christians throughout the ages have naively looked to religio-political authorities to honor the legacy of Jesus, to pass down through the ages the genuine, unadulterated, factually correct teachings of Jesus.

The convoluted history of human distortion of Jesus' command that his followers become vegetarian commenced with Paul when Paul instigated and popularized his own version of Christianity in order to meet the least resistance when persuading and swaying foreign populations to revere him as the leader of Christianity.

Progressively, the masses corrupted, eclipsed and extinguished Jesus' high-minded, all-inclusive, compassionate vegetarian teachings which upheld the sacredness of all life forms. Jesus' teachings condemned the murder of all animals, human and non-human and advocated universal non-violence. Jesus' profound vegetarian teachings became obscured smothered and silenced sharing the same fate as the historically earlier, yet same spiritually developed vegetarian teachings of the Buddha.

The Buddha's Vegetarianism (6th Century BC.)

This brings to mind the sorrowful, far-sighted prediction of the Lord Buddha, named Siddhattha Gotama. This spiritually elevated soul lived in northern India in the 6th century BC. He prophesied that in the future after his death some of his followers, bowing to their own cruel, grossly spiritually inferior, 'human' food preferences, would distort and extinguish the Buddha's pacifist, all-embracing, compassionate vegetarian teachings by eating animal flesh and mistakenly call themselves Buddhists.

The first fundamental step for all sincere spiritual devotees of all religious persuasions is to live a vegetarian lifestyle. By ruthlessly and pitilessly ignoring vegetarian commands, a person negates the attainment of spiritual advancement because an integral by-product of vegetarianism is that progressively over time it teaches each and every human soul to develop and internalize compassion for all animals, human and non-human.

Taken from the Lankavatara Sutras, which are the preserved direct quotations of the Lord Buddha, the Buddha predicted the future domination of cruel, deeply flawed, human food preferences extinguishing his spiritually advanced vegetarian commands:

"In the future, meat-eaters, speaking out of ignorance, will say that the Buddha permitted the eating of meat, and that he taught there was no sin in doing so."

Crucially, there are countless exhortations of the Buddha revealing his boundless compassion for each and every life form no matter how small or seemingly insignificant. It is factually known that the Buddha gave direct instructions to his monks that they strain their water before drinking preventing them from carelessly killing any single minute micro-organism.

Certainly, the Buddha showed compassion for microscopic organisms comparable to bacteria. Unsurprisingly authentic ancient accounts tell us that he was devastated, broken-hearted and distraught by the suffering and murder of fellow sentient, feeling, flesh and blood animals, who are far more evolved than bacteria, being emotional and consciously aware.

He condemned those hypocrites who exploited animals by having them killed on their behalf by others for the sake of their own merciless, unsympathetic, human food preferences. These individuals were perceived as being just as guilty as those who murdered the animal, without the receiver the animal would not be killed in the first place. Consequently, Buddhism classes them as accomplices, coconspirators and collaborators.

Tragically, many Buddhists and Christians have lost touch with their prophetic founder's original, morally advanced, compassionate vegetarian teachings. Authentic quotations from the Buddha including his teachings, demonstrating his vegetarianism and his all-inclusive compassion for animals, human and non-human, will be discussed in later pages, illustrating the background to the predominantly vegetarian world in which Jesus lived.

Notably, Buddhism is known as Buddha-sasana and Buddha-Dhamma, translated these mean, 'the Way of life or discipline of the Awakened-One' and 'the eternal truth of the Awakened One,' namely the Buddha. Buddhists believe that a Buddha will appear at intervals throughout human history whenever humankind has become ignorant, straying away from the Buddha's fundamental, far-sighted, compassionate, ethically elevated, vegetarian spiritual directives.

Saul/Paul

Returning to Jesus' first followers, the Jewish-Christians, who lived six centuries after the death of the Buddha, they were determined to remain faithful to Jesus' uncorrupted vegetarian teachings. Notably, it will be shown that the sermons of Jesus' loyal apostles were often less popular than Paul's more marketable, non-vegetarian version of Christianity. The following summary gives further clarification of Paul due to his pivotal significance for the distortion of Jesus' original vegetarian Christianity, all of which will be discussed in detail in later pages.

In a sharp and dramatic divergence to the disciples, hand-picked and trained by Jesus himself, Paul never lived, loved and discussed with Jesus, nor had Paul absorbed into his own spiritual consciousness, into his very soul, Jesus' all-embracing, compassionate, non-violent vegetarian message.

Paul, the mass-murderer, became the usurping, self-proclaimed, religio-political leader of early Jewish-Christianity. Paul had never met or studied under the tutelage of the man Jesus, yet most Christians have at least heard of Paul and certainly practice Paul's non-vegetarian form of Christianity. Most Christians know nothing of James, Jesus' brother, the long-term leader of the early church who faithfully continued Jesus' vegetarian tradition!

It is important to remember that prior to his self-appointment as an early Jewish-Christian leader, Paul had zealously and most proficiently persecuted early Jewish-Christian families, having these poor oppressed souls dragged out of their houses and murdered in large numbers. Paul had none of the advantages of the disciples, chosen by Jesus himself, who had been adopted into Jesus' close, spiritual family. Nor did Paul seek to adopt, internalize and protect Jesus' authentic ministry in its entire and original form as transmitted by Jesus to his very own disciples.

Instead, when the disciples met Paul at a time when word had reached them of his toleration and support of non-vegetarianism and his further distortions of Jesus' teachings, these faithful, impassioned devotees had outraged clashes with him, all of which will be discussed later in this serialized volume. It will become increasingly clear in later pages that many of these historic religious records illustrating the apostles' opposition to Paul have been destroyed or deliberately omitted by orthodoxy from the biblical canon.

Most other accounts of this animosity have been fully or partially suppressed through editing, being reworked by biblical scribes ordered to conceal the fact that the apostles who loyally transmitted Jesus' doctrines, including Jesus' vegetarianism, vehemently refuted many aspects of Pauline Christianity.

Sadly, Pauline Christianity was spreading far and wide overseas among the gentiles, eclipsing fundamental components of Jesus' authentic teachings, most particularly Jesus' vegetarianism. However, authentic ancient texts and biblical accounts clearly illustrating Jesus' vegetarianism and the apostles' clashes with Paul over his dilution of and opposition to vegetarianism will be provided later.

Little Known Facts about Paul

At this juncture, in view of the fact that Paul spread his version of Christianity to the gentiles far and wide, it is valuable to expose some little known facts about Paul. Many Christians today are unaware that it took Paul three years after his apparent conversion to Christianity before he returned to Jerusalem and finally met some of the disciples who had become the authentic Apostles of Jesus.

After a mere two weeks Paul left, again heading north. Astonishingly, Paul chose not to meet the apostle Peter or the other original church elders, all of whom were tutored by Jesus until ten years later!

Paul's Sacrificial Doctrine Popularized the Eating of Animal Flesh

During this decade Paul created his own popularized version of Christianity in which he included Jesus as a sacrificial victim. By publicizing the concept that the highly esteemed Jesus, was himself, a necessary sacrificial victim, Paul smoothly paved the way for his new, lesser informed, overseas converts not to be inconvenienced and to continue their age old traditions of eating animal flesh. Other early Christians progressively came to accept the murder of animals as necessary sacrificial victims to be eaten not only as permissible food but as authorized food preferences.

By approving the sacrifice of animals, a deceitful custom synonymous with animal slaughter for food, Paul sanctioned, endorsed and validated this cruelty which became a historical tradition perpetuated by global slaughterhouses today. The fact that many early church fathers remained faithful to Jesus' vegetarianism will be discussed later as further evidence of the vegetarianism of Jesus' first followers, the early Jewish-Christians, led from Jerusalem.

Condemning animal sacrifice including the eating of their flesh afterwards, the 7th and 8th century prophets together with Jesus, James, the remaining apostles and the early Jewish-Christians guided from Jerusalem, had nothing in common with Paul's homespun sacrificial Christianity: J.R.Hyland in God's Covenant with Animals clarifies: "The God whom Jesus came to earth to reveal was nothing like the God of Paul's understanding: A God who needed the sacrifice of countless animals, or of His own son, in order to be reconciled to a sinful humanity." *4*

Raising awareness of such insidious brainwashing that has gone on for over two thousand years helps us to understand how good people have been and still are, oblivious to the suffering and murder of animals, most of whom are trapped, entombed, enslaved and incarcerated in the historical and on-going extremely profitable animal slaughter industry.

From the outset Paul opposed Jesus by having many of Jesus' first followers killed. Incredibly, later he appointed himself as an apostle and relentlessly sought to challenge the leadership of James and the other apostles, whilst he spread a non-vegetarian message!

Illustrating Paul's total flouting and contravention of Jesus' and the 7th and 8th century BC prophets' condemnation of animal sacrifice including eating their flesh afterwards, Paul introduced and propagated Jesus as a sacrificial victim, creating a further component of Pauline theology, practically making it an article of faith to eat animal flesh. J.R.Hyland adds:

"...Paul, like his Jewish ancestors and Christian descendants, had to ignore the biblical texts that denounced any kind of sacrifice-animal or human. And although Christianity had no tradition of animal sacrifice to justify, through Paul it retained and built upon the orthodox Jewish insistence that this bloody worship was divinely ordained. Christianity validated the concept of sacrificial religion, and then decreed that the death of Jesus was a sacrifice of such magnitude that it finally satisfied the "justice" of a God who had not been propitiated by the shed of blood of countless animals.

In the centuries that followed the writing of Paul's Epistles, various spokesmen built their own theories on the unstable foundation of his conjectures. And early churchmen like Ireneus, Justin, Tertullian, and Augustine presented variations on the theme of Christ's propitiary death, claiming that the sacrifice of animals was the God-ordained prototype of that death." 5

Jesus' 'Works' Negated Paul's Animal Consumption and Blind Faith

The Orthodox Church absorbed and accepted Pauline doctrines and was increasingly responsible for creating entrenched historic and on-going indoctrination, fostering unquestioning obliviousness amongst pious, yet unsuspecting Christians. Tragically, from the earliest days, the faithful apostles were enraged with Paul for teaching converts that they could eat animal flesh and that they should actively demonstrate blind faith, to the Pauline doctrines he gave them!

Clearly, Paul and his successors demanded and cultivated unquestioning obedience amongst those they converted and led. Ultimately deviation from docile compliance was branded heretical, the legacy of which has spanned and impacted over two thousand years, cultivating a series of flawed beliefs including the tragically inaccurate, non-vegetarian beliefs of millions of Christians world-wide. Thankfully, this issue is finally being redressed here in the 21st century.

66

Jesus and his passionately dedicated disciples fulfilled the 7th and 8th century prophetic ancestors' teachings, reaffirming that it is imperative to express their devotion to spirituality through their "works," by spiritual actions, not Paul's further doctrine demanding 'blind faith' replace 'works' for his gentile converts. Obviously, Paul's blind faith doctrine was and will always be, intensely susceptible to abuse, leading to the indoctrination and exploitation of all unsuspecting devotees, who may naively accept unquestioned man-made dogmas, which, in turn, would increase the power and grip of religio-political church leaders.

Notably "works," in contrast to the vacuous belief in blind faith in unquestioned man-made religious dogmas, creeds and doctrines which become articles of faith, involves daily spiritual thought processes, choices and actions. Spiritual actions progressively encompass, becoming totally integrated into a person's spiritual life-style and are illustrated by the demonstration of respect, sensitivity and empathy to the needs of others, helpfulness and compassion to all animals, human and non-human.

Markedly "works," is all-inclusive, compassionate action; Jesus taught his followers to love his/her neighbor and all beings are a person's neighbor. 'Works' is a concept that is in sharp contrast to hiding behind the deeply flawed, empty and murderous animal sacrifice ceremonies, tragically killing conscious and aware, sentient, feeling, flesh and blood, terrified sacrificial victims, in the ludicrous belief that these condemned, evil, bloodthirsty ritualistic homicides will paradoxically extinguish probably lesser past sins.

Jesus' concept of 'works' was in sharp contrast to Paul's absurd doctrine tragically endorsed the sacrifice of animals likening them to a cleverly distorted version of Jesus as a 'Sacrificial Lamb of God.'

Paul through Gentile Converts Overthrew Jesus' Vegetarianism

It will now be apparent that this introductory chapter is providing a brief overview of how Jesus' authentic vegetarian teachings were under attack from the very beginning, whilst Christianity was in its infancy. Jesus' vegetarianism was watered down and distorted, suppressed, opposed and cumulatively forgotten becoming lost throughout the centuries, ultimately creating our contemporary Christian ignorance and our utter obliviousness that Jesus' vegetarian teachings ever existed.

This astonishing summary introduces some of the historical facts that have had the utmost tragic consequences for our related animals, namely our fellow living souls, and the reduced level of spirituality of humankind. To reiterate, all points summarily raised here will be discussed in detail with supportive evidence in later pages in this serialized volume.

Notably, the suppression of Jesus' vegetarian doctrines began with Saul, who was infamous for his tyrannical persecution of the first followers, of Jesus's original, undistorted, vegetarian teachings. Realizing, that this religious movement was burgeoning and relentless, Saul became Paul and subsequently changed tactics. Paul's next objective was to lead and shape this unstoppable, potentially revolutionary spiritual movement.

Shocking and alarming the disciples, Paul appointed himself as an apostle, becoming the only self-appointed apostle! Paul claimed he had experienced a spiritual transformation and unlike other converts instead of following Jesus' ministry as faithfully transmitted by the authentic disciples, now proclaimed as genuine apostles, arrogantly he sought to lead the movement, utilizing and building upon his own earlier theological training.

This was the nature of Paul's fierce and uncompromising character. Angered by the respect converts attributed to James and the remaining legitimate apostles, Paul astonished them by rivaling, attacking, sarcastically denigrating and criticizing them and amending Jesus' doctrines amongst Paul's own gentile converts, in contrast to those dutifully preserved and propagated by the apostles.

Typically, a person would expect a convert, particularly the blood-stained Paul, to feel guilt-ridden after a genuine, spiritually transformative mediumistic experience of Jesus, which he said occurred on the road to Damascus. Notably, the following years are characterized not by a remorseful, repentant Paul, seeking deeper extensive knowledge of Jesus' doctrines from Jesus' apostles, in view of his previous murderous conduct. Significantly, Paul was not transformed into a committed obedient, modest and humble convert.

Instead, from the outset, as outlined earlier, Paul had exceedingly little to do with Jesus' pious, mutually supportive apostles. It cannot be over emphasized, whilst Paul was further afield, converting the gentiles, he actively challenged, defied, rivaled, in effect attempting to usurp, the dedicated Jerusalem leadership of the first followers of Jesus, bequeathed by Jesus to his own brother, James.

Amongst Paul's gentile converts, including those overseas, at an early stage in the Jesus-trained disciples' ministry, later pages will detail how Paul competed with many of Jesus' original doctrines which were devotedly defended and safeguarded by the over-lordship of James and the remaining steadfast apostles.

Paul accomplished this despite these dutiful apostles' strongest, heartfelt protestations, that Paul was wrongly gaining misinformed converts by popularizing and watering-down Jesus' vegetarian doctrines and distorting and suppressing other fundamental components of Jesus' original teachings.

Incredibly, some of the apostles complained that Paul's popularized, distortions of Jesus' message was more acceptable to the public than their teachings, shockingly resulting in the apostles losing authority and influence. Inevitably, heated clashes and angry confrontations occurred between Paul and the dedicated and trustworthy apostles, which will be discussed in later pages.

Jesus Executed for Freeing the Animals

This detailed introduction to the Animal Souls serialization is seeking to make clear that this serialized volume will progressively offer the reader detailed proof that Jesus taught all-inclusive vegetarian compassion embracing all fellow animals. This was prominently demonstrated by his deliberate public liberation of the animals in the temple and his staunch vegetarianism as recorded in a number of ancient authentic reliable texts, which will be introduced in a moment.

Contravening the norms set out by the religio-political authorities of his day, Jesus' pre-planned extremely public display of animal liberation, instilled in him the expectation that this compassionate and rebellious public spectacle would inevitably lead to punishment by execution.

Attempting to alleviate his disciples' forthcoming, looming grief, Jesus forewarned them, by predicting his impending death. Aware that his public deliverance of the vulnerable enslaved animals tragically destined for deceitful sacrificial slaughter for food, would both provoke and enrage the authorities, Jesus remained bravely committed to his planned, rebellious, all-embracing, kind-hearted exhibition for the edification of all future generations of converts.

Tragically, being the eminent spiritual leader that he was, Jesus dearly hoped that all his future followers would become vegetarian like him, demonstrating compassion, empathy, mercy and respect to all living souls, all animals, human and non-human.

As mentioned earlier, Jesus' heartfelt emancipation of the pitiful, innocent animals condemned to death fulfilled the long forgotten, compassionate animal teachings from Jesus' prophetic heritage; merciful and benevolent teachings with which Jesus would most certainly have been fluent.

Jesus' actions did breathe new life into the humane pleas of his 7th and 8th century BC prophetic forefathers and indeed accomplish them. Their ancient echoes were indeed fulfilled by Jesus' actions, they had scolded the populace, informing them that God loathed and despised the slaughter of fellow flesh and blood animals, who were eaten afterwards.

Indeed, Jesus' brave and compassionate actions were in accord with the teachings of his revered 7th and 8th century BC prophetic predecessors, who had vigorously denounced the abhorrent temple animal sacrifice practices, drenching the temple

70

with the blood of its defenseless emotional victims, having much in common with present-day, merciless slaughterhouses.

Demonstrating his solidarity with, sharing in and fulfilling the spiritual missions of each of his prophetic predecessors, Jesus brought their teachings back to life by reintroducing them. Jesus took matters further by fulfilling their spiritual goals by actually stopping the animal sacrifice in the temple, which they so abhorred.

They, like Jesus, had condemned animal sacrifice which led to the animal being eaten afterwards. Historically, these compassionate prophets and Jesus were as unpopular with the authorities as are modern-day, humanitarian animal charities. They likewise denounce the countless, cruel, most profitable animal exploitation, transport and slaughter traditions of our day. Throughout the centuries such practices have continued to make the formidable establishment rich and powerful.

Clearly, in return for the false, illusory and ridiculous, 'man-made' promise, that God would delete a person's sins, if they paid for the sacrificial murder of animals, the unsuspecting masses were successfully, profitably indoctrinated and manipulated into committing more sins! Compelled to buy animals associated with the prosperous temple authorities and then pay again for their repulsive animal slaughter, the flesh of these sentient beings fed the authorities afterwards.

Each of these terror-stricken animals trembled uncontrollably as they watched each other's gory, blood-splattered murder. Tragically, the odorous stench of death filled the temple which had become nothing more than a stinking modern-day slaughterhouse, empowering, enriching and feeding those who were already prosperous and powerful.

Jesus Prohibited Converts from Sitting at the Tables' of Devils/Non-Vegetarians

Authentic biblical and non-biblical accounts clearly proving the disciples'/apostles' condemnation of Paul's distortion and ultimate rejection of Jesus' fundamental vegetarian doctrines,

71

will be discussed in detail later. Awareness will be raised regarding the often censored, extinguished and long forgotten outright vegetarian content of these texts.

These ancient chronicles will reveal how Paul's own version of Christianity, Pauline Christianity, clouded, diluted, corrupted and overturned Jesus' central vegetarian teachings, prompting the loyal apostles' heartfelt, furious resistance.

This serialized volume will reveal that the apostles were appalled and outspoken in their opposition to Paul, condemning Paul's own practice of eating animal flesh and Paul's submission to and compliance with others who ate animal-flesh. Paul further demonstrated his opposition to Jesus' original vegetarian teachings by sitting at the forbidden non-vegetarian "tables' of devils." Crucially, the act of eating animal flesh and the act of sitting at the table of those who ate animal flesh, 'the tables of devils,' were undertakings expressly prohibited by Jesus.

Jesus' Teachings: Tables' of Devils were Eaters of Animal Flesh

This introduction has now made it apparent that the first devout followers of Jesus' undistorted teachings were the Jewish-Christians who Jesus vehemently forbade from eating animal flesh. Indeed, the callous act of eating animal-flesh endorses and perpetuates violence, cruelty and suffering among fellow, aware, sentient animal, 'living souls.'

This brutal deed was considered to sabotage and negate from the outset any person's attempted acquisition of spiritual advancement, being in total opposition to Jesus' all-encompassing, compassionate, vegetarian message, fostering empathy and kindness within all those seeking to pursue a spiritual path.

Eating animal flesh, a heartless, callous and coldblooded act, was considered to be entirely hostile to the central tenet of Jesus' advanced spirituality. As such, eating animal flesh was expressly prohibited by Jesus himself. Vegetarianism was practiced by Jesus, Jesus' family, his own disciples and by each of their converts and indeed vegetarianism was loyally copied for several centuries by oppressed, dedicated Christian devotees.

None of whom would sit at the prohibited "tables of devils," namely, 'the tables of animal flesh eaters.' Sitting with non-vegetarians would condone the irreligious act of cruelty, violence and murder of self-aware, conscious, feeling, emotional, fellow 'living souls.'

It will be cumulatively proven throughout this serialized volume that soon after Jesus passed away, Jesus' trained and newly proselytizing apostles, demonstrated that they were fully conversant with the term, "the tables' of devils," rulings obviously given to them directly by Jesus himself. This vivid and emotive branding irrefutably condemned hard-hearted individuals, lacking in compassion, who ate animal flesh. Significantly, Jesus' and his apostles' abhorrence to the merciless practice of eating animal flesh was extended to Christian vegetarians sharing the same tables as animal flesh eaters, the tables of 'devils!'

Later chapters will prove that Jesus' disciples, leading the first groups of dedicated followers, clearly did not eat animal flesh, as they were imbued with Jesus' impassioned all-inclusive, compassionate, empathetic, non-violent beliefs embodied in the practice of vegetarianism. Notably, the disciples' vociferous and passionately held vegetarian stance will be illustrated by accounts revealing they would not countenance any genuine follower of Jesus to eat animal flesh or sit at the same table as a person who eats animal flesh!

In the early years it was common knowledge that the disciples practicing Jesus' spiritual vegetarian ideology clashed with Paul's distorted version of Christianity, leading to heated documented confrontations between the two parties. One particularly fraught clash over Paul's acceptance of eating animal flesh, occurred in Antioch, as recorded in the biblical book of Galatians. This passionate altercation involving a number of Jesus' leading vegetarian apostles and the non-vegetarian Paul will be detailed later.

Due to orthodoxy's destruction, suppression and editing of historic religious records outlining Jesus', his family's and devoted followers' vegetarianism and orthodoxy's endorsement of non-vegetarian Pauline doctrines, fortunately we can utilize invaluable, authentic, ancient 3rd century AD manuscripts which categorically teach us about the vegetarianism of Jesus, his apostles, his first followers, namely the Jewish-Christians and a succession of early church leaders.

Recognitions of Clement, the Clementine Homilies and the Panarion of Epiphanius of Salamis

Notably, the precious ancient writings known as the Recognitions of Clement, the Clementine Homilies and the Panarion of Epiphanius of Salamis are perhaps even more important than the Dead Sea Scrolls and the Nag Hammadi documents, providing us with an open window into the past, clearly revealing the genuine and original vegetarian teachings of Jesus as practiced by Jesus' loyal and oppressed, first followers.

Crucially, modern day academics universally agree that the above named irreplaceable ancient historical records, part of the pseudo-Clementine literature, which markedly clarify and confirm the fact of Jewish-Christian vegetarianism are indeed authentic, originating from ancient Jewish-Christian and Ebionite sources.

It is of the utmost importance to raise public awareness that increasing numbers of highly respectable scholars are universally agreed that the Ebionites were amongst the earliest, loyal and devout followers of Jesus' authentic vegetarian teachings and were undeniably vegetarian. Importantly, the names of some of these eminent scholars whose research has led them to the fact of vegetarianism amongst Jesus' earliest followers include:

F. Stanley Jones, author of An Ancient Jewish Christian Source, James Tabor, author of The Jesus Dynasty, Hans-Joachim Schoeps, author of Jewish Christianity, Robert Eisenman, author of James, the Brother of Jesus, Keith Akers, author of The Lost Religion of Jesus, Mr. James, the translator of The Apocryphal New Testament and A.F. Klijn, the author of the Jewish-Christian Gospel Tradition.

One of the above mentioned authors, Epiphanius, writer of the Panarion of Epiphanius of Salamis, was a contemporary of the first followers of Jesus, the early Jewish-Christians, yet he opposed them. Consequently, Epiphanius' writings, describing their vegetarian traditions, emanating from Jesus himself, are, of the utmost historical value.

Significantly, Jewish-Christians were called Ebionites, Ossaeans, Elchasaites, Nazoraeans and Nasaraeans. Each of these mutually cooperative and supportive Jewish-Christian sects was irrefutably vegetarian. I believe my research progressively set out in this serialized volume will provide conclusive proof that the Ebionites/Nazoraeans/Nasaraeans were vegetarian and indeed followed Jesus' vegetarian ministry.

The Vegetarianism of the Ebionites/ Nazoraeans/ Nasaraeans

With reference to the above mentioned ancient manuscripts, Epiphanius' writings discuss in particular, the vegetarianism of the Ebionites, who were frequently called the 'Nazoraeans.' Both of the ancient reputable writers named Jerome and Theodoret, confirm that the 'Ebionite' vegetarian sect was another name for the 'Nazoraeans.' Remarkably, Jesus was known as 'Jesus, the Nazoraean,' the very name of this vegetarian sect providing further evidence of Jesus and his family's vegetarian background.

Decisively, Jesus' parents, Jesus and his siblings and larger family belonged to the Ebionite/Nazoraean vegetarian sect, a fact that is further conclusively substantiated by reliable texts, to be discussed later, informing us that James, Jesus' brother, was a vegetarian since birth. This fact obviously proves that Mary and Joseph, Jesus' and James' parents must have been vegetarian in order to bring James and Jesus up as vegetarians since birth! Fortunately orthodoxy failed to destroy all the authentic ancient records some of which continue to exist today.

Irrefutably, Jesus was also a vegetarian since birth! Notably, intertwined with their vegetarian tradition, the

75

Ebionites/Nazoraeans passionately rejected animal sacrifice, adhering to the teachings of the prophets of the 7th and 8th century BC and God's first and foremost commands for humanity to be vegetarian, transmitted in the Garden of Eden, recorded in the first biblical book of Genesis. To reiterate, all of which was fulfilled by Jesus's own ministry and perpetuated by his faithful disciples.

Vegetarian Ebionites, Hindus, Pythagoreans, Buddhists, Confucians

The earlier chapters of this serialized volume will illustrate that the world before the birth of Jesus, during his lifetime and for centuries after his death was predominantly vegetarian revealing that Jesus' vegetarian teachings were not isolated or in a vacuum but part of a continuum of ethically advanced spirituality. Indeed, this spiritually transformative vegetarian revelation was received by countless spiritually elevated leaders as will be shown shortly.

Significantly, the vegetarian teachings of the Ebionites/Nazoraeans disseminated by Jesus' ministry were in harmony with the spiritually advanced vegetarian teachings of: Hinduism: Buddhism: Pythagoras including many centuries of Greek vegetarian spiritual philosophers and Confucius to name but a few. Each of these spiritually orientated memorable vegetarian teachers gave the world widespread global vegetarian traditions, which flourished before, during and after Jesus' birth.

Pythagoras was called 'Man/the Man' ~ Jesus called himself 'the Son of Man/the Man'

It will be shown that Jesus' vegetarian teachings and spiritual doctrines share astonishingly close parallels with those of his famed 6th century BC, Greek predecessor, Pythagoras, the vegetarian spiritual philosopher and polymath. Introducing and summarizing below the beliefs and practices of Pythagoras and his schools of followers, has incredible similarities to those of Jesus and his converts.

76

Importantly, countless generations of students who attended the famous Pythagorean vegetarian, esoteric schools, following the spiritual example set by their eminent founder, condemned animal sacrifice and abstained from eating animal flesh, which, in harmony with Judaism, remained fundamentally prohibited and intertwined practices.

Pythagoreans abstained from eating beans, wore white linen instead of wool, lived in simple, pacifist communes, avoided luxurious living and wore their hair long, Jesus and his converts who lived several centuries later lived in overt solidarity with Pythagoreans!

Pythagoras' vegetarianism inspired countless Greek vegetarian spiritual philosophers who lived in future centuries. They each continued to enthuse their students with Pythagorean vegetarian beliefs and practices. Pythagoras shaped spiritual vegetarian schools of thought far beyond the shores of Greece and his influence on the geographically widespread perpetuation of the non-animal flesh diet became colossal.

Consequently, Pythagoras, famed for his vegetarianism, his name became synonymous with vegetarianism across the globe for two and a half thousand years until modern times! Until comparatively recently many vegetarians throughout the world were called Pythagoreans.

Astonishingly, the above description of Pythagorean doctrines, equally describe many Ebionite/Nazoraean teachings perpetuated by Jesus' own ministry and that of his loyal apostles. Importantly, the Ebionites/Nazoraeans and Pythagoreans shared the same fundamental spiritually advanced vegetarian principles.

Furthermore, both the Pythagorean and Ebionite/Nazoraean schools of thought were emphatic that people should not use oaths to emphatically swear to their honesty. Upholding all people as honorable, each taught that everyone should be believed for their truthfulness, without the use of oaths.

Historically, the celebrated and legendary Pythagoras was heralded as, 'the Man' or 'Man.' Incredibly most people today are unaware of the significance associated with Jesus' choice of name for himself which was, 'the Son of the Man,' and the 'Son of Man,' clearly illustrating Jesus' wholehearted support, fulfillment and perpetuation of Pythagoras' spiritually elevated vegetarian doctrines. The teachings of Jesus and his eminently famous vegetarian Greek predecessor will be discussed in later pages, which will progressively reveal the global vegetarian background to Jesus' own vegetarian ministry.

Vegetarianism Interwoven with Condemnation of Animal Sacrifice

The first followers of Jesus, the original Jewish-Christians, also known as the Ebionites/Nazoraeans, painstakingly passed Jesus' all-encompassing compassionate vegetarian traditions down through the generations until these followers of Jesus' original and authentic vegetarian doctrines were all but wiped out in the 4th century AD due to orthodoxy's repeated suppression of them. Importantly, these early Christians of the 4th century AD had mirrored, remaining faithful to the true and original vegetarian traditions of their earliest 1st century AD Jewish-Christian predecessors.

Significantly, echoing the 7th and 8th century BC prophets' powerful denunciations of the cruel brutality of animal sacrifice and the consumption of animals afterwards, likewise the ancient, though later authors of the Recognitions and Homilies also reiterate the teachings of their prophetic predecessors, clearly illustrating, that the doctrine of vegetarianism was indeed fundamentally and intricately interwoven with the denunciation of animal sacrifice.

Notably, the above prophets who lived almost one thousand years earlier likewise transmitted to humankind, God's profound compassion for animals, including God's outrage that these defenseless fellow, 'living souls,' were being murdered, in the profoundly misguided and absurd attempt to have God forgive earlier sins, contravening both the first commandment 'not to kill' and God's first and foremost commands ordering humanity to eat a vegetarian diet.

Importantly vegetarianism, which will be cumulatively proven to be a genuine, original and foundational tenet of Jesus' teachings, was required of all Jesus' faithful followers. Epiphanius, a contemporary of Jesus' first converts, informs us in his ancient and reputable writings, the Panarion of Epiphanius of Salamis 30.18.9, that he asked one of Jesus' converts why he had become vegetarian. This devout Jewish-Christian gave a simple reply stating Jesus had taught all of his followers to be vegetarian, avowing: "Christ revealed it to me."

Keith Akers in The Lost Religion of Jesus points out that: "Many of the Jewish Christian themes in these documents are also described in the New Testament – such as attacks on animal sacrifice, the virtue of simple living, hostility toward Paul, vegetarianism, and allegiance to the law. In all these ancient texts, we see reflections of a dissident Jewish-Christianity – a Christianity which was the ancestor of the Protestant, Catholic and Orthodox Churches of today." *6*

Crucially, the above named trustworthy and highly regarded texts of Jewish-Christian literature record the vegetarianism of the first, original followers of Jesus and the blossoming of the yet oppressed initial, vegetarian Jewish-Christian movement. Within these writings, table fellowship, including the prohibition of sitting at the tables of devils are discussed at great length. Keith Akers following comments illustrate the passion with which the first followers of Jesus condemned those who eat animal flesh and those who sat at 'the tables of these [non-vegetarian] devils':

"The Recognitions repeatedly refers to the necessity of being baptized before it is possible to eat at the same tables as Christians (1.9, 2.71-72, 7.34, 7.36; see also Homilies 13.9, 13.11). This is not a reference to a kosher regulation or to some other Jewish food law, but rather to a Christian food law. Peter in the Recognitions declines table fellowship even with earnest seekers after the truth, before they have been baptized…a remnant of this attitude [can be found in] modern Christianity, in the celebration of communion or the Eucharist…for the Jewish Christians, every meal was treated like…a communion meal…to be eaten only with believers….The rationale for this insistence on eating only with believers is interesting.

The Jewish Christians believed that eating at the "table of devils" was a grave error because this act of eating [animal flesh] gave the demons power over you. Demons are powerless over a person until that person becomes their table companion; the demons get power through food. (Homilies 8.20, 9.9). The "table of devils" is considered virtually any table with meat on it.... (Recognitions 4.16, 2.71). Demons are expressly allowed by God to take possession of a person who sheds blood, tastes dead flesh, or eats something cut or strangled (Homilies 8.19)." 7

Akers continues: "And the things which are well pleasing to God are these: to pray to Him, to ask from Him, recognizing that He is the giver of all things, and gives with discriminating law; to abstain from the table of devils, not to taste dead flesh, not to touch blood ... (Homilies 7.4) 8

Akers lists the injunctions carefully set out by the apostolic council, headed by James the apostle, who led the first followers of Jesus from Jerusalem, in accordance with Jesus' ministry. Notably, these injunctions command all genuine contemporary and future followers of Jesus to prohibit the eating of animal flesh and disallow converts from sitting at the 'tables of animal-flesh eating devils:'

"And this is the service He [God] has appointed: To worship Him only, and trust only in the Prophet of truth, and to be baptized for the remission of sins, and thus by this pure baptism to be born again unto God by saving water: to abstain from the table of devils, that is, from food offered to idols, from dead carcasses, from animals which have been suffocated or caught by wild beasts, and from blood; not to live any longer impurely..." (Homilies 7.8) 9

The above named precious, authentic, ancient writings, which have been briefly introduced here, will be shown to categorically command all faithful followers of Jesus' original teachings to strictly adhere to a vegetarian diet and to condemn animal sacrifice; characteristically both commands are fundamentally interwoven. It is of the utmost importance to all truth-seekers today, that these authentic early writings emphatically prove that the first Jewish-Christians, known as the Ebionites/Nazoraeans, were rigorous vegetarians.

To emphasize this point further: Homilies 7.4 implores people, "...not to taste dead flesh." Homilies 3.45 tells us that God "...was displeased with the slaughtering of animals, not wishing them to be slain, [and] did not ordain [animal] sacrifices."

Fortunately for posterity, the writer Epiphanius, was conversant with the Ebionite gospels and equally acquainted with members of the vegetarian Ebionite sect. Momentously, Epiphanius preserved for all future generations including us today, excerpts from these inimitable, irreplaceable gospels. Revealing orthodoxy's deliberate and scandalous suppression of Jesus' original vegetarian teachings by re-working and editing original religious narratives, Epiphanius' reliable, non-biblical, historical accounts teach us that, the authentic, historic, vegetarian Jesus emphatically refused to accept Passover flesh! Biblical accounts edited by orthodoxy make no mention of this!

In reality, Jesus's vegetarian spirituality had much in common with the compassionate 7th and 8th century BC prophets whose impassioned teachings condemning animal sacrifice and consumption he wished to fulfill; the vegetarian doctrines of the Ebionites/Nazarenes, including the Greek and Buddhist vegetarian cultures. Indeed, Epiphanius' above writings inform us that the genuine Jesus refused Passover animal flesh, stating: "I have come to destroy sacrifices."

Interestingly, historically, Jesus' vegetarianism was expressed in terms of destroying sacrifices, a conviction that echoes and fulfills the sentiments of his prophetic pioneering ancestors who likewise condemned the killing of animals in the name of misguided, revolting sacrificial customs as a mere excuse to eat animal flesh afterwards.

Again we see that historically, the condemnation of animal sacrifice/ killing animals was inextricably interwoven with the command to become vegetarian. All of Jesus' converts were vegetarians, fully conversant with Jesus' vegetarianism, none would countenance sitting at the tables of those who ate animal flesh. Tragically, until recent times the fact of Jesus' vegetarianism had become lost!

Importantly, scholars are universally agreed that the excerpts from the Ebionite/Nazoraean gospels provided by

Epiphanius, all of which emphasize the necessity of being vegetarian and condemn animal sacrifice, are dependable, authentic originals from the ancient Ebionite/Nazoraean gospels. Furthermore, the ancient reliable texts known as the Recognitions and Homilies also clearly describe Ebionite/Nazoraean vegetarianism, further substantiating Epiphanius' claims that the Ebionites/Nazoraeans were vegetarian.

Notably, from a date almost contemporary with Jesus, Paul is documented as being critical of Ebionite/Nazoraean vegetarianism recorded in Romans 14 and 1 Corinthians 8-10 which will be detailed in later pages. To reiterate, the Ebionites/Nazoraeans were the names given to Jesus' first followers, namely the Jewish-Christians, Jesus was also known as the Nazoraean.

Significantly, these invaluable writings including excerpts from the Ebionite/Nazoraean gospels provided by Epiphanius, and those texts known as the Recognitions and Homilies, graphically illustrate the original vegetarian commands dutifully followed by the first converts of Jesus and the apostles which despite oppression continued for several centuries, until they were overcome by opposition and their writings were hidden, destroyed and edited.

It is tragic for the animals, Jesus, his early converts and the majority of historic to present day devoted Christians, who have never been told of the existence of these authentic ancient vegetarian writings or have never read them. Thankfully this situation is currently being redressed today by my research and that of other scholars.

Jesus, the Good Shepherd

Acclaimed for being the Good Shepherd, Jesus used illustrative, didactic language, appealing for all-inclusive love and compassion, for all animals, human and non-human, inevitably, inescapably and unavoidably demonstrated through vegetarianism. Conspicuously, fostering kindness and empathy for animals amongst his followers, Jesus cleverly intertwined the plight of all animals, human and non-human, in many of his parables. Poignantly and revealingly, Jesus interwove the need for kindness, empathy, sensitivity and mercy for each and every animal as all of whom are 'living souls.'

In truth, Jesus would have been acutely aware that the very nature of true compassion spontaneously arouses the deepest heartfelt emotions for the plight of any deprived, disadvantaged, destitute animal, human and non-human. Jesus would have known that once a person genuinely internalized his teachings, it would lead to the progressive or sudden activation of whole-hearted, all-embracing kindness.

Instinctively and effortlessly a genuine convert cannot feel and demonstrate compassion to a person without feeling and doing the same for a fellow non-human animal. Naturally, they should feel the same empathy, sorrow and love for the distress, hunger, thirst, homelessness, insecurity, anguish, anxiety, fear or suffering of any other fellow animal, all of whom are innocent, emotional babes.

The outpourings of honest, authentic compassion cannot be turned on and off, empathizing with the distress of two-legged beings and not that of four-legged, sentient, conscious, aware, flesh and blood beings and all other organisms. When referring to God's knowledge of and empathy with, the plight of even the smallest sparrow, Jesus taught that kindness and respect should be demonstrated to even the strangest and tiniest life form. Crucially these beings, perhaps possessing minimum intelligence, still enjoy life which should be respected and protected and certainly they feel pain, suffering and murder.

God's Parental Love for all Beings

Later pages of this research will elucidate that Jesus demonstrated and commanded his followers to exhibit, God's parental love for even the most despised outcasts of his day, including lepers, prostitutes, taxmen, Samaritans and all non-human animals. Countless examples of Jesus' teachings reveal that his pleas for compassion and mercy were inextricably linked to all fellow beings, including our related animals; no being was excluded. Railing against the human sense of superiority, prejudice and self-centeredness, acting as God's mouthpiece, Jesus' vegetarian teachings demanded compassionate treatment for the 'living souls' of all animals created by their parent God.

Crucially, Jesus taught that the Father-Mother God is the creative, loving parent of all beings and inevitably God's parental love and concern for the emotional, mental, spiritual and physical welfare of every individual 'living soul,' no matter how small or unassuming is boundless.

The New Testament Gospel of Luke reminds us of Jesus' spiritual insights into the creator parent God's devotion to each of God's offspring. Recording Jesus' explanation, that no matter how apparently lowly, any being appears, the happiness and well-being of each and every soul is of paramount importance to the creative parent God, Luke chronicles Jesus' words below:

Luke 12:6 records Jesus as explaining: "Are not five sparrows sold for two pennies? And not one of them is forgotten before God."

Illustrating the importance of even the tiniest non-human being Jesus uses the analogy of God's love and awareness of the plight of even the tiniest sparrow similarly, documented by Mathew in the New Testament Gospel, Matthew 10:29: Mathew verifies Jesus' emphasis that God loves and actually feels the difficulties and pains of every life-form, all of whom are the children of God' creation:

"Are not two sparrows sold for a farthing? And one of them shall not fall on the ground without your Father [knowing and feeling it]." Of the utmost importance, the Gospel of John 10:11, quotes Jesus passionately teaching his followers that the righteous person would courageously give up his/her life to save any one of his/her animals. Jesus states: "I am the good shepherd. The good shepherd lays down his life for his sheep."

Significantly, this is exactly what Jesus did, by freeing the downtrodden animals Jesus attempted to teach all future converts the endless depths of his all-embracing compassion for the helpless animal victims. Jesus did, indeed, lay down his life for

84

these traumatized emotional babes, who were fearfully dreading slaughter in the temple.

By untying the animals and saving their lives, Jesus attempted to teach humanity how precious and important each of these living souls are and that his converts should likewise demonstrate the utmost compassion and mercy for all animals, human and non-human. Importantly, as alluded to earlier, to make this point, Jesus deliberately chose to free the animals, not during the earlier quiet, deserted night, but in full crowded and bustling daytime view.

Enraging the powerful temple authorities, by his courageous opposition to their intended sacrificial murder and consumption of the animals, scholars universally agree that it was this act that inevitably led to Jesus' execution. Indeed, Jesus was aware that his planned public liberation of the animals would so infuriate the temple authorities that it would lead to his death.

Forewarning his disciples of his impending death sentence, events proved the accuracy of his prediction. Indeed Jesus was arrested and crucified as a result of this emphatic, selfless and compassionate vegetarian statement for the edification of all future generations of humankind.

Jesus' Appeals for All-Embracing Compassion

Chosen from a myriad of Jesus' all-inclusive didactic appeals, sensitively and cleverly highlighting and interweaving the shared suffering and shared need for mercy and compassion for all animals, human and non-human, alike Jesus taught his followers that all animals feel and fear the overburdening strain of any form of yoke, drudgery, suffering and murder. Illustrating this point, the Gospel of Matthew 11:28-30 records Jesus as saying:

"Come to me, all you who are weary and burdened, and I will give you rest. Take my yoke upon you and learn from me, for I am gentle and humble in heart and you will find rest for your souls. For my yoke is easy and my burden is light."

Deliberately and specifically, Jesus was born surrounded by the comforting murmurs and companionship of fellow, aware, flesh and blood animals including goats, cows, oxen, sheep and donkeys as described in Luke 2:7. It was no coincidence that Jesus was born amongst the animals for whom he would later lay down his life. The biblical author's description of the nativity scene illustrates a typical barn populated with a whole host of animals.

Uniquely, no other ethically elevated prophetic spiritual teacher's life began in a stable surrounded by an extensive range of animals. This research will prove that throughout the course of Jesus' spiritually advanced vegetarian ministry, he passionately commanded all future generations of his sincere followers to exhibit compassion and mercy to all fellow animals demonstrated by their pious vegetarianism.

God's Foremost Vegetarian Command

Intensely immersed since childhood in the Jewish scriptures, undoubtedly Jesus would have been acutely aware of God's first communications with the human spiritual consciousness, which demanded vegetarianism. The first commands transmitted by God to the animals, human and non-human, reflect God's primary and most pressing concerns, those dearest to the creative parent God's heart. The first of humanity, represented by Adam and Eve were accompanied by their animal brethren in the Garden of Eden.

God's instructions to them, recorded in the Book of Genesis, as found in the Jewish Torah and first book of the Christian Bible, commanded from the beginning that both human and non-human animals, live side by side, happily and healthily in universal and never ending non-violence, peace and harmony, eating a vegetarian diet.

Crucially, this vital, wise, far-sighted, spiritually advanced ethos, teaches the precious sanctity of all life-forms. This spiritual wisdom is fundamentally entwined with all-embracing compassion, respect, preservation and the long-term continuation of the rich spectrum of life on this planet.

God's command to eat a vegetarian diet spotlights God's burning, first and foremost, most urgent, persistent and paramount concern. God commanded the living souls of all beings to respect each other, living in non-violent concord, murder being condemned, no life was to be taken, no matter who they are, as every living soul is precious to the loving parent God and humanity was meant to learn this fact. The author of Genesis 1:29-30 records God as saying:

"Behold, I have given you every herb yielding seed which is upon the face of all of the earth, and every tree that has seed-yielding fruit - to you it shall be for food. And to every beast of the earth, and to every fowl of the air, and to everything that creepeth upon the earth, wherein thee is a living soul, [I have given] every green herb for food."

All of Creation was commanded to live a vegetarian lifestyle, after which we learn that God was pleased, thereby God set in motion the peaceful, respectful, spiritually elevated compassionate vegetarian order in which the taking of any life was prohibited. Genesis 1:31 informs us that God was pleased with the vegetarian order:

"…Behold, it was very good." Many other references to God's commands for all members of Creation to eat a vegetarian diet can be found, two further examples follow: Genesis 2:16 states: "And the Lord God commanded the man, saying; "…of every tree of the garden, thou mayest freely eat…" and Genesis 3:18 records God's command: "Thou shalt eat the herbs of the field."

Jesus certainly raised human awareness by breathing life back into these forgotten, first, imperative unyielding Divine vegetarian commands, including those transmitted by God many centuries later to Jesus' prophetic ancestors. They too, acted as Gods' mouthpieces, fervently condemning the misled custom of murderous animal sacrifice, a deceitful excuse to eat animal flesh. As alluded to earlier, this denunciation was typically interwoven and integrally associated with vegetarianism.

Ancient Prophets Condemned Animal Sacrifice and Consumption

Deeply engaged in the teachings of his 7th and 8th century BC prophetic forebears, Jesus and his trained disciples frequently quoted from Jeremiah's, Isaiah's, Hosea's, Amos's and Micah's compassionate animal teachings which passionately condemned the homicidal, fraudulent and faithless killing of animals as tragic sacrifices, to gratify human food preferences.

These prophets will be discussed in detail later however the following offers a brief insight into their teachings which Jesus sought to fulfill. Although revered in name only, sadly and progressively, many emissaries of their exhortations requesting 'works,' not animal sacrifice and consumption, had, over the centuries, become forgotten, neglected and thereby rejected.

Acting as God's inspired envoys these ancient Jewish prophetic agents had reprimanded, chastised and cautioned the populace, informing them that God sought their righteous acts, in all their dealings, throughout their lives, not empty, ritualistic, murderous, animal sacrifice and animal flesh consumption.

As God's ambassadors, they declared that God was repulsed by these evil and hollow acts, murdering defenseless, harmless, trusting, innocent animals, whose tragic bodies, the life drained out of them were eaten afterwards.

Paradoxically, as noted, animals were killed and eaten afterwards as the result of the preposterous and deeply flawed indoctrination of the masses by the temple authorities that both this merciless, murderous demonstration and other sins would be forgiven! Inspired as God's representatives on earth, these devastated and impassioned divine mouthpieces, fiercely condemned these disgusting temple practices, making it nothing more than a greedy, industrious slaughterhouse drenched in blood.

Communicating on God's behalf as God's envoys, Jesus' prophetic ancestors condemned the errant and misled population for murdering and eating defenseless animals. These divinely appointed spokespersons passionately extolled the parent God's utter abhorrence and revulsion by the murder and eating of such unfortunate, emotional, childlike, animal victims.

As early as the 7th century BC, Jeremiah's heartfelt warnings to the people, graphically illustrated the creative parent God's abhorrence and detestation of the sacrificial murder and suffering of traumatized, innocent, vulnerable, animal living souls. Enthused as God's messenger, Jeremiah cautioned that if they continued killing and eating animals, God would take the land away from the people and gift the land to the animals alone!

Astounding the masses, Jeremiah revealed how ignorant and misinformed the people had become by educating them that in ancient times God granted original mutual covenants with the people. God promised to lead the tribes as their God in exchange for their ethical obedience, including the time God liberated the disparate Hebrew tribes from Egyptian slavery.

Jeremiah clarified that on all such momentous, historic occasions, God never once, requested the sacrificial murder of animals, thereby all such acts were grossly mistaken and imported from other cultures!

Jeremiah 7:22 records Jeremiah's edifying comments: "For I spake not unto your fathers, nor commanded them in the day that I brought them out of the land of Egypt concerning burnt offerings or sacrifices." As God's ambassador, Jeremiah sought to correct the above misinformed beliefs, teaching the populace that they had long lost sight of God's first and foremost original commands.

During the exodus journey out of Egypt, across the desert to the Promised Land, the newly liberated tribal rabble progressively welded together as an increasingly united people. Importantly, despite repeated infidelity, God's objective was to fuse these disparate tribes together, gradually unifying them as a nation, defined by its obedience to God's commands which, as people matured spiritually, were understood to be increasingly ethical.

However, repeatedly before and after reaching the Promised Land they were rebuked for their unfaithfulness, straying away from God's original laws and importing and adopting the repugnant animal sacrifice traditions and animal flesh eating food preferences of ancestral and neighboring peoples.

Later pages will show that in ancient Egypt, the eating of animal flesh was rare, however some fish were eaten. Indeed there was a prevalent strain of vegetarian ancient Egyptian priests and priestesses, holding a high status, confirming that the Hebrew slaves would not have typically eaten animal flesh whilst in ancient Egypt.

By the 8th century BC, Isaiah was likewise 'called' by God to act as God's representative. He continued to illustrate God's revulsion at the thought of the nation's cruelty to animals. Isaiah 1:11-13 clarifies God's scorn:

"To what purpose is the multitude of your sacrifice to me? Saith the Lord; I am full of the burnt offerings of rams, And the fat of fed beasts, And I delight not in the blood of bullocks, or of lambs, or of he-goats…Bring no more vain oblations; It is an offering of abomination unto me." Isaiah 66:3 offers a further example recording Isaiah's attacks on those who harm animals:

"He that killeth an ox is as if he slew a man. He that sacrificeth a lamb as if he broke a dog's neck."

Called by God to speak on God's behalf, Amos, who also lived in the 8th century BC, tells us repeatedly in the biblical book of Amos that God hated animal slaughter and consumption and sought the demonstration of spirituality in all their deeds, instead. Amos 5:21-24 illustrates this fact:

"I hate, I despise your feasts, and I will take no delight in your solemn assemblies. Yea, though ye offer me burnt-offerings and your meal-offerings I will not accept them. Neither will I regard the peace offerings of your fat beasts…But let justice well up as waters. And righteousness as a mighty stream."

Jesus Fulfills Prophetic Ancestors' Missions

As alluded, to earlier, by revivifying and acting upon the Jewish prophets' spiritually all-embracing, compassionate animal message, transmitted to them by God, Jesus fulfilled their teachings. Jesus literally gave up his physical life as the result of his public liberation of the tragic animals who dreaded slaughter in the temple.

Living as a vegetarian, Jesus further integrated all-inclusive compassion and vegetarianism into the spiritual consciousness of his followers demonstrated by his own vegetarian ministry, continued by James' long-term vegetarian leadership and the proselytizing of the remaining faithful vegetarian apostles.

Jesus believed that awareness needed to be raised along with meaningful clarification regarding the profundity of the prophets' forgotten and thereby rejected teachings. If a person allows any animal to be harmed or killed they can equally allow a person to be harmed or killed, as the gift of life itself is not valued as sacrosanct.

Hearts and souls therefore become hardened to the suffering of all beings, murder becomes an integral, on-going and accepted part of life that strikes back at us like a double edged sword. As a consequence of the lack of compassion and respect for all animals, hostility and violence is bred and the continued existence of all of the world's inhabitants, human and non-human remains dangerously precarious.

Jesus schooled his disciples in his prophetic ancestors' teachings, replete with exhortations commanding humanity to show mercy, empathy and compassion to all animals and fiercely condemning the murder and ingesting of animals. Jesus, followed by his devoted apostles reminded the populace of Isaiah's above vivid words which emphasize that the killing of an animal is as vile and abhorrent to God as the killing of a human animal. Jesus would also have been acutely aware of the religious texts quoted at the outset of this introduction.

In keeping with his assertions during his sermon on the mount, Jesus' spiritual mission, resurrected and breathed new life into the forgotten pleas for spirituality and compassion for animals of his prophetic predecessors and fulfilled them. They, in harmony with Jesus, transmitted the sentiments of God. Jesus reinvigorated his passionately merciful ancestors' lone voices, who cried out their opposition to animal sacrifice and feasting on their carcasses afterwards, echoing the sentiments of vegetarianism.

It becomes increasingly clear that Jesus' compassionate liberation of the horrified animals dreading murder in the temple was in total accord with the teachings of his prophetic forebears who had likewise condemned the cruel, misguided masses for animal slaughter and consumption and their lack of spirituality. As noted earlier Jesus was emphatic regarding the importance of compassion for all animals, human and non-human, no matter how apparently insignificant or small, with reference to the benevolent, creative parent God's empathy with the struggles of even the tiniest bird.

Perilously and heroically, Jesus acted upon these suppressed compassionate teachings by publically releasing the animals in the Jerusalem Temple during the Jewish Passover holiday which was a particularly emotional and bustling time. Overflowing with incoming, exhausted and excited pilgrims the Jerusalem Temple dominated by the wealthy temple authorities had become the focal point.

The Roman leadership fought to maintain control of the commotion of unruly, lively multitudes as tempers became frayed when tired, lost and confused newcomers, notably, incoming emotionally and financially manipulated pilgrims, converged on the local inhabitants and the temple itself. Due to the prosperity this sacrificial tradition brought in, the common man was duped, swindled and led astray by their own religio-political authorities, governed by the acquisition and retention of personal profit and power.

Vegetarianism Fashioned Jesus' World

Jesus' ethically advanced compassionate vegetarian doctrines will be clearly evidenced by the research contained in this serialized volume. Jesus' vegetarianism will be supported by the vegetarian teachings of his many global, spiritual, vegetarian predecessors, contemporaries and successors, each pleading for vegetarian compassion. Jesus' vegetarianism was comparable to and in harmony with the many ethically advanced vegetarian religions and spiritual philosophies which proliferated and flourished, dominating the world many centuries before, during and after Jesus' birth.

Due to the distortion and suppression of Jesus' vegetarian ministry for practically two thousand years, to help the reader become acquainted with Jesus' vegetarian ministry, this serialized volume will begin by outlining and summarizing the spiritually elevated compassionate, vegetarian ideologies that proliferated many centuries before the birth of Jesus and continued to burgeon and circulate after his death. The vegetarian world in which Jesus lived includes the profound and far-flung vegetarian teachings of generations of Greek spiritual philosophers, Confucius in China, and the authors of the Hindu Vedas and the Buddha.

For those who are shocked by the revelation of Jesus' vegetarian ministry, preaching compassion and respect for all animals, human and non-human, it will become clear that this elevated spirituality was not exceptional in the sense of being rare.

Jesus' vegetarianism was not in a global vacuum but in harmony with and part of a multiplying continuum of elevated human spirituality, exhibiting kindness to fellow animals. Indeed, it will be shown that there were many ethical vegetarian spiritual ideologies which shaped the world in which Jesus lived.

These spiritual philosophies each recognized that vegetarianism is an exalted spiritual value, teaching humanity about the sanctity of each individual life-form, which is imperative for the survival of all animals, human and non-human, on this planet. Notably, vegetarianism is a pacifist, non-violent philosophy, which values the life of all beings, as sacred.

Vegetarianism: The First Spiritual Step for Spiritual Truth-Seekers

Each thriving, principled vegetarian belief system including that of Jesus, taught that vegetarianism is an essential first step to progressively obtaining and internalizing the virtue of compassion. Vegetarianism cannot be omitted or avoided by any person committed to spiritual advancement. Step by step on the unfolding spiritual journey, the practice of vegetarianism teaches each individual a new, spiritually elevated norm, in accord with a religious conversion.

If vegetarianism is carried out for compassionate reasons rather than for the many personal health benefits a vegetarian diet offers, a person will find they cannot return to cannibalistic flesh eating. Practicing non-violence by their compassionate food choices, progressively, converts become used to not taking away the incalculable animal lifetimes of fellow, emotional, aware, feeling, flesh and blood, living souls.

Progressively, each increasingly compassionate spiritual vegetarian convert learns that it is wrong to be the cause of untold misery, exploitation and suffering by having animals killed on his/her behalf. Present day materialist indoctrination and blinkers removed, they progressively, sensitively and compassionately empathize with the unspeakable plight of all fellow beings as themselves, thereby each individual, advances his/her level of spirituality.

The longer a person has practiced vegetarianism, the thought of eating fellow traumatized beings and smelling the stench of their cooking, flesh and blood carcasses, hidden and dressed up by the sauces and recipes of indoctrinating, propagandizing and brainwashing, flesh-eating cookery programs, becomes increasingly heart-breaking, disgusting and nauseating,

Progressively, spiritually orientated vegetarians sympathize with all animals' indescribable and unimaginable suffering, murder and consumption. They are saddened by other humans who thoughtlessly continue repulsive cannibalistic, Neanderthal traditions. Increasing numbers of scientific studies are revealing that flesh-eaters invariably and inevitably suffer, later in life, from the multiplicity of associated detrimental health consequences an animal flesh diet brings.

When a person eats a fellow related animal they devour bodies filled with cholesterol which is responsible for a wide range of chronic human ailments, to mention a few here, these include strokes, heart disease and attacks, they also consume a variety of chemicals and hormones such as anti-biotics, growth and other artificial hormones and de-licing chemicals (fish).

94

Blood is Inseparable from Flesh

Some people eat flesh believing it does not contain blood. It is important to clarify that flesh and blood cannot be separated, in effect flesh and blood are synonymous. Blood is permanently and irreversibly contained in skin cells, blood is therefore impossible to separate from flesh. Importantly, the smallest unit of any tissue is a cell, on a microscopic level each cell is clearly seen to be surrounded by capillaries which contain blood, therefore it is impossible to remove blood from flesh, a fact proven at a cellular level, the two, flesh and blood are ceaselessly intertwined. The term flesh and blood therefore refers to a living soul.

This fact is extremely relevant for those who have animals murdered on their behalf associated with Muslim halal and Jewish kosher methods of slaughter. This type of murder is typically carried out without having the acutely aware animals stunned. They are hung upside down whilst their throats are slit, sometime after, dying slowly, their blood and life gradually drains from their necks.

Some are seen to die hung upside down in the back of travelling vehicles in transit to those who wish to eat them. Crucially, blood is synonymous with flesh and flesh is synonymous with blood: the prohibition of consuming blood is in truth, the prohibition of consuming flesh, the prohibition of eating a living soul.

A person would expect, as humanity advanced spiritually, traditions would reflect progressively elevated, moral and humane codes of conduct, including a ban on causing animals to suffer and the prohibition of killing and eating animals. Ironically, it was in the ancient past including the centuries before and after Jesus's birth that the world was largely vegetarian, in contrast to more recent centuries, however today vegetarianism is fast spreading across the planet.

However, an increasing 21st century sea change is resulting in vast numbers of people from all global religions returning to the spiritually elevated vegetarian diet of their ancestors. Spiritual truth-seekers, taking this life-changing, non-violent, health promoting decision, learn that vegetarianism has far-reaching and immeasurably valuable consequences for the spiritual and physical health of each spiritual devotee and animal alike.

It is paradoxical that the revelation of Jesus' vegetarianism, the vegetarianism of his devout disciples, including the vegetarianism of the first centuries of loyal Jewish-Christian followers, is shocking to many 21st century Christians especially in view of the fact that Jesus is revered for being the Good Shepherd and acclaimed for his fathomless depths of all-embracing compassion.

However, not all of Jesus' historic and contemporary followers have deeply integrated the enormous profundity of his message into their spiritual consciousness. They have lacked awareness that the fundamental vegetarian core of his all-inclusive, loving teachings incorporating all animals, human and non-human were suppressed whilst Christianity was an emergent religion.

Summarizing Topics within Proof Animals Have Souls

Each installment of this research will progressively raise awareness of Jesus' vegetarian teachings and that of his first followers. For several centuries, they dutifully copied Jesus their leader, through their vegetarianism. During these centuries these oppressed, loyal followers fought against suppression, persecution and the corruption and distortion of their master's all-embracing, compassionate, vegetarian teachings.

Having briefly introduced some of the many revelations contained within the whole of this serialized research, the following is a brief overview of the topics contained in this first installment named Proof Animals Have Souls.

The main themes we will explore are as follows: the interconnected and interdependent relationship between all animals, human and non-human: our astonishingly ancient relationship with companion animals, proven through archaeological discoveries: and a number of the global vegetarian spiritual philosophies commanding humankind not to harm fellow animals but to show them kindness and respect.

These discussions set the scene, prior to the provision of evidence revealing a far deeper and much more accurate understanding of Jesus's all-inclusive, compassionate vegetarian ministry. This was reflected in his empathetic, heartfelt concern for our related, animal companions.

This first installment: Proof Animals Have Souls commences this voyage of discovery with a synopsis of the science proving all 'living souls,' all animals, human and non-human are interconnected and unified. This fascinating summary reveals that the multitudes of 'living souls' human and non-human, who, equally have families and conceive of this planet as 'home,' belong to a single, interdependent and interrelated earth family, all originating from a single, shared common ancestor. Contemplating the timeless, endless, black oceans of outer space, home to billions of stars, suns and planets, should help us grasp the limitations of human understanding of this fathomless universe in which all life forms live.

The belief in God is left to the personal opinion of the reader. However, arguably, for those who do believe in God, they should beware of assigning the term 'God' to the gaps in human knowledge, as increasingly, the gaps are being filled in and this flawed, limited understanding of God, pushes the concept of 'God' ever further back. Arguably, just because the scientific discovery of evolution offers us, an inkling into the processes of creation once set in motion, it does not, in my opinion preclude the existence of an enigmatic, creator God.

Quantum physicists admit that we know and understand very little regarding the laws of nature at the sub atomic level. Astonishing and baffling new discoveries at this level of existence continue to overturn and defy all we previously understood in physics. Refraining from assigning the term 'God' to the gaps in our knowledge, this book's examination of the magnificent process of evolution does not in my opinion necessarily negate an originator, a creative, parent God.

It is important to be aware of the fact that when Charles Darwin first announced his theory of evolution to his academic peers in 19th century England, due to the uncompromising and limited scope of the religious political and scientific personalities of that time, it caused these positions to become dogmatically opposed and polarized.

Following on from the discussion of the evolution of all beings from a common ancestor we will then explore an archaeological examination of humankind's earliest friendship with our related animal brethren who have shared this planet with us from the beginning of time. Precious archaeological discoveries prove that ancient companion dogs and cats befriended and walked side by side with many of the first humans.

Leaving their loyal remains in cave dwellings, archaeological finds confirm that these dog and cat friends, guides, aides and bodyguards were typically buried with those children and adults whom they had selflessly cherished and protected and for whom they would have willingly sacrificed their own lives.

Following the meandering river of time into the long forgotten and distant past, this research continues by surveying the extensive, multi-ethnic, vegetarian practices of the ancient world, illustrating the widespread vegetarianism that shaped Jesus' world. Shining a light into the distant past, into the lost annals of history, these pages illustrate that Jesus's vegetarianism was part of a continuum of spiritually elevated vegetarian doctrines, widespread across the globe.

Surveying the global profusion of vegetarian spiritual philosophies, setting the worldwide vegetarian scene before and during the life of Jesus, clearly illustrates the vegetarian background to Jesus' ministry. The serialized review documents a fascinating and enlightening survey of diverse global vegetarian teachings emanating from ancient Egypt, Ancient Greece, Vedic Hinduism, Hinduism, Buddhism, Judaism and Confucianism each acting as precursors for Jesus' vegetarianism.

Progressively this exploration sets out the worldwide vegetarian teachings advocating compassionate vegetarianism and respect for animals which shaped the world in which Jesus lived, many remained contemporaneous with Jesus' own spiritual ministry. Acting as a finely tuned religio-historical detective, I continue by presenting the long lost and ignored facts that irrefutably evidence a clearer understanding of the original, undistorted vegetarian teachings of Jesus.

The many global vegetarian cultures, religions and spiritual philosophies to be discussed, each commanded humankind not to harm our fellow animals, in contrast they are to treat them with compassion and respect; spiritual qualities embodied in the ethically elevated practice of vegetarianism.

The prodigious ancient eastern cultures are discussed, summarizing the fundamental vegetarian components of Hinduism and Buddhism. Incredibly, Vedic Hinduism embraced vegetarianism as early as 1500 BC, extensively spreading this pacifist vegetarian way of life throughout India. By the 6th century BC Hinduism was challenged by the competing and flourishing vegetarian religions of Buddhism and Jainism.

Synopses are given regarding the vegetarian teachings of the Greek polymaths, the founders of modern-day academia, who, from at least the 6th century BC for approximately one thousand years, taught an elevated vegetarian spiritual philosophy. Incredibly, in the 6th century BC, Pythagoras, the celebrated Greek sage, genius and vegetarian spiritual philosopher sought to enhance his knowledge by becoming a student of the long-term vegetarian ancient Egyptian priestly sects who safeguarded ancient Egyptian wisdom.

The eminent Greek teachers lived centuries before the birth of Jesus and the Greek vegetarian spiritual philosophy survived, like that of the early vegetarian Christians, for several centuries after Jesus' death. Countless generations of memorable Greek intellects established flourishing academies of students. These bountiful universities perpetuated and spread vegetarianism, far and wide, which was integral to their ethically advanced spiritual philosophy and intellects.

Moving on to ancient China, the vegetarian teachings of the highly esteemed Confucius (551-479 BC) will be discussed and also the Jewish vegetarian teachings, some of which were integral to Jesus' Jewish heritage. It is fair to say that for countless centuries a large part of the ancient world was predominantly vegetarian.

99

Increasingly, archaeological evidence is revealing that ancient cultures, vast distances apart, were not isolated but linked by extensive and courageous land and sea trade routes. These densely populated merchant caravans and ships, not only carried merchandise and people over vast geographical expanses but spread vegetarian spiritual beliefs across man-made borders.

Importantly, the research set out in the early part of this serialized volume, populates and sets the stage, graphically illustrating the vegetarian background to the world in which Jesus lived, highlighting the fact that vegetarianism is not a recent phenomenon but has an extensive global heritage of which Jesus was an integral part. Jesus lived in a long forgotten, predominantly spiritually orientated vegetarian world. These discussions prepare the reader for the research which sets out proof that Jesus' elevated spirituality was likewise fundamentally based on vegetarianism.

This exploration will reveal the most spiritually elevated strands of the major world religions and spiritual philosophies commanding vegetarianism which predominated and flourished many centuries before and after Jesus' birth. The commonality of themes will be shown; each commanding humankind to act towards fellow animals the same as we request of God, as benevolent, parental guardians who empathize with the needs of these infant living souls' ensuring their welfare, happiness, health and safety.

These same world religions and spiritual philosophies continue today, teaching their adherents to live vegetarian lives, having no share in the responsibility for the genocide which befalls our fellow animals. For the entirety of their lives, these emotional children who are unable to speak human languages have great difficulty communicating to the insensitive human animal, their thoughts, feelings and emotions. Sadly, most of which, go unheeded by humans, hardened, oblivious and unresponsive to their diverse communicating sounds, including facial and body language. Genuine spirituality instructs us to show them compassion and respect in all our dealings.

We are even warned by the most ethically elevated teachings of the Greek spiritual philosophers and religions such as

100

Hinduism and Buddhism, that as a result of the cycle of reincarnation, (the rebirth process through which all living souls have the opportunity to progressively attain spiritual evolution), the animal flesh a person eats, will sooner or later, belong to his/her 'deceased' beloved family member, now reincarnated as a non-human animal.

These global and historic vegetarian spiritual teachings tell us that countless newly incarnated individuals reincarnate as non-human animals in order to gain first hand empathy with the exploitative plight, suffering and destiny of animals. Living as animals, thereby identifying and commiserating with animals, these incarnations ultimately enhance each living souls' level of spirituality as they learn and internalize the dire need for spiritually evolved all-embracing qualities demonstrating mercy and compassion.

The concept of the transmigration of the soul between the bodies of human and non-human is accepted by large proportion of the globe. A life as an animal perhaps acts as a catalyst to enhanced soul growth. Many pet owners would testify to their belief that many animals offer unconditional, limitless love and devotion being more faithful and compassionate than humans. Members of these religions believe that those who eat animal flesh share in the responsibility for the appalling cruelty, immense suffering, exploitation and murder of animals.

They believe their non-vegetarianism spontaneously incurs irrevocable karmic laws of nature drawing to them many negative events during their present life which also detrimentally shape their next incarnation. However, suffering lives of oppression, exploitation, sorrow and anguish themselves during non-human animal lifetimes, nurtures the growth of their kindness, teaching individuals to be merciful, compassionate vegetarians, elevating their spirituality, in turn, shaping happier, future incarnations.

Many fascinating subjects related to animals will be discussed throughout the course of this research, including the continuing influence today of Descartes, the ruthless first vivisectionist. Descartes' pitiless, barbaric, inhuman, long term and ongoing legacy continues today to cruelly indoctrinate the public with tragic consequences for all animals.

Animals screaming, nailed to his vivisection table, under-going live, conscious, wide-awake, vivisection, were disregarded by him as mere unfeeling machines. His followers were brainwashed by his philosophy, in preference to realizing that he was, indeed capable of performing such callous, torturous acts on feeling beings.

Mercilessly, in true psychopathic fashion, Descartes atrociously cut open their alert, attentive, emotional, sentient, flesh and blood bodies and took out their organs and body parts, one by one. The transition at death of these living souls brought them incredible relief from unimaginable suffering, ending their trauma.

Death arrived as a deep angelic anesthetic, as their souls re-awoke in the non-physical heavenly spirit realms of existence! All who eat animal flesh tragically appear to adhere to Descartes' absurd teachings that animals are like machines who do not feel pain. Proof Animals Have Souls now commences with a synopsis of the scientific evidence proving that all living souls, all beings, human and non-human, belong to a single, interrelated, interdependent earth family.

CHAPTER 3 – OUR SINGLE, INTERRELATED, INTERDEPENDENT, EARTH FAMILY

"A fire-mist and a planet,
A crystal and a cell,
A jellyfish and a saurian,
And caves where the cave men dwell;
Then a sense of law and beauty,
And a face turned from the clod-
Some call it Evolution,
And others call it God."

W.H. Carruth.

Through the processes of evolution, all beings share a common ancestor making them a single, interrelated, interdependent earth family. As the above poem suggests, I personally do not believe the process of evolution has to preclude the existence of an original, creative, parent God, however, this personal decision is left to the reader. I perceive evolution as the process through which God enabled all life to evolve, by setting the creation process in motion.

A wide range of scientific disciplines have universally proven that all life forms who make up the web of life on the bountiful but fragile, eco-system of our planet Earth, share a common ancestor. As a consequence of this, all life forms on

Earth are interrelated and interdependent at levels we are only just beginning to uncover.

We live in a dynamic universe, incredibly it was once much smaller than it is now. Gravity is the fabric of space and time and Einstein's insights lead us to the concept of the moment of creation. People prefer to think of the universe as eternal but in fact it has a beginning known as the Big Bang and it will have an end.

The universe is expanding and one day it will contract. However, science does not hold all the answers there are many equally important strands to knowledge which help us to make sense of the entirety of existence. Species depletion is occurring at an alarming rate far in excess of natural extinctions therefore it is imperative that we develop a spiritually based science.

Traditional Newtonian science, which is proving inadequate to explain all the profundities of the perceived physical and non-physical world, is in sharp contrast to the cutting edge breakthroughs of quantum science. Paradoxically, many natural sciences, often secular, are proving the correctness of the astute, intuitive and insightful wisdom inherent in the teachings of countless perceptive vegetarian spiritual teachers who lived throughout the millennia.

For the vast array of life to continue on this planet it is imperative to adhere to the compassionate and sagacious wisdom of our historic spiritual savants in order to safeguard all species. Compassionate vegetarian wisdom was fundamental to the vegetarian teachings of a long succession of vegetarian spiritual teachers including the authors of the Hindu Vedas, Buddha, the Greek spiritual philosophers, Jesus and many other ancient spiritual teachers.

The all-embracing merciful compassion of many ancient global prophets and spiritual philosophers is certainly spiritually elevated however they also demonstrate a multifaceted, far-sighted enlightenment. Scientists have become increasingly aware that if we harm any other species we also damage ourselves and our home, the earth, on many multi-dimensional levels. It has taken humanity eons to finally wake up to the fact that the loss of any one species can have dramatic negative, unseen repercussions on all other species, revealing an intricate chain reaction throughout the living world.

Despite the rich diversity of life forms on Earth, astonishingly all beings are made of the same components. Remarkably, all beings share the same building blocks of life, because they have a shared ancestor. Species differ because they have each evolved in different circumstances over millions of years.

Sadly, en masse, the human animal offers many fellow animal beings no compassion or respect, as they are slaughtered in their millions every year and many species due to human aggrandizement, become extinct. Typically, humankind shuns and rejects their unconscious awareness that every irreplaceable creature is precious and plays a vital role in the intricately related, interdependent web of life.

Endless examples can be given to demonstrate this point. However, let us here look at two examples of apparently humble species, which are usually disregarded as pests, namely bees and bats. Superficially judged, they, like many other species are rashly considered, criticized and frequently thought of as a nuisance. Fatefully, if the global bee population was to become extinct or to be severely reduced in numbers, there would be earth shattering consequences.

The demise of bees would cause the loss of pollination of the entire range of all vitally nutritious fruits, nuts, vegetables and cotton. Their loss would act as a catalyst to world-wide famine. Crucially, few people realize if the global bat population was to die out untold numbers of related beings on Earth would be overrun by disease conducting mosquitoes.

Returning to bees, importantly, bees act like barometers, measuring the damage caused by humanity to the health of the planet. Primarily through the bees' absorption of ever more powerful poisonous cocktails of herbicides, pesticides, insecticides and fungicides, bees particularly in agricultural areas, are fast dying out in incredible numbers.

The use of various chemicals may kill bees directly which would inevitably cause them pain, as pain is felt through the nervous systems of all creatures. Alternatively chemicals can lower bees' immune systems, making them vulnerable to viruses and other disorders.

Governments' sanctioning the use of nerve agent chemicals, poisonous to bees are particularly opposed by global conservation charities. These chemicals include neonicotinoid insecticides which are frequently sprayed, by farmers, in particular, on oilseed rape, despite an increasing corpus of evidence which proves this substance damages and blights the homing and foraging abilities of honey bees and bumblebees.

The number of honey bees has halved since the 1980's in Britain alone whilst three of the United Kingdom's twenty-five bumble bee species have already become extinct by the early part of the 21st century. This ever encroaching annihilation of bees and other wild pollinators can potentially demolish the essential pollination of much needed food leading to world-wide starvation.

Significantly, it is a known fact that bees fare a little better in urban areas where peoples' gardens provide welcome respite, acting as sanctuaries for bees along with a variety of supportive vegetation. It is believed the reason for this is that urban home gardens, located amongst town and city buildings, are not saturated to the same extent with the agricultural industry's increasingly lethal use of chemicals.

Bee destruction has become so alarming, that if the mass annihilation of bees goes unhalted, it is expected that by 2035 there will be no more bees left in the USA. Some indicators suggest that bees will become extinct much sooner. The anticipated loss of bees needs to be halted, as their annihilation threatens the globe with an impending, dire, food shortage during the very century that the world population is expected to double in size!

Incredibly, in contemporary times, bee hives are being hired out! Containerized, bees are flown in airplanes to fulfill vital pollination tasks in areas where bees have already become extinct. Incredulous bee keepers discover that many bees, once freed from their hives, appear to die quite quickly or through confused neurological signals, of manmade origin, they are unable to find their way back to their waiting hives. As a consequence they then die, never to be taken back home and never to be hired out to fly and pollinate again.

This sickness is often described as Colony Collapse Disorder or CCD. Significantly, some scientists believe this condition is caused by a dangerous combination of malnutrition and neuro-pesticides, a sorry state of affairs. Soil is not left fallow and fertilized as it was in the past consequently fruit and vegetables do not absorb or provide the same nutrients for any life form today.

Importantly, more than one third of all comparatively nutritious and tasty food eaten is given to us by the pollination work of bees. These foods include those that expert nutritionists tell us to eat the most, and keep in plentiful supply as they boost and sustain good health. These foods include nuts, fruit and vegetables. Significantly, without pollination humanity and other animal populations will be forced to eat gruel which is made of wheat and corn.

Incredibly bees pollinate over three million flowers in a single day. Farmers cannot hope to attempt to play the role of the honey bee as this gargantuan task would neither be practical or sustainable. Remarkably, bees, flowers, nuts, vegetables and fruit evolved closely and harmoniously together, again exemplifying the interrelated and interdependent evolution of the natural world. Notably, each of these closely related species cannot survive without the other as each belongs to the single, interrelated, interdependent, earth family.

Having analyzed honey samples obtained from bee hives, scientists are alarmed that some honey actually now contains a range of pesticides. Humanity has initiated and set in prolific motion destruction on an unprecedented scale. The human animal has become a proficient architect in causing mass extinctions and daily, global genocide of animals, human and non-human alike. Earth, as a living organism will heal over time from the human animal's terrifying air, sea and land pollution and consequent life threatening atmospheric changes.

In time, Mother Earth will also recover from the human animal's preoccupation with world-wide deforestation, detrimental to the atmosphere. This scarring of the landscape also causes the loss of irreplaceable habitats making countless species homeless, causing mass extinctions.

Our generous blue and fecund planet has throughout her long history healed herself many times before from incredibly dramatic, violent, fiery and tumultuous onslaughts originating from volcanoes and from outer space. After every furnace and firmament, shifting oceans and land masses, the Earth's revival process has taken millions of years, far beyond any physical individual's lifespan.

Significantly, each time the aftermath and repercussions of the event has led to a very differently adapted living world giving birth to very different species of living creatures and vegetation. Mother Earth, home to the natural world, will indeed heal and re-stabilize herself after humanity has tragically brought about its own extinction and that of other related species.

A person is reminded of the devastating extinction of the dinosaurs who, like humankind, had presumably taken their apparent domination of the Earth for granted. It is thought-provoking that these extinct, presumably less intelligent giants walked the earth for countless millennia, far longer than the human animal has achieved to date.

As reflected in the past, the future new, healing Earth, will have little in common to the one all present life forms now know, as 'home.' Her generosity to the human animal is not limitless and in its present form is all but spent. No organism can keep on taking without replenishing, nurturing and respecting the entire interdependent, interrelated earth family, who each sustain us all, sharing our planetary habitat.

Of necessity, humankind need to step up measures of conservation which include increasing breeding, protection and conservation programs for the multiplicity of endangered species and halting the exploitation and daily mass slaughter of defenseless miserable animals for food. We need to end the wretched putrid condemnation of cows, calves, sheep, lambs, pigs and poultry.

They suffer physical and mental anguish in dark, faeces-ridden, infernal, foul-smelling conditions, necessitating increasingly stronger daily cocktails of hormones and antibiotics in their food which have further debilitating consequences on human health. We also need to make a transition to wholly agricultural farming which will feed the globe thus ending starvation. Agricultural farming, per acre, feeds vastly more people than even, industrialized, factory 'farming' of animals can ever achieve.

In summary, for the mutual benefit of the human animal and all other related beings, all of whom are 'living souls', humanity needs to take heed of its closely interwoven and reciprocal relationship with the whole spectrum of life forms. Humankind need to learn empathy, which is the capacity to understand and sympathize with the feelings of others.

In return for acting as benevolent, respectful, compassionate guardians demonstrating kindness, empathy and respect for all members of the single earth family, all related species would mutually benefit. All toxic forms of land, sea and air pollution would be halted. Such changed priorities are imperative for the continued survival for all, in the world as we presently know her.

Billions of years old, Earth, its atmosphere and the evolution of all its related life forms operate and adapt on a timescale that is far longer than the lifespan of any single, physical being from any species. Today, we should not understand the problem facing each and every one of us as one in which we need to work to save Mother Earth, significantly, Mother Earth will survive but we will not! Tragically, as architects of our own destiny, we will take most if not all innocent, unsuspecting, vulnerable species with us.

The above facts are a timely reminder that, however seemingly insignificant any life form is, they are vital to the well-being of the entire living world, which inevitably includes the welfare of the human animal. Many of all present day beings and life forms will not survive the changes that are fast approaching. The dawning catastrophe requires us to work to save Mother Earth in the form in which all present life forms currently recognize and know her.

We need to strive to maintain the atmospheric conditions for which all present, related species have evolved and adapted to, as life enhancing. Our Mother Earth as we currently know her is fast becoming unrecognizable. She is changing from the planet on which humanity and all other interdependent living species have evolved to live on and know as home. As conditions on our earth-home rapidly change each year, cumulatively she will no longer support most of all present day related life-forms. Taking long overdue conservation measures is not striving to save Mother Earth, it is striving to save ourselves and all related sentient beings!

The human animal may achieve too little, too late, alleviating the destruction of our planetary habitats, temporarily saving themselves. They may find themselves surviving with great difficulty for a finite period of time on a barren wasteland, a desolate planet, devoid of glorious song birds who formerly decorated the skies and the abundance of wonderful fellow companion beings that progressively swam in the grossly polluted seas or walked this magnificent planet with us.

Charles Darwin's Scientific Revelation

A short summary of Charles Darwin's revolutionary evidence for evolution will be discussed in order to clarify the facts proving the shared ancestry and consequent relatedness and interdependence among the intricate web of life on earth. Darwin was an English naturalist who caused great indignation in 19th century Victorian society when he presented his accumulated evidence that humans and all other life forms share an ancient common ancestor.

In 1858 Darwin and Alfred Russell Wallace combined their efforts and produced a paper for the academic community concerning the processes of evolution. However, by the following year, 1859, fearful that Wallace would present his lesser evidence for evolution first, Darwin finally published his long-standing, in-depth research which he had been hesitant to make public for many years.

Darwin's major treatise called On the Origin of Species by Means of Natural Selection made a major impact on all branches of academia and has revolutionized the subject of biology ever since.

Darwin rather than Wallace is celebrated for presenting the concept of evolution to the world due to the fact that Darwin possessed decades of extensive research and fossil evidence which provided detailed support for his theory of evolution. It is Darwin who is acclaimed today as the father of this theory as it was Darwin's on-going evidential presentations and writings that raised awareness, educating his academic peers. At that time, although the research of Wallace and others also evidenced the processes of evolution their analysis of the evidence was much less detailed and incomplete.

Integral to Darwinian evolution is the concept and process of natural selection and common ancestry explained here.

"Surviving individuals, (living forms) which vary in some way that enables them to live longer and reproduce, pass on their advantage to succeeding generations...Part of the proof of evolution is in the fossil record, which shows a succession of gradually changing forms leading up to those known today. Structural similarities and similarities in embryonic development among living forms also point to common ancestry. Molecular biology (especially the study of genes and proteins) provides the most detailed evidence of evolutionary change." *1*

Darwin's biological theory revealed to the world, "...that the various types of plants, animals, and other living things on Earth have their origin in other pre-existing types and that the distinguishable differences are due to modifications in successive generations." *2*

Before my later provision of substantive details regarding the theory of evolution it should be pointed out that this discovery has been the most tested scientific theory ever. Importantly, the decades of research that led to this leap in human knowledge continues to be confirmed by the collection of diverse evidence over subsequent decades from many different scientific disciplines.

The proof underlying this wonderful insight of the interrelatedness and interdependence of all Earth's living organisms is overwhelming. This means that it is beyond any shadow of doubt that, the diversity of all 'living souls' whether they live on the land, fly in the skies or swim in our oceans share a common ancestor and are most significantly related members of the same family. We are all one singular, interrelated and interdependent earth family and each family member made of the same building blocks of life has descended from a shared ancient ancestor.

All Beings are Brothers, Sisters and Cousins

All beings and life forms are fellow inhabitants of our mutually shared home the Earth. Scientists are becoming increasingly aware that each species plays a significant, yet still little understood role in the maintenance and support of the complexity and diversity of the whole living world. If compassion for the plight of fellow animal 'living souls' does not motivate a person it is important for he/she to be aware that the survival and well-being of each species is vital for the well-being of all species as all are inter-related and interdependent.

During the long history of evolution of life on this planet, depending on how long ago any particular descendant lineage separated from another, some species can be considered cousins and brothers and sisters, whilst those who separated further back in time might be considered to be great-great grandparents. Consequently, each member of the single earth family who lives on the land, sea and skies, should be treated with the utmost compassion, empathy and admiration.

The abundant and enormous diversity of species that have lived and currently live on Earth is breath-taking yet as noted, all flora and all fauna share identical building blocks of life. The following gives an insight into the wide range involved. It is " ...incredible [due to differences] in size, shape, and way of life - from lowly bacteria...to stately sequoias [trees], rising [300 feet], ...[to] bacteria living in hot springs at temperatures near the boiling point of water to fungi and algae thriving on the ice masses of Antarctica and in saline pools at -23 degrees (- 9 degrees F); and from giant tube worms discovered near hydrothermal vents on the dark ocean floor to spiders and larkspur plants existing on the slopes of Mount Everest..." *3*

Discoveries Complement Faith

For those who believe in the existence of a parental, creator God, who permeates and dwells within all creatures, it is vital to understand that acknowledging the facts that support the theory of evolution does not inevitably imply that God does not exist. The process of evolution simply reveals that once the magnificent creative process was set in motion, typically called the Big Bang, it took more than the symbolic or estimated seven days hypothesized by the ancient scribes who wrote the Book of Genesis, the earliest book contained in the bible.

Historically, some followers of particular interpretations of religion have been afraid to accept the weight of the evidence for evolution fearing this advancement of human knowledge implied that an unfathomable, omniscient, omnipresent, omnipotent, parental creator God, could not exist. Arguably, the full concept of God will always remain beyond the level of our limited human understanding. Surely, if God does exist, God would work through tools such as natural events such as the Big Bang and natural laws.

Humanity is tasked to strive to continually enrich our knowledge and understanding of all things and should not be afraid of new developments. Learning to integrate and synthesize new knowledge, enhancing former beliefs is challenging, as at first, knowledge might be used as a weapon appearing to totally overturn earlier concepts. Hopefully, the progression of human knowledge should deepen and enliven newly synthesized personal beliefs, increasing our wonder, appreciation, compassion and respect for all life forms and the planet herself.

Ancient religious scribes sought to understand and explain to others how the diversity of life originated and proliferated on this planet. They ascribed the creation of the Earth and all the species upon it to be the creative work of a 'Parental Creator God.' Many people accept that an aspect of this enigmatic, celestial, omnipresent intelligence dwells within the soul all life forms as all of whom are the parent God's beloved children; all offspring are the children of creation.

The scribes taught that God is responsible for the design, creation and monitoring of all life forms including the Earth herself. However, these spiritually enlightened ancients had no way of knowing how old creation was or how long it took for life to be created and proliferate. They hypothesized that it took seven days. Their belief that God created all life forms does not have to be overturned by the insights gained from the discovery of the slow process of evolution which took far longer than seven days.

Disadvantaged by their lack of advanced scientific knowledge, gained by us through modern day scientific disciplines, these ancients did not possess scientific methods such as radiometric dating which accurately dates the evidential fossils including transitional fossils that we have accumulated today. Transitional fossils reflect naturally occurring sequential transitional developments amongst life forms providing us with visual evidence of how a particular species has evolved through incremental adaptations over time, often into structurally different or new species.

Countless illustrative, practically pictorial transitional fossils have been unearthed. Incredibly, some of these fossils of ancient creatures provide us with images which teach us about and prove the existence of beings such as walking whales, fish with fingers, fish with feet, human ape hybrids and many more. All of which evidence the relentless progression of the process of evolution, once the process of creation was enigmatically set in motion. Evidentially, it cannot be overstated all life forms on this planet belong to one, single, related, interdependent earth family made of the same building blocks of life.

Estimating time periods without modern day scientific and technological support, these pious ancients wrongly theorized that God created the universe in seven days. For those who believe in God, arguably, speed does not prove the existence of a God. Surely there is far more wonder aroused when we learn of the wonderful complexity of the slow, progressive, relentless, bountiful process of the procreation and multiplication of life

114

forms occurring over millions of years? Arguably it is more magnificent to be made aware that all beings, including all other life forms are collective members of one enormous, yet single, connected family.

There is no reason to think that if a creative parent God does exist surely God would consider all of His/Her offspring, namely all species, to be precious. The ancient writings of Hindus, Buddhists, Greeks, Chinese, Jews, Christians and Moslems implore humanity to demonstrate compassion to all human and non-human animals and life-forms. Indeed, Christians should be acutely mindful that Jesus taught his followers that God is aware of and empathizes with, the anxiety and suffering of all of the parent God's offspring, human and non-human, demonstrated by God feeling the sorrows of even the tiniest sparrow.

Significantly, the concept of evolution does not have to be interpreted in such a way as necessarily destroying a person's religious beliefs; including the belief that the diverse earth family which embraces all species, are the children of God's creation. Arguably, many theists accept that an omniscient, omnipresent, omnipotent, enigmatic, creative energy, namely God would be an integral part of all creatures, dwelling within them, and all creatures would be a fundamental part of the energy substance of God.

Crucially, many ancient scribes wrote as spiritual teachers not scientists, telling us in the Book of Genesis that God created the Heavens and the Earth and all life forms in seven days. Arguably, they should not be misjudged because they made an error regarding an assumed time period when they sought to convey a spiritual not scientific message.

Typically, the bible authors in keeping with the customs of many ancient peoples used numbers in a symbolic manner to flesh out their accounts. Notably, many traditional cultures used numbers in a symbolic way rather than using them to convey a specific factual number, a precise calendar date or an exact number of days or years.

Certain numbers or multiples of those numbers are regularly repeated, always with symbolic significance, throughout the books preserved in the bible. This is a common feature found among traditional cultures to this day. In effect, if God created the shared common ancestor of all life forms then God is the source of the evolutionary process which radiated out, diversifying and proliferating over the millennia into majestic numbers of species.

Dennis Bratcher, a highly respected authority on biblical studies clarifies that:

"A great many numbers in both Testaments are used symbolically, are stylized for other purposes than simple counting, or are approximate numbers based on different cultural ways of reckoning…the number three (often used…to mark the passage of a short period of time or extent without intending specifics; Jon 3:3, 1:7), seven (symbolizing completion; Gen 2:2, Gen 29, Matt 15:35), twelve (symbolizing wholeness and community; Gen. 35:22, Jud 19:29) and forty (a schematized number used for a generation or simply an unspecified long period of time; Gen 7:4, Ex 16:35)." *4*

The unparalleled magnitude and majesty of the universe and the incredible diversity of life on Earth is awe inspiring. Discovering that it has taken millions of years for Earth to become the planet with which we are familiar and that it has supported infinite numbers of evolving species, simply reveals we cannot take the scribes' limited grasp of the time period of subsequent creation as literal.

As stated, these ancients were disadvantaged they did not have the numerous scientific disciplines we have today. Consequently, their estimate of the period of time for creation to occur should be understood in symbolic, not literal terms.

If a person believes in God, the process of evolution does not destroy belief in God it simply provides the detail for belief. The theory of evolution does immensely increase our respect for the magnificent, interdependent, interrelated web of life engendered through the workings of the processes of creation.

If a person believes in God then the theory of evolution should increase their awe with respect to the breathtaking process of creation set in motion by the wondrous energy of God, millions of years ago. This belief should enhance our respect for the benevolent, abundant yet sensitive ecosystem of our planet and all the intricately related life forms living upon it.

116

Improving our understanding of the processes of the natural world, which we have termed the laws of nature, should not be the cause of a believer ceasing to believe in God. The concept of God should not be applied as the answer to only the gaps in our knowledge.

That form of understanding of God is flawed because as new scientific discoveries progressively unlock knowledge that had hitherto remained a mystery, God would be pushed ever further back to the diminishing gaps in our knowledge. This flawed concept of God would become progressively dissolved as the mysteries of life become better understood. Such is the error of applying the concept of God merely to the gaps in human knowledge.

Arguably, if a person believes in God then an improved understanding of the systems of the natural world leads to a better understanding of the magnificence of God as an all-powerful energy that set in motion the processes of creation. Some people believe that the living world is a system of matter governed by natural laws, not God.

It should be pointed out that improving our understanding of the creation process is no different to understanding other systems of matter, processes of the natural world, such as the sun rises every morning, if you drop something, gravity will cause it to fall, the tides of the sea, ebb and flow and vegetation dies every winter and returns to life every spring.

Understanding the processes of the natural world, should not rob a person of their belief in God any more than an improved understanding of how life evolved should deprive a person of their belief in God. The natural world and its processes can be viewed as the tools through which God operates as a creative energy, dwelling within all life forms, all created beings, not as an anthropomorphic, bountiful, old man akin to Father Christmas. For those who believe in God, God can be understood as the creative energy catalyst which initiated the evolutionary process, the creator who set the creation process in motion, enabling all life forms to evolve.

Orthodoxy Wrongly Feared Discoveries

Historically, many learned people have tragically become martyrs after their discoveries extended the limitations of human knowledge. One example is Galileo, (1564-1642), the Italian scientist who was the first to use the telescope to investigate the earth's position in the solar system. This physicist, mathematician and astronomer confirmed the same earlier 15th century heliocentric findings of Copernicus, showing that the planets circle the Sun rather than the Earth.

This 'new' knowledge challenged and eventually ended centuries of Orthodox Church dogma which forced people to believe the planets circled the earth and not the sun! Galileo, the genius, had the traumatic experience of facing the powerful Church appointed Roman Inquisition.

These much feared and dangerous men regularly tortured people forcing them to renounce unpopular beliefs. Orthodoxy denounced Galileo as a heretic. Fortunately, they did not murder him however they prevented this great mind from carrying out further research, forcing him to live the remaining part of his life under house arrest. This example highlights human misunderstandings, ignorance and insecurities.

The universally celebrated genius, Albert Einstein, made contributions to human knowledge regarding gravity, as the fabric of space and time, which has led us to the realization that our earth is not eternal but has a beginning and an end.

Incredibly, we are now aware that approximately 14 billion years ago the universe was smaller than the smallest part of an atom, revealing that the universe is not static but dynamic, that it is progressively expanding and will one day contract. Significantly, all discoveries ultimately open new vistas of understanding as long as we are genuine truth seekers who are open-mined enough to see them. Instead of being challenged by the fact that the universe is not eternal we can deduce from Einstein's discoveries that there was indeed a moment of creation!

The findings of this 20th century mathematician and physicist who developed the theory of relativity have contributed to human knowledge extending our horizons. Successively others are supplementing and perfecting Einstein's discoveries.

Importantly, a word to believers, gaining knowledge does not have to negate a person's belief in the existence of a creative energy known as God. However, the attainment of new knowledge may force people to extend their limited understanding and horizons regarding the concept of an eternal, all-powerful, creator God.

Theologians and Evolution

Significantly, perhaps through fear and misplaced, though commendable loyalty, still today in the 21st century, there are diverse communities of organized Church members and other believers who are not church goers who reject, outright the facts of the academically celebrated theory of evolution instead of integrating that knowledge into their paradigms of thought.

Some theologians and believers alike, past and present, feel that the only way to express their loyalty to God is to argue that the universe was created in seven days, because the ancient writers of the book of Genesis symbolically suggested or wrongly told us this was the case.

Arguably, for believers the important thing is that the ancient scribes taught that the world was created by God, not how long they estimated God took to create it.

For those who believe in the existence of a parental creator God, it is best not to limit a person's concept of God nor take the scribes' erroneous seven day creation account literally, information that was beyond the knowledge of these ancients.

Historically, in the same way, devout churchmen of Galileo's day were wrongly misled into believing that Galileo's inspired discoveries were heretical. Galileo revealed the correct relationship of the earth to the sun, exposing the flawed teachings of the Orthodox Church, negating its authority. The leaders of this dogmatic institution wrongly claimed that Galileo's findings challenged the very existence of God!

In effect, Galileo was simply adding to the font of human knowledge and the precise relationship of the sun to the earth was insignificant to the concept of God. In 1992 Pope John Paul II admitted that the Church was wrong for opposing the findings of this 16th century Italian genius. In modern times, it is futile to counter the momentous and overwhelming evidence which proves that creation, once set in motion, evolved over millions of years.

Evidence proving the facts of evolution continues to be stock piled by the multifarious relevant scientific disciplines to this day. Crucially, all biological sciences have proven the shared common ancestry of all life forms. "The evolutionary origin of organisms is today a scientific conclusion established with the kind of certainty attributable to such scientific concepts as the roundness of the earth, the motions of the planets and the molecular composition of matter." *5*

Based on their literal interpretation of the biblical Book of Genesis, both historically and today, some theologians wrongly teach their church membership that all life-forms were created simultaneously and every species has remained totally unchanged for millions of years. They believe that to accept the magnificent process of evolution that has taken place over millions of years is to reject God, yet God can be perceived as being the original prime mover, the creative source of evolution. Below Pope John Paul II, in 1981 sought to redress their fears saying:

"The Bible itself speaks to us of the origin of the universe and its make-up, not in order to provide us with a scientific treatise but in order to state the correct relationships of man with God and with the universe. Sacred scripture wishes simply to declare that the world was created by God, and in order to teach this truth it expresses itself in the terms of the cosmology in use at the time of the writer. Any other teaching about the origin and make-up of the universe is alien to the intentions of the Bible, which does not wish to teach how the heavens were made but how one goes to heaven." *6*

Early Beliefs How Life Began

As stated, comparatively large numbers of people even in the 21st century refuse to accept the conclusive findings of evolution based on perceived religious objections. Significantly, the evolutionary process reveals how all creatures are related, interdependent and belong to a single earth family. The findings of evolution do not have to negate the belief in a creative parent God who began the creative process.

By rejecting the theory of evolution out of hand, some theists (believers in a God) inadvertently disadvantage animals and all other species, throwing the baby out with the bath water. By appreciating the fact of our relatedness with all species, a person learns the importance of showing all of our relatives the utmost compassion and respect, as affirmed and commanded by global religious texts.

Early Beliefs and Developments

The study of how the building blocks of life originated on this planet has a long and fascinating history. Prior to the 19th century discovery of the processes of evolution, most people took all religious texts literally, accepting the beliefs of the ancients' that life formed spontaneously from non-living matter. Historically, people supposed that complex living organisms are born from decaying organic substances.

According to this bygone, mistaken 'spontaneous generation theory' mice were believed to be spontaneously generated by grain and likewise maggots were spontaneously to have been generated by decaying meat.

In the late 17th century Anthony van Leeuwenhoek's discoveries introduced the world to micro-organisms namely protozoa and bacteria. Inevitably, his findings fuelled interest amongst his scientific peers who were interested in the newly visible and enigmatic world observed through the microscope.

Around the same time Francesco Redi showed the world that if rotten meat is kept free of flies which hatch eggs then maggots will never appear in the meat. The discoveries of van Leeuwenhoek, followed by those in the mid-19th century of Charles Darwin and Louis Pasteur proved that the belief based on erroneous religious dogma in the spontaneous generation of life forms was most gravely flawed.

On February 1, 1871 Darwin suggested in a letter to Joseph Dalton Hooker that the first presence of life possibly began in a; "warm little pond, with all sorts of ammonia and phosphoric salts, lights, heat, electricity, etc. present, so that a protein compound was chemically formed ready to undergo still more complex changes... [Darwin noted that] at the present day such matter would be instantly devoured or absorbed, which would not have been the case before living creatures were formed." 7

With the publication of his book, The Origins of Life, in 1924, Aleksandra Ivanovich Oparin provided his scientific peers with extensive knowledge regarding how life emerged on this planet. 8 Oparin taught that atmospheric oxygen obstructed the synthesis of organic molecules. These molecules are the essential building blocks for the evolution of life. He deduced that a primeval soup of organic molecules could be created in an oxygen-free atmosphere due to the interplay of sunlight.

Oparin explained that these molecules would combine in an increasingly complex manner, eventually forming coacervate droplets. Due to fusion with other droplets, the original droplets would grow and through the process of fission, daughter droplets would be created which would reproduce. This process would provide them with a primitive metabolism, in which the factors which create cell integrity would survive and those that did not would die off and become extinct.

In the mid 1920's J.B.S. Haldane described the Earth's pre-biotic oceans as a 'hot dilute soup.' Haldane reasoned that organic compounds which are the building blocks of life would have been generated in these ancient oceans. Haldane also deduced that living matter could evolve from self-replicating but non-living molecules. 9

Modern day scientists universally agree that the origin of life on earth was generated from the following chemicals, methane, ammonia, water, hydrogen sulphide, carbon dioxide or carbon monoxide and phosphate. It is believed that molecular oxygen and ozone was either scarce or not found at all in primordial times.

Life Created from Chemicals

In 1953 Stanley Miller and Harold Urey fascinated both the global academic community and the world's populace with their experiment which proved that life can be created from chemicals. Miller and Urey's experiment began with a simulation of the chemical environment of the primitive earth. They demonstrated to the academic community that organic molecules which are the components of all life forms could have been spontaneously generated by inorganic precursors, namely chemicals.

In the 1980's Gunter Wachtershauser reasoned that the biochemistry of all life forms, scientifically known as organic compounds, including all those creatures that have become extinct, have their ancestral route in primitive chemical reactions on the early earth.

Various theories have been forwarded attempting to explain how organic molecules evolved into a protocell, (an early basic life form) which further evolved into more complex multicellular organisms such as amoeba-like life forms. Further evolution took place over millions of years leading to the diverse life forms that we have on earth today.

It is not necessary here to provide a detailed discussion of the various theories seeking to explain the origins of life on earth. Suffice it to say, typically scientists belong to three camps, they believe evidence indicates that life began in the oceans or alternatively that life began several kilometers beneath the surface of the planet or instead that life was introduced to the earth from other planets, arriving here through travelling inter-space, planetary bodies such as comets.

Scientific discoveries do not have to overturn a person's beliefs. I believe it is plausible for a person to accept that God committed the initial act of creation, utilizing the natural laws of nature, working through natural events. Science emphatically proves rather than disproves that the universe certainly had a beginning – an initial creative moment – known as the Big Bang.

Moses and the fleeing Hebrew slaves shared the belief which became a fundamental characteristic of Judaism and later Christianity that all God's activities are inevitably carried out through natural events, working through, rather than contravening the laws of nature.

Some examples follow, illustrating the Hebrew religious belief that God helped them by working through natural events. Moses predicted and utilized the onset of plagues and natural disasters to persuade pharaoh to free the Hebrew slaves: due to the opportune choice of route of departure from Egypt when pharaoh changed his mind and sent Egyptian chariots to retrieve the newly liberated, fleeing slaves, the marshy, muddy water-bed engulfed the wheels of the chariots saving Hebrew lives, supporting their escape (exodus via Sea of Reeds).

Alternatively, these timely and exceptionally shallow waters facilitated the Hebrews' successful escape from Egyptian bondage (exodus via Red Sea). When the newly released Hebrews faced starvation in the desert, most timely and miraculously a natural food substance was carried to them on the wind preventing outright famine.

Clearly, all life forms on this planet are related, share a common ancestor and originate from natural processes, (laws of nature) through the interaction of chemical compounds and gaseous vapors. From this all life forms were ultimately born, continuing to evolve and diversify according to their own innate structures. Amazingly, the shared common ancestor who gave birth to all life forms came into being billions of years ago.

"The virtually infinite variations on life are the fruit of the evolutionary process. All living creatures are related by descent from common ancestors. Humans and other mammals descend from shrew-like creatures that lived more than 150 million years ago; mammals, [which include humans], birds, reptiles, amphibians and fishes share as ancestors aquatic worms that lived 600 million years ago and all plants and animals derive from bacteria-like micro-organisms that originated more than 300 billion years ago. Biological evolution is a process of descent with modification. Lineages of organisms change through generations; diversity arises because the lineages that descend from common ancestors diverge through time." *10*

Shared Common Traits Explained by Evolution: Natural Selection

Darwin's long-term and extensive research included his analysis of the ancient fossils of extinct life forms, including those of transitional fossils which are particularly informative and illustrative. Darwin's investigations included the examination of the geographic distribution of species together with the comparative study of living species.

The results of Darwin's dedicated research led him to reveal to the world that all organisms (life forms) traditionally evolve in a progressive manner in contrast to earlier beliefs, previously summarized, that the process was static and unchanging.

Darwin provided detailed reasons supported by evidence, why each life form possesses distinct physical features such as wings, each of which enable every life form to carry out specific functions. Notably, Darwin introduced the world to the concept of natural selection, a model which explains why life forms possessing the most advantageous characteristics such as keener vision or faster mobility, typically survive longer than life forms without these advantages. Those species who live longer, predictably generate more abundant numbers of offspring than disadvantaged counterparts.

Those life forms with the most advantages typically survive, successfully increasing in numbers whilst disadvantaged life-forms progressively reduce in numbers and eventually become extinct. It is for this reason that the process of natural selection is often described as 'the survival of the fittest,' indicating that the processes of the natural world habitually select the fittest specimens to survive, reproduce and proliferate.

All Sciences Confirm the Concept of Evolution

The on-going and cumulative activity, of teams of scientists, from a wide spectrum of scientific disciplines, progressively, corroborates and supplements Darwin's insightful and revolutionary findings. For example the comparatively young science of genetics, arising in the 20th century, now provides us with detailed genetic evidence which further authenticates the fact that the process of natural selection does indeed take place.

The findings of yet a further young science, known as molecular biology, instituted in the second half of the 20th century, has facilitated further validation together with momentous leaps forward in our understanding of biological evolution.

Incredibly, molecular biologists possess the technology to analyze the genes of different individual life forms. Not only this, they can assess the closeness of the familial relationships between different species, providing indisputable proof that all life forms are related to each other with differing degrees of closeness. In layman's terms, through analysis of each and every life form's genes molecular biologists can reveal whether each species, all of whom are related, should be considered to be a person's great great grandparent or more distant cousin.

This fact is illustrated by the following example, molecular biologists have discovered that the genes of humans and chimpanzees are remarkably similar, differing in only 1-2% of the units of which the genes are comprised.

Although chimpanzees do not speak any of the diverse human languages, they do indeed, clearly use facial and body language and utilize many other vocal and tonal displays of language to communicate with each other, corroborating how remarkably close and alike we are. Human animals are gaining the sensitivity and patience to painstakingly observe the diverse methods employed by other non-human animals to communicate with each other.

For this reason it is expected that within five years we will be able to use the vocal communication we have gained through observation, together with the use of technology, to allow us to effectively communicate with dolphins. Regarding the relatedness of all living beings:

"Since Darwin's time, the evidence from [diverse sciences] has become considerably stronger and more comprehensive, while biological disciplines that emerged more recently, genetics, biochemistry, physiology, ecology, animal behavior (ethology), and especially molecular biology have supplied powerful additional evidence and detailed confirmation.

The amount of information about evolutionary history stored in the DNA and proteins of living things is virtually unlimited; scientists can reconstruct and detail the evolutionary history of life by investing sufficient time and laboratory resources. Evolutionists no longer are concerned with obtaining evidence to support the fact of evolution but rather are concerned with what sorts of knowledge can be obtained from different sources of evidence." *11*

The reader may wish to refer to the timescale diagram located at the back of this book, as we continue in the next chapter to examine further astonishing, thought-provoking proof of the interrelatedness and interconnectedness of all animals, (all life-forms) human and non-human, including all flora and fauna life forms.

CHAPTER 4 - TRANSITIONAL FOSSILS PROVE SHARED COMMON ANCESTOR

"I suggest that in proportion as man is truly "humanized," not by schools of cookery but by schools of thought, he will abandon the barbarous habit of his flesh-eating ancestors and will make gradual progress towards a purer, simpler, more humane and therefore more civilized diet-system."

Henry S. Salt, (1851-1939).

Fossils

The process of fossilization itself is comparatively rare due to the usual rapid decomposition of living organisms. When fossilization is successful it occurs as the result of natural processes which have accidently protected fossils for millions of years.

Fossilization takes place when a life form has been frozen and covered by sediment soon after its demise or alternatively its life terminated in an oxygen-free location which, likewise, preserves organisms as a fossil. Hard bodied fossils of life-forms and beings that lived for a longer epoch of the earth's history are inevitably, the most commonly occurring fossils to be unearthed.

In contrast, soft tissue fossils such as jelly-fish are extremely rare as the soft tissue is more prone to disappear without trace than the tissue of creatures that possessed more protective hard body parts. The fossil record compiled to date, commences with organisms that date back to the earliest times and have typically been petrified in rock. Paleontologists study extinct and early fossilized life forms which they continue to unearth. Remarkably, nature has preserved these to different degrees through natural events. Paleontologists work closely with evolutionary biologists and molecular biologists together these scientists systematically trace the historical record of lineages (family trees) of life forms back to the earliest historic epochs.

The evidence they provide offers further proof of the common ancestry and relatedness of all species, namely the entire earth family. The combined multidisciplinary scientific effort of countless teams of scientists continues to accrue detailed evidence, authenticating beyond doubt that the evolutionary diversification of life forms resulting in all the species known today, originated with a shared common ancestor.

The cumulative discovery of a diverse range of fossils of varying sizes from many eras and geographic locations has led to the creation by the scientific community of a historical fossil record, enormously advancing our knowledge of the most ancient life forms.

Such relentless and tireless research teaches us how different life forms either became extinct or progressively evolved throughout the millennia. Their evolution would have occurred as the result of evolutionary processes such as natural selection summarized earlier and/or sequential adaptations to the changing environment, at intervals giving birth to further related yet different species.

The fossil record, "shows successions of organisms through time manifesting their transition from one form to another...[Radiometric dating measures] the amounts of natural radioactive atoms that remain in certain minerals to determine the elapsed time since they were constituted - make it possible to estimate the time period when the rocks and the fossils associated with them, were formed." *1*

Incredibly, through the process of radiometric dating, scientists have discovered that our earth is 4.5 billion years old. Scientists from a wide range of scientific disciplines are constantly unearthing supportive supplementary evidence to corroborate the originally incomplete Darwinian theory of evolution and the initially unfinished fossil record. The fossil record is an ongoing and fragmentary jigsaw puzzle ranging over millions of years and the globe, its compilation is an enormous task.

A diverse range of scientific fields are continuously providing humankind with an ever increasing history of the evolution and adaptation of diverse life forms on Earth, a process that has taken place over millions of years. The magnitude of the scientific task is considerable as each discipline adds its evidential pieces to the increasingly complete jigsaw puzzle picture. This momentous task is progressively being accomplished with fastidious precision providing us with knowledge such as:

"The earliest fossils resemble micro-organisms such as bacteria and cyanobacteria (blue-green algae); the oldest of these fossils appear in rocks 3.5 billion, years old. The oldest known animal fossils, about 700 million years old, come from the so-called Ediacara fauna, small wormlike creatures with soft bodies.

Numerous fossils belonging to many living phyla and exhibiting mineralized skeletons appear in rocks about 540 million years old. These different organisms are different from organisms living now and from those living at intervening times. Some are so radically different that paleontologists have created new phyla in order to classify them. The first vertebrates, animals with backbones, appeared 400 million years ago; the first mammals, less than 200 million years ago." *2*

Evidence from Transitional Fossils Proves Evolution

Impressively, transitional fossils provide us with a frozen moment in time. From these specimens we can observe how the descendent of one life form evolved into a related but slightly different life form providing us with a sharper understanding of how life forms adapted, diversified and proliferated. Paleontologists have discovered prolific examples of fossils which capture and clearly illustrate these phenomena demonstrating for us the step by step evolutionary transition of countless species, including primates, various hominids also known as proto-humans, being the ancestors of present day humans. For example, transitional fossils of whales that walked the land and fish possessing fingers have been unearthed.

Transitional fossils illustrate how descendants of known organisms (life forms) have developed transitional forms or features, throughout their evolutionary journey, creating new, historically divergent lineages, generally evolving into new pathways of adaptation to the environment.

The term 'missing link' is characteristically applied to transitional fossils as they link individual organisms to their more ancient relatives, revealing connections to a single, yet extensive, earth family tree. It is highly improbable that every transitional fossil linking all organisms together will ever be discovered due their incredibly ancient nature. However, the fact that countless transitional fossils have been unearthed testifies to the existence of such highly illuminating missing link phenomena.

The transitional fossil remains of walking whales graphically portray a time when whales walked on the land. However, some migrated back to life in the oceans, where life originated. Over time, the gap in the relationship between these land and sea groups widened, each demonstrating common evolutionary processes associated with the environment they lived in and other factors.

Clearly, whales once bore a closer resemblance to their related land dwelling mammals who continued to evolve on the land. Incredibly, although these gigantic mammals returned to the seas, whales continue to this day to breathe oxygen, returning to the surface to breathe out carbon dioxide.

When a whale dives in the cold oceans its heart rate slows which is an extreme example of the diving reflex humans still have in vestigial form, indicating humans swam under water once too, during an ancient epoch in our evolutionary history. Significantly, whale fins also retain to this day the boney vestiges of their mammalian land ancestors. Astoundingly, whales have more brain spindle cells than humans indicating that they have significantly deeper and more profound use of language, self-awareness, feelings, emotion and compassion than humans, as brain spindle cells are responsible for these highly evolved attributes.

Interestingly, those other magnificent beings who live in contemporary waters, namely crocodiles, have an ancestry dating back 200 million years. Due to the fact they can go without food for some months at a time as a result of having slow metabolisms and can swim deep into the waters, they avoided extinction in contrast to the dinosaurs.

Incredibly, transitional fossils of fish with fingers have been brought to light, revealing an astonishing period in the distant past when fish bore a closer family relationship to land dwelling organisms. Their evolutionary destiny remained on the land in contrast to the fate of fish who continued to evolve in rivers, lakes and oceans.

The reconstruction of a comprehensive and exhaustive fossil record of all life forms is ongoing by scientists. Detailed information is now readily available regarding the evolution and relatedness of countless life forms however records are more complete for some life forms than others. Scientists are piecing together the missing links between the human mammal and other mammals, particularly those that have the most in common with the human animal.

The "... succession of forms over time has been reconstructed in detail. One example is the evolution of the horse...The horse can be traced to an animal the size of a dog having several toes on each foot and teeth appropriate for browsing; this animal called the dawn horse...lived more than 50 million years ago. The most recent form the modern horse ...is much larger in size, is one-toed, and has teeth appropriate for grazing. The transitional forms are well preserved as fossils, as are many other kinds of extinct horses that evolved in different directions and left no descendants."

Transitional Fossils of Human Ancestors

Many transitional fossils have been unearthed revealing the ancient lineage of many historic and present day species.

Ancient transitional fossils clearly reveal a number of life forms who acted as intermediaries between present day apes and humans. Extraordinarily, many intermediate fossils, graphically illustrating the stages between primates linked to the human lineage and intermediate human animals known as hominins have been found.

Bizarrely, even today, in the 21st century, some humans are born with actual tails, mirroring their ancient ancestors. These are photographed and amputated soon after birth. This genetic throw-back to the human animal's ancient past demonstrates a living transitional fossil or missing link. Many medical photographs of contemporary human babies born with intact tails can be readily viewed in medical books and on the internet.

"The oldest known fossil hominins – i.e. primates belonging to the human lineage after it separated from lineages going to the apes - are 6 million to 7 million years old, [they] come from Africa, and are known as Sahelanthropus and Orrorin…which were predominantly bipedal [walked on 2 legs] when on the ground, which had small brains." *4*

We know a great deal about the lineage that led to the present day human animal. The following excerpt from the Encyclopedia Britannica offers an excellent summary regarding the historical evolution of the human animal.

"Ardipithecus lived about 4.4 million years ago, also in Africa. Numerous fossil remains from diverse African origins are known as Australopithecus, a hominin that appeared between 3 million and 4 million years ago. Australopithecus had an upright human stance but a cranial capacity of less than 500 cc…comparable to that of a gorilla or a chimpanzee and about one-third that of humans.

Its head displayed a mixture of ape and human characteristics - a low forehead and a long apelike face but with teeth proportioned like those of humans. Other early hominins partly contemporaneous with Australopithecus include Kenyanthropus and Paranthropus; both had comparatively small brains, although some species of Paranthropus had larger bodies.

Paranthropus represents a side branch in the hominin lineage that became extinct. Along with increased cranial capacity, other human characteristics have been found in Homo habilis, which lived about 1.5 million to 2 million years ago in Africa and had a cranial capacity of more than 600 cc (brain weight of 600 grams), and in H. erectus, which lived between 0.5 million and more than 1.5 million years ago, apparently ranged widely over Africa, Asia, and Europe, and had a cranial capacity of 800-1,100 cc…The brain sizes of H. ergaster, H. antecessor, and H. heidelbergensis were roughly that of the brain of H. erectus, some of which species were partly contemporaneous, though they lived in different regions of the Eastern Hemisphere." *5*

Major Evolutionary Processes

All life forms on earth share an ancient common ancestor and are therefore related; a fact that has been authenticated beyond doubt. "There is probably no other notion in any field of science that has been as extensively tested and as thoroughly corroborated as the evolutionary origin of living organisms." *6*

In order to help the reader understand this discovery let us take a brief look at the major evolutionary processes which caused diversification leading to the contemporary multiplicity of species, discovered by Darwin and validated by teams of multidisciplinary scientists, proving the web of life on earth belongs to a single, related, earth family.

Typically, evolution occurs as a gradual, though continuous process of change within lineages over time. This occurs due to gene substitutions caused by the process of natural selection, mutation, genetic drift and further genetic processes associated with the specific life form. There are also the evolutionary processes of both origination and extinction of species. However, fossil evidence seems to suggest that some species do actually appear suddenly whilst most other species manifest more gradually.

Examples of evolution can be found when analyzing: "The forelimbs of mammals [which] are normally adapted for walking, but they are adapted for shoveling earth in moles and other mammals that live mostly underground, for climbing and grasping in arboreal monkeys and apes, for swimming in dolphins and whales, and for flying in bats.

The forelimbs of reptiles became wings in their bird descendants. Feathers appear to have served first for regulating temperature but eventually were co-opted for flying and became incorporated into wings....While the evolution of the forelimbs - for walking - into the wings of birds or the arms and hands of primates may seem more like changes in function, the evolution of eyes exemplifies gradual advancement of the same function - seeing. " 7

Darwin's theory of evolution is composed of three interrelated issues: Firstly, all life forms share a common ancestor: Secondly his theory pertains to the evolutionary historical record such as when lineages of different species separated from each other and how each lineage went on to make successive changes: Thirdly his theory relates to the processes that create evolutionary changes.

Hereditary Variation

At the heart of Darwin's theory beginning the whole process of evolution is the mechanism of hereditary variation. Advantageous variations in an organism enhance the chances of an organism's struggle for survival and reproduction. Consequently, those organisms possessing favorable variations successfully continue to survive and reproduce most effectively from one generation to the next. Those organisms with the least favorable variations progressively become extinct.

Two important processes underlie the functioning of evolution, after hereditary variation occurs natural selection selects the advantageous genetic variants that will be inherited by successive generations.

"Hereditary variation also entails 2 mechanisms - the spontaneous mutation of 1 variant into another and the sexual process that recombines those variants to form a multitude of variations." *8* New species typically emerge as a result of slow, yet continuous processes which cause, "...gradual change prompted by natural selection. Environments are continuously changing in time, and they differ from place to place. Natural selection, therefore, favors different characteristics in different situations. The accumulation of the differences eventually yields different species." *9*

Adaptation

Scientists have verified that the product of natural selection has generated features such as eyes and wings. As noted, the process of natural selection favors advantageous genes, beneficial to each life form, assisting it in its particular environment. Natural selection allows these favorable genes to multiply whilst disadvantageous genes detrimental to survival progressively become extinct.

"Darwin accepted the facts of adaptation - hands are for grasping, eyes for seeing, lungs for breathing. But he showed that the multiplicity of plants and animals, with their exquisite and varied adaptations, could be explained by a process of natural selection.... Natural selection was proposed by Darwin primarily to account for the adaptive organization of living beings; it is a process that promotes or maintains adaptation. Evolutionary change through time and evolutionary diversification [multiplication of species] are not directly promoted by natural selection, but they often ensue as by-products of natural selection as it fosters adaptation to different environments." *10*

Genetic Drift

A further mechanism inherent in the evolutionary process is genetic drift, defined by the Encyclopedia Britannica as: "A change in the gene pool of a small population that takes place strictly by chance. Genetic drift can result in genetic traits being lost from a population or becoming widespread in a population without respect to the survival or reproductive value of the alleles

involved. A random statistical effect, genetic drift can occur only in small, isolated populations in which the gene pool is small enough that chance events can change its makeup substantially."
11

Speciation

Speciation is a further integral process inherent in the methods utilized by evolution. This is the means by which one species becomes split into two or more species because the original species finds itself reproductively isolated from the remaining members of the same species. This situation can occur due to changes in the landscape which can unwittingly separate same species groups from the remaining members of the same species.

For example, one group of the same species may find themselves quite by chance on an isolated land mass, alienated from the larger group as the result of natural events, such as topographical changes causing the disappearance of a land bridge to the mainland. The emergence of the sea, a river, a lake or a mountain range would then act as a barrier to same species reunions, effectively separating single or multiple groups from the same species.

Now found at separate locations with differing environments to contend with, each separated group and its future generations of descendants progressively evolve and adapt differently to the original group. As a result of each groups' evolutionary changes, the relationship gap widens and increasingly they become reproductively isolated from one another. Over the course of millions of years, due to the detached evolution of each group of life forms, they become two or more independent evolutionary units.

"Evolution can take place by anagenesis, in which changes occur within a lineage, or by cladogenesis, in which a lineage splits into two or more separate lines. Anagenetic evolution has doubled the size of the human cranium over the course of two million years; in the lineage of the horse it has reduced the number of toes from four to one. Cladogenetic evolution has produced the extraordinary diversity of the living world, with its more than two million species of animals, plants, fungi, and micro-organisms." *12*

Since the 1960's, molecular biologists can make: "Comparisons of the amino acid sequences of corresponding proteins in different species [providing] quantitatively precise measures of the divergence among species evolved from common ancestors, a considerable improvement over the typically qualitative evaluations obtained by comparative anatomy and other evolutionary sub-disciplines." *13*

In 1968, the Japanese geneticist named, Motoo Kimura, presented the details of his neutrality theory regarding molecular evolution to the academic world. He suggested that a 'molecular clock' of evolution can be traced back in time relating to all species. Motoo suggested that:

"The degree to which amino acid or nucleotide sequences diverge between species should provide a reliable estimate of the time since the species diverged. This would make it possible to reconstruct an evolutionary history that would reveal the order of branching of different lineages, such as those leading to humans, chimpanzees, and orang-utans, as well as the time in the past when the lineages split from one another....the molecular clock is not exact...into the early 21st century it continued to provide the most reliable evidence for reconstructing evolutionary history." *14*

The second and third features of Darwin's theory of evolution relates to the "evolutionary relationships between" [specific life forms and the] "events of evolutionary history, as well as how and why evolution takes place – [these] are matters of active scientific investigation." *15*

With reference to the earlier reference to the closely relatedness of the human to the chimpanzee, scientific evidence proves that humans are more closely related to the chimpanzee and the gorilla, than the human, chimpanzee and gorilla are to monkeys and baboons. Notably, individuals should be aware that humans are classified as animals, mammals and indeed primates. Primates are the highest order of mammals which include lemurs, monkeys, anthropoid apes and humanity.

Mutation

The evolutionary process of mutation is typically regarded as the predominant cause of genetic variation, creating the building blocks of life for future generations which are filtered through the process of natural selection. Mutations are random changes that can be beneficial or detrimental to an organism. The Encyclopedia Britannica defines mutation as:

"An alteration in the genetic material (the genome) of a cell of a living organism or a virus that is more or less permanent and that can be transmitted to the cell's or virus's descendants....Mutations result either from accidents during the normal chemical transactions of DNA, often during replication, or from exposure to high-energy electromagnetic radiation (e.g., ultraviolet light or X-rays) or particle radiation or to highly reactive chemicals in the environment." *16*

All Life Forms are Related Proven by Structural Correspondences

Further evidence upholding the fact that all life forms are related, sharing a common ancestor, is provided by the analysis of skeletons from a diverse range of sentient beings, living in enormously different environments and leading extremely different lives, yet each have very similar skeletons. "The correspondence, bone by bone, can easily be seen not only in the limbs but also in every other part of the body.

From a purely practical point of view, it is incomprehensible that a turtle should swim a horse run, a person write, and a bird or a bat fly with forelimb structures built of the same bones. An engineer could design better limbs in each case. But if it is accepted that all of these skeletons inherited their structures from a common ancestor and became modified only as they adapted to different ways of life, the similarity of their structures makes sense." *17*

All Life Forms are Related Proven by Comparative Anatomy

Comparative anatomy scientists have compiled further evidence that all living organisms of the land, sea and air, share a common ancestor and belong to a single earth family. All are therefore, related 'living souls.' These scientists analyze the inherited structural similarities between different life forms, proving descent from a common ancestor, known as homology. They analyze and assess bone structures and other similarities in the bodies of all living organisms.

"The correspondence of structures is typically very close among some organisms - the different varieties of songbirds, for instance - but becomes less so as the organisms being compared are less closely related in their evolutionary history. The similarities are less between mammals and birds than they are among mammals, and they are still less between mammals and fishes. Similarities in structure, therefore, not only manifest evolution but also help to reconstruct the phylogeny, or evolutionary history, of organisms." *18*

If a contemporary engineer was tasked to create each present day life form as an absolute, finished creation, perfectly designed to suit each life form's specific way of life, each species would not possess the flaws that we readily find in them. Notably, "...the forelimbs of turtles, horses, humans, birds, and bats, an organism's body parts are less than perfectly adapted because they are modified from an inherited structure, rather than designed from completely "raw" materials for a specific purpose." *19*

Due to the universal descent from an ancient, shared, common ancestor, all life forms are related however numerous more obvious structural similarities have been found amongst the more closely related species namely humans, dogs, whales and bats.

Many structural similarities have been confirmed between the forelimbs of humans, dogs, whales and bats, remarkably proving their particular brand of relatedness. The forelimb skeletons of these different, yet related animals (mammals) exhibit

140

many strikingly similar structural parallels, evidencing their particularly close, yet often unheeded relationship.

All Life Forms are Related Proven by Embryology

Scientists specializing in the field of embryology, analyze each stage in the development of an organism, from the moment an egg is fertilized to the time the infant hatches or is born. It is of extraordinary importance, though most people are unaware of it, the embryos of fish, lizards and humans, demonstrate a striking similarity due to the fact all share a common ancestor.

Incredibly, these closely shared features are most apparent during their early developmental stages; visual images are available on the internet. However, as each of these embryos progress to maturity, fewer similarities are exhibited. Significantly, the more closely related species are, such as humans (classified as primates/mammals/animals) and other primates, the similarities in the development of the embryos continue for far longer.

"Common developmental patterns reflect evolutionary kinship. Lizards and humans share a developmental pattern inherited from their remote common ancestor; the inherited pattern of each was modified only as the separate descendent lineages evolved in different directions. The common embryonic stages of the two creatures reflect the constraints imposed by this common inheritance, which prevents changes that have not been necessitated by their diverging environments and ways of life." *20*

Again, the majority of people today have become ignorant of the fact that human embryos possess gill slits similarly the embryos of all other vertebrate (back boned) land animals, each possess gill slits too. This fact, further verifying our relatedness, is of momentous importance.

These family members, including the human animal, are known as non-aquatic vertebrates, possessing back bones but not sea dwellers. However, this diverse range of land animal embryos, never breathe through their gill slits. Significantly, the shared possession of gill slits, demonstrates that all vertebrate, land animals are descendants of the fish. The fish is therefore the shared common ancestor of an extensive range which includes humans, dogs, cats, cows, calves, sheep, lambs, horses, goats, pigs, foxes and many more.

It was mentioned earlier when discussing transitional fossils that even today, in the 21st century some humans are born with tails. Notably, it is a startling fact that all human embryos have a clearly visible tail by the fourth week of their gestation in the mother's womb. The human tail is at its longest in the sixth week of the baby's embryonic development. Mammals who exhibit embryonic tails include humans, monkeys, dogs and horses.

Typically, human embryonic tails progressively reduce in size as the embryo develops and is usually no longer visible after birth, the last vestige of which is the coccyx. Land vertebrates have more recent ancestors than the fish. These ancestors possessed tails, a fact that is still clearly obvious in human embryos, yet this ancient feature, reminding us that we too will always remain and be classified as animals, mammals and primates is not commonly known. All the more reason why we should not divorce ourselves from our fellow, related animals!

Notably, the science of embryology has revealed to us that many species including humans that appear visibly different to each other once they have reached maturity actually possess extremely close similarities to each other when they are embryos! The revelations gained from embryological research graphically illustrate the shared common features and similarities, exhibited by different species who, generation after generation, continue to display these hereditary genetic family resemblances, inherited from our most ancient shared common ancestor. Sharing this age-old, evolutionary kinship, all beings are related members of the same family.

Historically all Humans were Vegetarian

It is an extraordinary fact that most people are unaware that historically, human animals were unanimously, entirely vegetarian. Humans originated as vegetarians! This fact is demonstrated by the presence of the vermiform appendix found in the human animal today, a component of the human anatomy which clearly shows that our human ancestors were most certainly herbivores, namely vegetarians.

The vermiform appendix is a: "...functionless vestige of a fully developed organ present in other mammals, such as the rabbit and other herbivores, where a large cecum and appendix store vegetable cellulose to enable its digestion with the help of other bacteria." *21*

As later generations of our human ancestors made the transition from a totally vegetarian diet to an increasingly flesh eating diet, progressively their appendix became unused, ceasing to function, it remained in our human animal bodies. World leaders guided by intellectual 'think-tanks' are aware that the human animal will cumulatively be forced to return to a solely vegetarian lifestyle as the non-flesh diet is the most efficient for maximizing food production and distribution, preventing starvation in a world population set to double in size within the next one to two centuries.

Returning from flesh eating to a wholly vegetarian diet, the mammalian human body will reap the scientifically proven medical health benefits of vegetarianism and increasingly evolve in that direction. Medical think tanks are increasingly aware that the health benefits of vegetarianism are legion. Eating animal flesh has been proven to be responsible for the contemporary prevalence of heart disease, heart attacks, strokes, certain cancers and dementia including other chronic and potentially fatal ailments. With the absence of animal flesh in the human diet, which causes problematic high cholesterol levels, cholesterol induced diseases will be vastly reduced.

All Life Forms are Related Proven by Biogeography

Biogeographic scientists provide us with further evidence for the shared common ancestry and on-going relatedness of all life forms. It is a fact that each continent of the world is home to plants and animals that are unique to each continent. Significantly, the plants and animals found in one continent could equally be supported by a different continent that is characterized by a similar temperature and environment. The following example clarifies this point.

Although the continents of Africa and South America are found at the same latitudes, sharing similar temperatures and environments, the indigenous animals and plants of these two continents differ. Rhinoceroses and lions are found in Africa and not in South America similarly, South America rather than Africa is home to jaguars and llamas. The question arises, why did a specific range of animals and plants originate and flourish in one continent and not another continent, yet both continents share a similar climate and environment?

The processes of evolution holds the key to the solution: "This absence of many species from a hospitable environment in which an extraordinary variety of other species flourish can be explained by the theory of evolution, which holds that species can exist and evolve only in geographic areas that were colonized by their ancestors." *22*

All Life Forms are Related Proven by Molecular Biology

Relentlessly, molecular biologists are making enormous strides, mapping the historical, descendant lineages of all life forms on Earth, ultimately right back to the most ancient shared common ancestor. "In its unveiling of the nature of DNA and the workings of organisms at the level of enzymes and other protein molecules, it has shown that these molecules hold information about an organism's ancestry…molecular evolution has shown all living organisms, from bacteria to humans, to be related by descent from common ancestors." *23*

Astonishingly, this field of academic research has revealed that the molecular makeup of all life forms on earth, including bacteria, plants, animals and human animals, is astoundingly similar, obviously due to their familial relatedness. This is

144

revealed; "...in the nature of the components as well as in the ways in which they are assembled and used. In bacteria, plants, animals, and humans, the DNA comprises a different sequence of the same four component nucleotides, and all the various proteins are synthesized from different combinations and sequences of the same 20 amino acids, although several hundred other amino acids do exist." *24*

Impressively, molecular biologists have also discovered that the nucleotide genetic code which synthesizes proteins is virtually the same in all life forms on earth despite the apparent differences between species. Incredibly, they teach us that despite the enormous diversity of life on earth, apparent differences are only superficial, as astonishingly these scientists have also found that remarkably similar metabolic pathways (the organism's method for manipulating energy) exist in all life forms.

Repeatedly the findings of molecular biology prove that all life forms share a number of fundamental common features irrefutably proving the shared family relationship of all life forms, verifying that they are members of one single, related earth family, sharing the same common ancestor.

"This unity reveals the genetic continuity and common ancestry of all organisms. There is no other rational way to account for their molecular uniformity when numerous alternative structures are equally likely. The genetic code serves as an example. Each particular sequence of three nucleotides in the nuclear DNA acts as a pattern for the production of exactly the same amino acid in all organisms.

This is no more necessary than it is for a language to use a particular combination of letters to represent a particular object. If it is found that certain sequences of letters – planet, tree, and woman - are used with identical meanings in a number of different books, one can be sure that the languages used in those books are of common origin." *25*

Incredibly, molecular biology can assess the recency of common ancestry through analysis of the nucleotides or amino acids between any given organism, (life form/sentient being). Importantly, scientists have discovered that the more similar the sequence of amino acids between any given species, the nearer in time these species shared a common ancestry. Exemplifying the close relatedness, of the human to other mammals, the human animal and chimpanzees share 104 amino acids, possessing them in exactly the same sequence, differing from horses by only 11 additional amino acids.

Remarkably, human relatedness to chimpanzees, horses and other fellow mammal brethren, who are closely related, fellow sentient beings, is breathe-taking. Most people who have ever adopted an animal as part of their family, including primates, dogs, cats, horses and pigs, soon become intuitively aware of the animal's never ending displays of cognitive functions and emotions shared by us, their human animal counterparts. We each are part of each other as equal parts of the whole.

Antibiotics and Biological Adaptation

The world-wide scientific community is universally convinced by the wealth of multi-disciplinary evidence that the evolution of all life forms on earth from a shared common ancestor has been proven beyond dispute. Scientists are aware that the evolutionary process of biological adaptation is a fact of life for all species including bacterium and insects. The following example helps to illustrate this point. It is a known fact that bacteria regularly develop resistance against antibiotics when exposed over long periods to those antibiotics.

This occurs as a result of the chance evolutionary development of a bacterium that survives the effects of antibiotics, it is known as a resistant strain. Inevitably, due to the effects of the antibiotics, the other bacteria die off. Despite the presence of antibiotics, the resistant strain then multiplies becoming the prevalent strain until a new antibiotic is developed and focused against this resistant strain. In this way the relentless evolutionary cycle of adaptation continues.

This evolutionary process of bacterial resistance is accelerated by the fact that farm animals typically living in dirty, cramped pens in overcrowded conditions are fed antibiotics, daily mixed in with their food. This is obviously an unnatural chemical additive which has inevitable health consequences for all those who eat their flesh.

Most factory-farm animals live on a permanent diet of antibiotics, keeping them alive to suffer incarceration in filthy, deafeningly noisy, dark, overcrowded, stinking, squashed, indeed hellish conditions, often consisting of cramped small cages and pens or cow and pig rape racks used for regular artificial insemination, in which they live securely fastened, unable to move, let alone, rest, sit, lie down or turn.

The atmosphere in such tragic, heart-breaking, gloomy, earsplitting, heaving factory-farms is filled with the continuous, individual, spontaneous, heartfelt, torturous pleading cries, of the condemned but no human responds! Antibiotics are made increasingly ever stronger in order to salvage these wrecks of sentient beings, preserving them for typically slow, piece by piece dismemberment, slaughter and butchery.

Due to the tragic and disgusting manner in which animals are kept, resulting in the need to provide them with daily cocktails of antibiotics in their food, preserving them for slaughter, humans who eat their dead carcasses which are riddled with antibiotics are also bombarded with antibiotics. This state of animal affairs has resulted today, in the 21st century, in the need to create new antibiotics as animals human and non-human are becoming immune to the good effects of these drugs, taking us back many centuries! Following the rules of karma, the original scientific breakthrough of antibiotics is becoming lost and useless.

These flesh and blood beings, possessing the same nerve endings as human animals which convey the pain and suffering to the brain, sharing many other human features, are 'processed' for genocide as though they were inanimate tins of factory produce. Experiencing an unimaginable, painful, merciless incarceration and transportation no thought is spared for these living souls and no respite is given to them.

No mercy or compassion is shown to these fellow related mammals, who have barely survived their lifelong ordeal, living in vile, foul smelling, unventilated, noxious, verminous, festering, germ-laden factory-farms, often, knee deep in filthy disease-ridden faeces. In contrast to these dark endless sheds of hell, even farmed vegetables live their lives in sunlight and fresh air.

Throughout these unbearable conditions, these emotionally shattered and immensely deprived beings suffer days of overcrowded, relentless, joint-aching, exhausting transportation. The gross discomfort denies them sleep, water, food, exercise, respite, rest and relaxation.

For those alive when they arrive at the slaughter house destination, they are typically propelled off the lorry. One end of the truck's floor mechanically rises up like an enormous seesaw, slide or shoot, literally tipping these agonized, skidding, flesh and blood beings, dropping them, cracking their bones on the harsh ground several feet below.

The strong minded personalities, injured with ruptured organs and shattered limbs, remain determined to survive, wrongly believing this ordeal, being so unbelievably bad has to get better. Tragically and ironically these brave, herd-community leaders find they have survived all this, only to be slowly hacked to death, piece by piece, as slaughterhouse workers describe and admit.

Due to leg and shoulder fractures and dislocations, inevitably caused by this barbaric transportation and delivery, these broken hearts and souls crumple on the ground, these beings can no longer walk. These acutely aware and responsive fellow living souls are then prodded intensely with Taser-like rods which electrocute them, by fierce slaughterhouse men, unbelievably forcing these bloodied living souls to hobble and crawl on their broken knees to a merciless gradual bloodbath slaughter.

Typically, governments across the globe oppose on-going pleas by world-wide animal charities for cameras to be permanently erected in slaughterhouses and factory-farms allowing conditions to be monitored and raising public awareness of how animals are axed, sawed, spliced, butchered and dressed-up as pounds of bloody flesh for human dinner plates!

Living lives typically deprived of vital life-promoting sunlight, the caress of the breeze and the welcome texture of grass underfoot, bacteria builds up within these incarcerated animals with arguably, karmic repercussions on humankind, their oppressive jailers and murderers.

Typically, cows, sheep and pigs live on a daily, life-long diet of cocktails of antibiotics knowing nothing more than suffering throughout their tragic and wasted lives. This bacteria inevitably develops resistance to antibiotics and multiplies within these factory-farmed, emotional, flesh and blood beings whose nervous systems feel pain and suffering just like ours.

These same bacteria may be pathogenic making both the animal and human animal ill, the bacteria will inevitably, overtime, become resistant to the same antibiotics which are given to both humans and fellow animals, consequently neither will be helped to recover from the sickness caused by the bacteria using the shared antibiotics. Increasingly antibiotics are proving to be inadequate to fight disease in human animals and other animals because the evolutionary adaptations made by the bacteria, is outpacing the development of antibiotics.

The same evolutionary phenomena of adaptation, paralleling bacteria, explained briefly earlier, can be seen in the way insects evolve resistance against concoctions of pesticides, successively surviving these ever stronger, increasingly lethal poisonous chemicals. A chance evolution of a pesticide resistant insect within a species enables that insect to survive, reproduce and flourish. This flourishing insect passes on its pesticide resistant genes through its reproduction consequently this entire living species becomes resistant to the pesticide replacing those insects which lacked resistance.

Notably, pesticides are typically, deadly, toxic chemicals known to damage the complex interrelated, interdependent, ecological systems on which all earth's life forms depend for survival. Damage to any aspect of this intricate web of life has far-reaching, chain reaction, cause and effect repercussions, we as yet do not fully understand. Pesticides are successively becoming inadequate due to the evolutionary repercussions that have now been outlined.

Surely, it is best not to continue on the current frantic road of concocting ever more powerful, poisonous pesticides in order to perpetuate factory-farming, in view of their enormously damaging toxic effects on all life forms and the complex and diverse planetary environment. Without fail, due to the complex evolutionary process discussed individuals within any given species will continue to exhibit their resistance to every new pesticide, as they flourish they make the ever-increasing, deadly pesticides useless, yet damaging to the environment.

This fact proves that using increasingly powerful poisonous pesticides and increasingly stronger antibiotics is flawed, yet sadly antibiotics are a way of life preserving factory-farmed animals for slaughter. The answer is to stop factory farming animals and even vegetarianism.

Compassionate Vegetarianism is Good for Us

In contrast to the above descriptions, animals should live natural, organic healthy lives, grazing on green farm pastures in sunlight and fresh air and kept warm, comfortable and sheltered in the winter months. Today they are artificially inseminated creating millions of cruelly abused and mass slaughtered fellow animals. Healthy, organic, agricultural farming should be the norm as this method of farming can feed the globe most efficiently eradicating starvation, hunger and famine.

Televised interviews with farmers confirm that many of them are opposed to their continuous need to purchase ever-more expensive, new, increasingly powerful pesticides and antibiotics. Such destructive farming typically increases the profits of multinational corporations who manufacture these chemicals.

Together with the slaughter and transportation of these fellow, related animals, a highly profitable, annual multibillion dollar industry busily continues. Notably, farmers are also reporting adverse personal health conditions including cancers some believe to be caused by working with such toxins. If we demonstrate vegetarian compassion we can end this toxic way of life for farmers, all other life-forms and the planet.

All Creatures are Brothers, Sisters and Cousins

Many human beings are either unaware or have lost sight of the fact that humans are scientifically classified as mammals, animals and primates. This is perpetuated by the typical and deliberate coining of the phrase the 'human being' rather than the 'human animal.' Consequently, tragically, most humans live in an illusory pitiless bubble of falsely perceived separateness, mercilessly, mentally and emotionally divorcing themselves from the rest of their related animal brethren. This callously indifferent mental construct perpetuates the endless untold suffering of our brothers, sisters and cousins throughout their tragic lives ending in hellish slaughterhouses.

Mammals, the group to which humans belong, are an incredibly diverse animal, reflected in their variety of sizes, functions and habitats. It is estimated that there are 5,000 species of living mammals that are found on the land, sea and air. Mammals can be as small as the tiniest shrew living on the land and as large as the blue whale swimming in the oceans.

It is not possible to list all 5000 species of mammal here several examples include rodents, bats, cats, dogs, pigs, sheep, cows, horses, elephants, rhinoceroses, humans and other primates. Some of the major defining characteristics of mammals follow. All mammals are vertebrate animals (possessing a backbone) who suckle their young with milk produced by their mothers' mammary glands. Mammals also possess hair.

Significantly, the whale is a mammal which possesses hair only in the fetal stage in the womb. The offspring of mammals are born live except for echidnas which includes the duck billed platypus, these mammals lay eggs. Mammals are further distinguished by the fact that their mature red blood cells do not possess a nucleus. All other vertebrate life forms possess nucleated red blood cells.

151

Earth's Interrelated, Interdependent, Family Tree

David Attenborough, now in his late 80's, has made nature documentaries for approximately sixty years, observing and filming thousands of different species across the globe. However, he never ceases to be fascinated by the fact that all life on Earth is related, descending from creatures who scuttled out of the water on to dry land.

Speaking to 'What's On TV' magazine in an article called 'My Cousin the Chimp,' about his two part documentary program named, 'Attenborough: 60 Years in the Wild,' (shown on BBC2 in the United Kingdom, late 2012), Attenborough stated:

"We share 200 of our genes with those early life forms... There are some genes which are common to every single species on the planet....We share 95% of our DNA with chimpanzees.

Chimps use up to 20 types of different tools. Manufacturing tools in such a way had until then been thought to be something only human beings could do. Each community of chimps has their own culture and that was thought to be uniquely human too. Discussing humankind's genetic similarities proving we are related to all other species Attenborough point out that: "All life is interrelated, having come from a common origin. Our [human] DNA extends in an unbroken chain right to the beginning of life 4000 million years ago."

As has become clear, all life forms are members of Earth's related family tree. An overview of the progressive evolution and closer to more distant relationship of all organisms can be gained by consulting the countless illustrative family tree diagrams known as genealogic trees or phylogenetic trees, constructed by scientists based on similarities of appearance, embryology and molecular data.

For example, molecular biologists analyze the similarities and differences between species by analyzing their genetic and protein sequences, thereby pinpointing the historical closeness of different life forms. Importantly, all genealogic tree mappings constructed from the research results of diverse scientific disciplines have each turned out to be the same diagram, proving the accuracy of the genealogic trees with which we presently work.

These pictorial charts clearly reveal the relatedness of all life forms on Earth, presenting, the historical family tree record of every life form, including plants and trees. Notably, most of these family trees look more like a bush than a tree, as they trace the separate historical lineages back to the prehistoric, shared common ancestor of all living organisms. These illuminating diagrams or mappings clarify the separate descendant family lineages of all species tracing them back to a single first life form that came into existence at the beginning of all life on this planet.

These family tree illustrations clearly reveal how, through the evolutionary process, this single enigmatic life form diversified and proliferated into increasingly numerous species over millions of years; diversification resulted in each species radiating out from the single primordial common ancestor, forming ever more, new, related species. The ancestors of fish, plants, reptiles, birds and animals including the human animal replicated and diversified from the original, single, primordial, common ancestor, forming multitudinous branches of species all belonging to the single, variously related Earth family.

Having shown that our Earth indeed had a beginning and will have an end, the miracle of the multiplicity of all interrelated, interdependent life-forms dwelling on Earth, their endangered condition, sadly threatened with extinction and/or multi-billion dollar annual genocide, vanishing and suffering due to humanity's lack of compassion, arguably we should make the most of each and every life-span, including that of the Earth herself.

For the compassionate preservation of all living souls, it is therefore vital, that humankind reconnect with the rest of its relations in the living world. As will be shown later the spiritual teachings of prophets and philosophers embodied this far-sighted, compassionate wisdom for all animals, human and non-human and the Earth herself.

Isolating ourselves from the rest of the living world is detrimental to ourselves, all other life forms and the Earth herself. As we try to reconnect with our related brothers, sisters, and cousins let us now look at some of the remarkable archaeological evidence proving our earliest friendships with our animal relatives.

CHAPTER 5 -HUMANKIND'S MOST ANCIENT FRIENDS: DOGS AND CATS

"I believe in my heart that faith in Jesus Christ can and will lead us beyond an exclusive concern for the wellbeing of other human beings to a broader concern for the well-being of the birds in our backyards, the fish in our rivers and every living creature on the face of the earth."

John Wesley (1703-1791).

Having established the fact that all life forms are related, sharing a common ancestor, belonging to one enormous, interdependent, interrelated earth family let us now look at the ancient and enduring friendship between humans and fellow animals that began at the dawn of humankind. Importantly, compassion and sensitivity to one another's needs and respect between human animal and related animal are not curtailed to any one particular historical era. A kind, respectful and considerate man or woman in the 21st century AD has the same tender heart as a kind man or woman who lived in the 8th century BC or many centuries before.

The times and technology change but the best and worst of human characteristics and emotions are timeless and span the millennia. Just as a cruel, greedy materialist person today treads on all others craving money and power as their god, many ancient men and women were criticized for the same vices and personality defects by prophets many centuries before the birth of Jesus Christ.

Human characteristics demonstrated to each other and to fellow animals have remained the same throughout the passage of endless centuries. These range from the most elevated, moral qualities such as compassion, empathy, sensitivity, mercy, thoughtfulness and respect to the most depraved personality disorders, characteristics typically found among the many degrees of psychopathy, found amongst human psychopaths who are literally emotionally 'not in.'

Typically, psychopaths are flawed inadequate, self-obsessed individuals lacking the attribute of empathy. However they are often intelligent and ambitious and copy the emotional behavior of others in order to blend in socially. Due to the fact that there are many levels of psychopathy inherent in many human personalities they are by no means all murderers. Without empathy they are incapable of understanding and sympathizing with the feelings, anguish and suffering of others, consequently they possess little or no mercy, sensitivity, thoughtfulness and compassion.

Consequently, many have difficulty developing or maintaining relationships with others. For example some could torture, torment, drown or kill an animal. They could throw an animal out of a car or walk by and ignore a suffering animal that may have been knocked down by a car or neglect a starving homeless orphaned animal soul.

Those grossly defective, individuals who demonstrate the worst instances or more pronounced levels of psychopathy are unable to sensitively feel the emotional, mental or physical suffering of any animal, human or non-human, hence they could typically work in blood and guts slaughterhouses, killing countless living souls every working day! Inflicting pain on others can be a deliberate deed or alternatively through careless, callous indifference and neglect. The wise proverb is equally true that bad things happen when so-called 'good' people do nothing!

As the human animal, classified also as a primate and mammal, has demonstrated the same range of characteristics throughout the millennia, likewise, our present-day four-legged

156

animal relatives share many of the same characteristics as their ancestors. Typically they offer love, protection, loyalty and companionship and with amazing regularity, from the dawn of time, gallantly lay down their lives to protect their human animal family and other animal companions with whom they live or have just met!

Throughout history animals have acted as utterly devoted, self-sacrificing companions and faithful protectors of the human animal. In order to breathe life back into our ancient relationship with dogs soon to be discussed, let us first look at their heroic deeds illustrated by the following brief contemporary news accounts revealing the passionate and selfless nature of dogs.

Let us commence by honoring the elderly nine year old, male Jack Russell terrier named George, who lived until 2007, in Taranaki in the town of Manaia, New Zealand. One fateful day he was asked to play out in the park and walk to the dairy with a group of five local children of various ages. This day had tragic consequences when two aggressive pit bull terrier dogs openly attacked his human friends.

Nobly and altruistically, George ran at these larger, heavier, stronger and more powerful aggressors, defending and deliberately deflecting them from his human children friends. This act of selfless courage, laying down his life for his friends gave them time to flee in terror. Horrified onlookers watched George get ripped to pieces. They were incredulous at the elderly George's self-sacrificing gallantry.

They were mindful of the fact that George, a small, aged, vulnerable Jack Russell dog, had not for one moment instinctively thought to run away from this obvious slaughter and save himself. To run away as the children did, would have been totally understandable. George's foremost spontaneous thoughts were to save the children giving them time to flee the bloodbath. Those who finally dragged the pit bulls off George were appalled to see that poor little George's barely breathing blood-drenched body had been horrifically mangled, contorted and broken by the ferocious pit bulls' savagery.

George was utterly brutalized by their totally unwarranted murderous onslaught. Due to the atrocious extent of injuries endured by George, inflicted on him by the pit bulls over a significant period of time, his agonized suffering had to be ended by a vet, who euthanized him, allowing this brave little hero to pass to spirit, his life cut short at the age of nine.

Tragically, noble George's anticipated carefree and happy walk with these children turned out to be his last. George, an emotional child himself, was equipped with the same selfless, heroic gallantry as history's elite, those honorable men and women who fought and died, often in warfare, laying down their lives to save the lives of others.

Accordingly, valiant George was awarded two posthumous medals. A committee appointed by the local Society for the Prevention of Cruelty to Animals (SPCA) unanimously confirmed that George had saved the children from severe injury and at least one life, that of the four year old boy on whom the two pit bulls had initially rounded and attacked.

The SSPCA (the Scottish Society for the Prevention of Cruelty to Animals) possess a medal designated for humans who have shown bravery in defense of a fellow animal, however this organization awarded the medal to George for his defense of humans. George was sent a second posthumous medal from a fellow protector of the innocent. The highly esteemed medal known as a purple heart was gifted to George by an American marine of thirty years named Jerrell Hudman. Hudman had received the award in 1967 for his service in Vietnam.

After reading on the internet about George's tremendous self-sacrificing courage and tragic fate, this veteran of Vietnam clearly recognized that George possessed the most elevated virtues rarely found in humanity as George had knowingly attempted to fight off two ferocious dogs, much stronger than himself virtually allowing himself to be savaged as a decoy whilst attempting to save the lives of others. In order to show their honor and admiration for George's self-sacrificial act of bravery and integrity, New Zealanders have had a statue of George erected in his memory.

A further account of yet another dog's heroism follows. Recently a visual and audio news video by SonnyRadio.com was sent to me by email. Sadly, this news reel filmed a dog who walked on to a busy highway and is tragically hit by a car. It appears the poor soul was hit again by further, thoughtless drivers of oncoming traffic. Remarkably, a second dog, presumably the tragic victim's beloved friend, ran on to the motorway, selflessly and hurriedly he/she dodges in and out of the speeding traffic, to the unconscious, injured dog's aid. Pulling the injured dog, the video informs us, "inch by inch," the savior uses his/her tightly grasped paws around the agonized dog's body in contrast to teeth. Incredibly, this deliverer without thought for his/her own safety, welfare and life drew the wounded dog to safety at the side of the road.

It is possible that this rescuer did not know the victim however this valiant dog was clearly prepared to lay down his/her own life to save that of another. Laying down one's own life for another is the highest attribute to which any animal, human or non-human animal can aspire. We later learn that both this road traffic victim and courageous champion survived. We can only hope that this brave, selfless and compassionate dog and this liberators injured friend were blessed by a kind person offering them both a permanent loving home.

A third, true, real-life news video in email circulation, films a desperately pleading dog; this distraught, solitary figure stands alone next to his dead dog friend in the middle of a busy road apparently in Asia. The depth of this tragic dog's heart rending grief is etched into the dog's distorted face and panicked body as it passionately paws its dead friend, clearly trying to bring him back to life, in doing so its heart is bursting as it lets out emotionally agonized cries.

Its friend had been hit by a car and the driver did not stop to help. Distraught, desperately nosing its dead friend, its broken hearted disbelief evident, he begs the dead dog to wake up, the depth of its love is overwhelming. The passionately loving dog refused to take himself to safety and leave the innocent victim's body alone in the road to be hit by yet another car. Risking his own life, he stood his ground hoping for a miracle.

Finally, a number of shocked drivers stopped their cars in incredulous disbelief at the spectacle. People began to crowd around and take photographs of the heartbroken dog's plight. The ever growing number of witnesses became deeply moved by the incredible depth and profundity of love this animal had for its tragically murdered friend. Again, hopefully a compassionate person will offer him a loving home and attempt to heal his emotional wounds.

A fourth video in email circulation anonymously sent to me shows an American news reel which has filmed a tragic dog, knocked down by a car and a second dog presumably his close friend is stood in the middle of the road refusing to leave his friend's side. The video shows authorities finally rescuing the road traffic victim, taking him/her away in a van.

Tragically and unbelievably they appear to drive off leaving his/her beloved friend behind. Alone, by the side of the road he/she watches the van pull away with his unconscious friend or relative inside. If this dog was indeed left behind, as a result of this apparent gross insensitivity by human animals, perhaps these two companions will never see each other again for the rest of their tormented lives.

Dogs have evolved in such close proximity with the human animal they can read a person's emotions, moods and body chemistry. Dogs are known to sense epileptic imbalances which produce seizures or fitting, warning their human companions before their onset. Dogs are aware of drops in blood sugar levels amongst diabetics and have been known to sniff out cancer amongst their human charges, whilst stroking a dog, drops a person's high blood pressure! It pays us to care for our dogs as we are only just learning how much they can do for us in return. Dogs are our companions, protectors and indeed healers.

It is believed there are 70 million pet dogs in the United States in modern times. Many human animals and fellow animals, both historically and today, demonstrate a spiritual depth often played out in their deep, emotionally fulfilling and healing relationships. These are often teacher student relationships, notably the spiritual teacher is most often not the human. Many photographs and videos show primates and dogs befriending one another, establishing long term, close relationships, notably humanity are biologically classified as primates.

160

Historic Pets were Honored

Peritas, Alexander the Great's Pet Dog

Following on from the above heart-rending contemporary accounts of heroic dogs, each of whom should be cherished by humanity, let us discuss two fascinating historic examples of the extremely close relationship between famous humans and their best friends, both the dog and horse, shining a light on how some humans have indeed honored their companion pets. These brief examples help to illustrate how pets have been loved, cared for and respected throughout the centuries and the globe, after which we will explore humankind's first most ancient friendship with domesticated animals.

Alexander III of Macedon (356-323 BC) more popularly known as Alexander the Great, had an Egyptian coastal city named after him, Alexandria. Believing he had to accomplish a divine commission to create a single world monarchy, this brilliant military genius responded to his perceived calling by conquering most of the civilized world.

Significantly, this stalwart and seasoned warrior spent a large part of his life fighting alongside countless men of high caliber who lived together for many years, bonding as brothers in war. Alexander was a well-educated general who had become astute in his judgment of the qualities and flaws inherent in others.

It is all the more telling that Alexander was filled with admiration, respect and love for his heroic, self-sacrificing, steadfast, courageous and loyal dog named Peritas who had demonstrated long-term exemplary qualities and virtues. Consequently, Alexander named a city, Peritas, in loving memory of his loving, cherished and treasured dog, rather than after a fellow human. In gratitude and awe of Peritas' fine and outstanding characteristics, Alexander rewarded Peritas in this way for his lifelong, sincere, faithful and devoted friendship.

It is believed Peritas regularly heroically protected his master during the savagery of warfare and that Peritas tragically died in Alexander's arms after Peritas' actions saved Alexander's life. The name Peritas is the Macedonian name for January, perhaps denoting the month of this heroic dog's birth.

The city of Peritas, thought to be located in India, housed a monument in its central square to pay tribute to Peritas' life and commemorate Peritas' courage. The city of Peritas is presumably situated near to the city of Bucephalus which was the name of Alexander's horse. Alexander named this further city after his loyal, brave and faithful horse and likewise commissioned and dedicated a central memorial monument to his steadfast horse. These cities would have fallen to Alexander and his troops after his defeat of King Porus at the Battle of Hydaspes.

Mongol Emperor Kublai Khan's Pet Dogs

Throughout the millennia and the globe humans have discovered that their pets gifted them with their loyal companionship together with their loving faithful hearts and souls. As the examples at the outset have shown, humans respond with various degrees of reciprocation, dependent on their often limited sensitivities reducing their ability to empathize with the needs of animals and understand indisputable animal communications utilizing sounds including facial and body language. Sadly, many humans are unable to demonstrate genuine love and compassion for these living souls.

Notably, historically, in the Far East some fortunate pets were provided for by rich masters who paid attendants to look after them. Servants of monarchs would care for pets given to their masters as highly prized gifts, in exchange for trade permits. Significantly, the Mongol Emperor Kublai Khan (1215-1294), grandson of the famed Genghis Khan, adopted, sheltered and fed 5000 dogs, each of whom were devoted to one another. To reward and safeguard them Kublai Khan had a palace built for them to live in! The Mongol Emperor Kublai Khan (1215-1294), is also renowned for finalizing the conquest of China in 1279 AD.

How the Human Canine Friendship Began

After early humans had killed an animal for food and clothing, wolves due to their heightened sense of smell would have inevitably been drawn to the same spot, searching for remnants of food left behind. As the humans began to butcher the animal, the patiently waiting wolves would have defended this position, keeping other wild animals away and from causing danger to the humans, a task for which the humans would have been grateful. Inevitably encouraging the wolves to stay and continue their self-appointed protective role, the humans would have thrown scraps of food to them as gratitude payments.

Over time, the wolves' and their descendant dogs clearly developed an increasingly symbiotic relationship with humans, as the wolves began to regularly protect the kill-spot and progressively share hunting missions with their fellow human hunters. In these ancient times dogs increasingly played the role of protector and watchdog, utilizing their keen sense of smell and efficient tracking and hunting abilities they led hunting missions, helping humans to trace food.

Naturally, ancient domesticated pet dogs acted as fiercely loyal, protective companions, watchdogs, trackers and hunters. With superior senses and speed they merged with and led their human families as they tracked and hunted prey for the joint canine and human community and working as a pack these dogs transported the fallen prey back home. Interestingly, the jewelry and tools of ancient peoples known as the Aurignacians, who lived 31,700 years ago, to be discussed later, were adorned with pictures of the large animals which they and their canine friends hunted.

One hypothesis is that the origin of the domesticated dog came from the human rearing of wolf cubs after the parent had been killed for food or clothing and over a short period of time humans domesticated them. Studies have shown that after merely ten generations of breeding silver foxes, whereby the breeder selects and mates the most docile for each successive future generation, significant morphological changes are seen to occur.

Surprisingly, the changes discovered not only relate to the offspring's increasingly affectionate, loyal and protective temperament towards humans but interestingly also clearly reveal marked changes in their physical coloring. Prior to domestication the above personality traits would have been exhibited towards their own species only.

The entire domestication process would not have taken long in view of the fact that at the young age of only one to two years the medium sized female canine can become pregnant, beginning her estrus cycle (heat) and pregnancies last only sixty three days. However, the dog may have quite naturally domesticated itself as a result of lines of more docile wolves being drawn to and breeding with other more docile wolves.

It may remain a mystery exactly how the dog became domesticated. Interestingly domestication could also be rapidly achieved with the many present-day highly intelligent, timid, emaciated and starving, often injured, urban foxes who, as a result of human proliferation and urbanization lead harshly disadvantaged lives, with a drastically curtailed life expectancy.

Approximately 6,000 years ago, at the close of the Middle Stone Age and on into the New Stone Age ancient Britons became less nomadic. Less dependent on hunting, they began to grow some basic crops and herd cattle and sheep. As the Bronze Age drew in, by 2200 BC Britons were increasingly settled. By this time dogs, performing the role of sentries, were taught to sound the alarm and defend the livestock from attack by wild predators.

The human community had for some considerable time become the dogs' community as dogs are by nature very much a social, family pack animal. The natural disposition of dogs is to live, sleep and eat together, collectively hunting as a team, this team now included the humans. Historically and today wild dogs hunt in unison in an intelligent coordinated manner whilst at least one dog is left behind from these forays to care for the puppies of the entire pack.

Remarkably, upon return these nannies are gifted with food by those dogs who went hunting, which is typically regurgitated or carried back for them as repayment for their protective baby-sitting role, caring for the community's infants whilst the parents were away.

In harmony with the original wolf pack/dog pack lifestyle, dogs together with our prehistoric ancestors, lived, ate, worked and slept together. Hunting as a well-organized team, all members began to appreciate the obvious mutual benefits of this arrangement. Dogs were also taught to round up and herd the sheep and cows, a trend that would have become increasingly common as human societies developed throughout the world.

Through the writings of Strabo (44 BC-23 AD) a Greek, who lived approximately 2000 years ago, who recorded geographical detail and historical events for posterity, we learn that Iron Age Britons, aware of the important qualities and skills of dogs, regularly exported a selection of them to Europe. The predominant role of the dog at the close of the Iron Age in Britain was that of watchdog and herder of livestock on farms.

Significantly Cunobelinus, the name of an Iron Age chieftain, means 'the Hound of Belinos,' when translated. This fact reveals that as a result of the fine, highly prized and admired canine qualities and skills with which humans had become familiar, certain dogs were increasingly held in particularly high esteem.

Notably, even a Celtic god possessed the same canine name of the Hound of Belinos, graphically demonstrating that dogs soon became highly regarded, admired and valued. This Celtic god was believed to be the embodiment of all that was respected in the dog, including self-sacrificing courageous protection, loyalty and devotion, steadfastness, determination, bravery, intelligence, uncomplaining stoicism, gratitude and playful mischievous humor.

From the earliest archaeological discoveries to the present day it has been proven that human animals and their companion animals have continued to share an extremely close, ancient and on-going history. The following summary of humankind's first religious beliefs, shaping our earliest human ancestor's relationships with animals, will cast some light on the ancientness of that intensely devoted and mutually fulfilling relationship.

Animism and Animals: Spontaneous Ancient Spiritual Consciousness

At this juncture, prior to examining archaeological and other evidence proving humanity had close bonds with fellow animals, it is helpful to have a brief look at the beliefs underlying animism, helping us to understand something of the earliest human belief systems relating to all animals, human and non-human, generated in the days of our prehistoric ancestors which are still inherent in global religious principles today.

Inevitably, animism arose as a result of humankind's most ancient, spontaneous spiritual consciousness and was found in the earliest human settlements throughout the globe. Notably, this ancient spiritual intuition has been dated to the Paleolithic age, which is as old as humankind itself.

The Latin word 'anima' meaning 'breath' or 'soul,' gave rise to the name animism, namely the earliest religious beliefs. It is believed that early humans noticed an animating life force/soul/spirit in all living beings that was lost at death. During the sleep state and in mediumistic visions they made contact with the spirits of the deceased and increasingly began to ask them for assistance for daily life issues often through the use of rituals.

Early tribal societies were typically animists, integral to this belief is that souls/spirits irrefutably dwell in humans, animals, plants and rocks including a range of geographic structures such as lakes, rivers, mountains and other aspects of the natural world such as thunder, wind and shadows.

Animists believe that all life forms such as the human animal, the non-human animal, including vegetation and non-living natural world phenomena, possess a spiritual essence and all are therefore sacred and should be honored and respected. Animism represents the belief that the non-physical spirits/souls of humans, animals, plants, stones, fire, water and wind are immortal. Animists believe that physical bodies merely house souls/spirits for a short and temporary period consequently spirits/souls live on, independently of the physical body.

Interestingly, many contemporary near death experiencers describe landscapes in the non-physical world populated with animals, birds, people, oceans, lakes and mountains which is certainly indicative that these ancients were right and that all the above phenomena do possess a spiritual essence that continues to exist in the non-physical realms. Animistic cultures past and present, typically accept as a norm, that they can contact deceased animals and relatives who, after death dwell in the regions of the spirit world. Sir Edward Tylor's book of 1871, named Primitive Culture, defined animism as "the general doctrine of souls and other spiritual beings in general."

It was believed that the soul animated all creatures including vegetation and that these souls/spirits could move from one living creature to another and even move into non-living things, representing ancient echoes of the belief in reincarnation and the transmigration of the soul. Notably, inherent within all religions to this day is some degree of animism. Animism represents humankind's pure, innate, spontaneous knowingness; a, spirituality, beyond and without organized religion with its religious denominations.

According to the animist world view, humans are typically considered to be of the same highly prized value as their fellow related animals. For animists, humans, other animals, birds, fish, vegetation and other environmental features are integral, sacrosanct related components of the natural world and importantly humans are inseparable from other members of the natural world. The author of Respecting the Living World Graham Harvey offers a definition: "Animism is the attempt to live respectfully as members of the diverse community of living persons [only some of whom are human] which we call the world or cosmos." *1*

Irrefutably, extraordinary respect and compassion was demonstrated to animals in animist cultures. Living animal bodies were also considered to house dead ancestors again this belief has much in common with later beliefs in reincarnation and the transmigration of the soul, which teach us that after physical death all spirits/souls repeatedly returns to live physical existences sometimes as an animal and sometimes as a human animal. Notably, animists believe each and every soul is a unique and distinct entity. Nick Herbert has coined the phrase of "quantum animism" as a means of describing how 'mind' who many would describe as God, pervades and infuses all levels and all components of reality.

Professor Rupert Sheldrake, writing in his books, The Rebirth of Nature: New Science and the Revival of Animism and secondly, the Science Delusion, offers his present day summary understanding of animism as a model that accepts all components of nature to be alive.

31,700 Year Old Belgian Pet Dog

Animistic beliefs, being as old as the first of humankind, were certainly expressed through humankind's most ancient and enduring friendship with increasingly domesticated companion animals. This friendship is mirrored today by our cousins, fellow primates, who form close bonds with dogs in particular.

Evidence from archaeological discoveries proves that domesticated dogs were committed, protective, unfaltering companions to the earliest of our humans ancestors in a range of countries throughout the ancient world including Persia, North America and North east Africa. Initially, it was thought that dogs have been human companions for 15,000 years.

Incredibly, the discovery of more ancient remains suggests that the close relationship between human and canine was on-going more than 31,700 years ago. Amazingly, DNA evidence suggests that present day dogs developed 100,000 years ago, indicating that the ancient ancestors of dogs and humans lived and worked together for 100,000 years in a mutually beneficial relationship. This surely adds tremendous weight to the claim that dogs are a human's best friend. Indeed it is a fact that dogs are humankind's oldest friend!

Significantly dogs lived, walked and worked with us when we lived as ancient cave dwelling nomads, hunting on foot we searched for food together. Dogs lived with us in ancient times when we paddled canoes, drove chariots and constructed the earliest seafaring galleons. Today, countless thousands of years later, dogs ride around with us in petrol and electric cars they fly overseas often sitting on our knees, in airplanes with us, travel on trains with us even crossing the sea via the channel tunnel train with us and travel the oceans by ship and cruise liner with us.

If, in the distant future, humans ever seek to inhabit an earth-like planet, dogs would certainly cross the galaxy travelling in rockets with us. They would continue to be loved and needed offering us their steadfast, loyal companionship and watchdog protection over us. As humans and canines evolved together, this most ancient and wonderful symbiotic relationship is characterized by the dogs' continued devotion in the 21st century, acting as humans' ever-present, closest and age-old companion.

Incredibly, the remains of a 31,700 year old Stone Age, pet dog have been unearthed in Goyet Cave in Belgium. This extensive period in human prehistory known as the Paleolithic era or Stone Age covers approximately from 2.5 million years ago to 20,000 years ago, beginning with early humans using basic tools made of stone and concluding with modern day human hunter gatherer societies. The Stone Age period provides us with the earliest archaeological remains whilst earlier discoveries fall into the field of paleontology.

The lengthy Paleolithic era has been divided into three classifications by academics based on the dating of epochs. The first is the Lower Paleolithic or Early Stone Age dated between 2.5 million-200,000 years ago. At this time the Hominin ancestors of humans, including Australopithecus, Homo habilis, homo erectus and homo ergaster inhabited the globe.

The second is the Middle Paleolithic or Middle Stone Age dated between 200,000-45,000 years ago, during which the Neanderthals and the first Homo sapiens emerged, notably, the latter possessed the first anatomically modern features and behavior patterns. Compassion was indeed a feature of these societies demonstrated by their care for older and infirm members of their societies and tools were more complex.

The third is the Upper Paleolithic or Late Stone Age dated between 45,000-10,000 years ago, notably Neanderthals decreased in numbers, diminishing in existence by 30,000 years ago. However, it is believed that many different 'species' of human ancestors may have interbred with one another and reproduced, creating the next hybrid generations of human ancestors. This epoch in human history reveals fully modern behavior patterns including the earlier noted compassion, illustrated by cave art, extensive stone, ivory and antler tool products and companion pets.

It is in the Late Stone Age era in which the bones of the 31,700 year old pet dog were found however it is believed that working dog, protective companion pets, presumably lived with humans at an earlier stage. Dogs living 31,700 years ago would have lived alongside the Aurignacian people who lived in Europe from the Upper Paleolithic era.

These dogs most resemble the Siberian husky however they were larger. Prior to the above 31,700 year old revealing discovery the oldest remains of ancient pet dogs were of those who lived in Russia dating back only 14,000 years ago, 18,000 years later than the confirmed date of 31,700 year old pet dogs.

Significantly, the results of the isotopic analysis of the bones of the 31,700 year old pet dog indicates, that these prehistoric pet dogs were fed horse, musk, ox and reindeer. Importantly, the food fed to these ancient domesticated dogs who led their human communities tracking and hunting was the same as that eaten by their human companions. It can be deduced that these domesticated dogs that lived and worked amongst the Aurignacian peoples were rewarded with their share of the same spoils, encouraging them to continue to perform their much needed duties for these ancient communities.

French Child's 26,000 Year Old Pet Dog

The ancient close relationship between human and dog is further supported by an exciting 26,000 year old archaeological discovery of the preserved footprints of a child and his/her companion dog, they walked side by side together through the dark labyrinthine passages in Chauvet Cave in France.

The child also left signs of a torch of fire as the pair made their way together through the dimly lit tunnels. Significantly, the child had accomplished a chore with his/her fiercely protective friend the dog, loyally by his/her side. However, it is believed that the above evidence proves that the reciprocal close bonds between canine and human developed much earlier, practically with the dawn of humanity.

15,000 Year Old British Pet Dogs

As stated earlier, the remains of ancient pet dogs have been found in many places throughout the globe. This fact suggests that the bones of domesticated dogs from prehistoric times have not been found in ancient inhabited areas due to the lack of natural forces needed to preserve ancient bones, a common problem, rather than the lack of the canine human symbiotic relationship.

Archaeologists have found the remains of 15,000 year old domesticated pet dogs in Gough Cave in Somerset, England in the United Kingdom, proving in yet another country, human and canine hunting partners lived and worked together since the earliest times. These domesticated dogs lived in England during the Old Stone Age, at the close of the last Ice Age.

Excavators also unearthed 9,500 year old bones of ancient pet dogs between the years 1949-1951, in Starr Carr in Yorkshire, England. This early period in Britain was known as the Middle Stone Age. Interestingly, these primordial, domesticated dogs, who were non-aggressive descendants from the wolf, still possessed large teeth.

Ancient Israelite Dogs were Highly Respected

The findings summarized in an article in The Journal for the Study of the Old Testament prove that a complete re-evaluation of the ancient Israelite attitude towards dogs is needed. While the term dog has been used as a criticism of a person, dogs themselves were shown to be highly-regarded, appreciated and respected as devoted protective companions in ancient Israel.

Dogs were invaluable, often working as sheep dogs. This precious warm-hearted aid lived and worked with the shepherd and sheep acting as an early warning system alerting both to danger and actively saving the lives of both shepherds and sheep.

Notably, the bible provides us with the story of Job, who thought more highly of his sheep dogs due to their obvious admirable characteristics than the fathers of certain young men who troubled him.

"But now they mock me, men younger than I, whose fathers I would have disdained to put with my sheep dogs." (Job 30.1) The same respect and high regard for dogs is demonstrated elsewhere in the ancient Jewish and Christian scriptures, two further examples include verses which can be found in the Book of Tobias 6:2 and 11:4.

12,000 Year Old Israelite Pet Dog

Incredibly, the remains of a 12,000 year old pet dog have been unearthed in Israel. This skeletal discovery was found in the Natufian site of Ein Mallaha in northern Israel. Significantly, this four or five month old dog was respectfully buried beside the bones of an aged human. The youthful dog had been sensitively and gently laid to rest immediately below the tender left hand of the human skeleton as if the human was still sympathetically and lovingly caressing his devoted childlike companion.

These two loving lifetime friends were carefully buried side by side, clearly evidencing the belief that these two devoted companions would make their transition after physical death to the next realms together, again awaking, reuniting and jointly entering and sharing life again in the after death realms together.

12,500 to 9,000 BC Year Old Israelite Pet Dogs

Incredibly, at a second site in the cave of Hayonim in Israel, the remains of a human and canine burial can be clearly seen, in this case, together with the human burial is evidence of

172

the burial of two companion canids. The Natufian culture has been dated to the close of the Pleistocene era approximately 12,500 to 9,000 BC.

These sedentary or semi-sedentary Mesolithic peoples lived in the Mediterranean territory of the Levant. Importantly, similar to many other ancient cultures these people would have needed dogs for protection, hunting and herding livestock, obvious bonds of mutual respect and love between the two would have developed, strikingly evidenced by such shared graves.

John Pickrell writing as a science journalist for the National Geographic Magazine on-line news informs us that: "In contrast to cats, intentional burials of dogs and puppies with humans occurred earlier and have been more common in the archaeological record. [Some of the] ... earliest are known from the Natufian stage, 12,000 years ago in Israel." *2*

9,500 Year Old Cypriot Pet Cat

A 9,500 year old Cypriot pet cat and its human companion were unearthed in 2001 by a team of French archaeologists conducting excavations on the Mediterranean island of Cyprus. Both cats and dogs are known as "commensal domesticates," a term that describes these animals' preference for living around humans and befriending them.

Consequently, historically, as in present day, mutual deep and loving companionships developed, that spanned life, both in the physical and non-physical realms, resulting in the most enduring gesture a person can make and that is to express their wish to share a grave with their beloved faithful animal friend. When a person was ready to pass to the after-life they obviously asked family and friends to ensure that they were buried in the same grave as their beloved animal companion, in some instances they may have died together at the same time.

Regarding human and animal shared graves, it is quite probable the animal companion died naturally at an earlier date and that our human ancestors stored their animals' bones so that they could be placed beside them in their graves at the time of their own demise. This was to ensure that their loving animals would remain close to them for eternity, travelling with them and continuing to live with them in the regions of the after-life.

In the dimmest, darkest past as far back as we can glimpse, in the history of human animals and non-human animals, dogs and cats have befriended humans. A shared love and companionship between the two most obviously developed. From the earliest times this mutual companionship of love, compassion and friendship gave rise to the exchange of affection, protection and loyalty. The shared lives of human, canine and cat has been evidenced by many archaeological discoveries, some of which are outlined here.

Significantly, this 9,500 year old Cypriot pet cat lived and loved with our human ancestors in prehistoric times, known as the Stone Age or Neolithic Period. The Neolithic period is thought to be 10,000-12,000 years ago in Europe whilst significantly, this stage of development occurred much earlier in other regions. John Pickrell informs us that:

"The carefully interred remains of a human and a cat were found buried with seashells, polished stones, and other decorative artifacts in a 9,500 year old grave site on the Mediterranean island of Cyprus. This new find, from the Neolithic village of Shillourokambos, predates early Egyptian art depicting cats by 4,000 years or more."*3*

In Pickrell's interview with Melinder Zeder, the curator of the Old World archaeology at the Smithsonian Institute in Washington, USA, Zeder said: "In the absence of a collar around its neck, the deliberate interment of this animal with a human makes a strong case that cats had a special place in the daily lives, and in the afterlives, of residents of Shillourokambos."*4*

The corpses of both the human and cat had been delicately and sensitively laid together in a symmetrical fashion with both of their heads pointing to the west. Importantly, both sets of remains were found to be in the same quality of preservation and both were accompanied by jewelry and stone tools. This ancient pet cat is thought to have died at the age of eight months and there is no evidence at all that it had been used for food.

174

Rather, with both heads directed towards the west and bejeweled it is believed the cat had a close relationship with the person with whom it was buried and both were expected to share the afterlife together. The tenderly buried cat belonged to the Felis silvestris species which is the species ancestor from whom all domesticated cats have sprung.

The French archaeologist, Jean-Denis Vigne, from the National Museum of Natural History in Paris clarified during Pickrell's interview that cats have most likely been human companions from an even more ancient date. Vigne commented on the fact that illustrations of cats have been discovered on 10,000 year old, Stone Age Neolithic Period engravings and pottery. This would indicate that late Stone Age people believed that cats had a spiritual significance as well as being valued as adored pets.

Apart from cat illustrations on pottery, the actual remains of cats on the island have also been dated to the late Stone Age, however, these cat remains were not found in graves. This does not indicate that cats were not pets in this early era or that they were not traditionally buried with their human companions. Historically cats, foxes, pigs, goats, deer and cattle were not native to Cyprus. Consequently, this range of animals must have been deliberately taken to the island by seafaring humans.

Astoundingly, 10,000 year old figurines of cats made of stone or clay have been unearthed in a number of countries including Israel, Turkey and Syria, revealing that cats were highly regarded as warm, loving and beautiful pets who may have been originally adopted to keep ancient homes clear of mice.

Pets in the Ancient Egyptian Civilization

Importantly, the discovery of the remains of the 9,500 year old pet cat in Cyprus predates the known domesticated pet cats of the majestic, ancient Egyptian civilization of approximately 5000 BC. However, archaeological evidence proves that the ancient Egyptians were devoted to their companion pets some of whom included cats, dogs, monkeys and gazelles and possibly birds.

Consequently, it is reasonable to assume that the earlier ancient Egyptian peoples, later known for their founding of a remarkable and enduring culture also had feline, canine and monkey companions prior to the establishment of the outstanding dynastic pharaohs.

This supposition is supported by the fact that if undeveloped communities cared for a variety of animals as pets at an earlier date than 5000 BC, then inevitably the precursor to the awe-inspiring Egyptian civilization did also; especially in view of the fact that the ancient Egyptian love, care, sympathy and playfulness with animals who possessed collars and leads is poignantly evidenced by countless tomb paintings and illustrations decorating ancient Egyptian artifacts.

Undoubtedly precious to the ancient Egyptians on many levels, these pets including birds were meticulously mummified often using the same precious materials that were used for the pharaohs and their royal families.

It is probable that the archaeological remains, evidencing the pre-Egyptian Empire's possession of pets at a historically earlier date has not been preserved or we simply have not yet found it. Importantly, the cats and dogs of the ancient Egyptians were not only family pets but they were also worshipped as gods. Certainly, all pets celebrated as gods would have been treated with the utmost compassion and respect, enjoying all the love, food, water, comfort, luxury and health care the adoptive pet family could offer.

Notably, cats were also perceived as being the bringers of good fortune. The ancient Egyptians painstakingly mummified a wide range of animals so that human animals and non-human animals could travel together to the after death realms, sharing and enriching each, others' lives again for eternity. If they traveled to the domains of the next life independently of each other, they believed they would again reunite in the afterlife landscapes and continue as the same inseparable companions as before.

Incredibly, primates have been found to share the same sarcophagus as the ancient Egyptian pet owner. These ancient compassionate individuals obviously treated their pet like the innocent, vulnerable child that it is, not only sharing a tomb together but also a coffin. Notably, at first sight, archaeologists thought the primates' bones were those of a human child.

The Ancient Egyptian Civilization Bejeweled and Clothed their Pets

Certainly dogs and cats were the first animals to work for humans and live amongst them, making them our longest lasting and enduring animal friends. These unbroken bonds that have endured for many thousands of years since humanity was in its infancy should be highly respected and valued. Most modern day people clothe their pet dogs in coats for rainy, windy and cold winter days and also provide them with beds and blankets.

They would be wrong to believe that because they are loving individuals who typically live in technologically advanced societies that they are the first to offer love, protective comfort including a whole range of animal welfare measures, health attention and burials for their pets.

Many contemporary pet owners would be surprised to learn that the ancient Egyptians were devoted to their pets, ensuring their animals' happiness, health, long-term welfare and funerary arrangements at death. Perhaps they were even more caring than many pet owners today. They took the necessary funeral measures according to ancient Egyptian religious beliefs to safeguard their mutually shared continued existence together in the afterlife.

It is fascinating to know that our human ancestors, living many thousands of years ago, responding to the reciprocal expression of empathy, love and devotion between them and their devoted pets, were the first to dress their beloved pets, protecting, adorning, beautifying and decorating their beloved pets in jewelry.

Significantly, ancient Egyptian illustrations show us that their dogs walked in highly decorated collars and leads and their monkeys who often carried out tricks to the sheer delight of their human friends and families, wore clothes and jewelry. Consequently, attending to the welfare and comfort of animals and giving them gifts are not lavish customs practiced by individuals from modern day, rich, indulgent societies but by the most ancient of societies including that of the ancient Egyptians.

This kindness and compassion clearly demonstrated to animals is indicative that the members of those societies, including those of the Egyptian civilization, were spiritually elevated individuals. Those who value the lives of fellow animals certainly value the lives of human beings. The Greek philosopher Plutarch's (46-120AD) words of wisdom clarify: "Were it only to learn benevolence to humankind, we should be merciful to other creatures."

The famous writer Francois Voltaire (1694-1778) reminds us that [we should]:
" regard other animals as our brothers, because they are endowed with life as we are, because they have the same principles of life, the same feelings. The same ideas, memory and industry - as we. [Human] speech alone is wanting to them. If they had it should we dare to kill and eat them? Should we dare to commit these fratricides?"

The writer Reverend Humphrey Primatt (1736-1779) adds: "Pain is pain, whether it is inflicted on man or on beast' and the creature that suffers it, whether man or beast, being sensible of the misery of it whilst it lasts, suffers Evil..."

Early Archaeological Egyptian Pet Dog Discoveries

Significantly, dogs are first mentioned in pre-dynastic Egypt, to give an idea of dates, the late Pre-dynastic Period ranges between approximately 3100-2950 BC, these were extremely ancient times. This would be before the early Egyptian dynastic period dated at approximately 3100-2686 BC which was followed by the Old Kingdom 2686-2181 BC. Due to the discovery of the preserved bones of ancient domesticated pet dogs found in the Egyptian region, ranging from approximately 5000 BC, we know that in later years pet dogs were indeed common.

Notably, the Egyptian artifact known as the Moscow Cup from the ancient Egyptian Badarian culture, dated at 4400-4000 BC, reveals illustrations of domesticated pet dogs. The Egyptian

Badarian culture identified by their last remaining artifacts, including metal and glazed objects, was an ancient 5th century BC farming culture whose small village settlements occupied areas in Upper Egypt.

Further Egyptian artifacts proving the close bond between dog and human since the most ancient of times is the Asmolean Palette and Hunting Palette. These ancient items from the later Naqada II period (3500-3200/3000 BC) provide us with illustrations of domesticated dogs wearing leather collars so that they could wear their names around their necks and be walked on leads.

In order to appreciate the more ancient nature of the above earlier Egyptian cultures which responded to the friendship offered by dogs, it is helpful to be reminded of the fact that even the early Egyptian dynastic period 3100-2686 BC followed by the Old Kingdom 2686-2181 BC were later eras than the lives of those who made these incredible, extremely ancient pet artifacts.

It is valuable to bear in mind that just because the bones of domesticated pet dogs have not been found in Egypt of equivalent age to those pets found in Cyprus it does not necessarily suggest that they did not exist, merely that natural forces did not preserve them.

Ancient Egyptian Collars Display Dog and Cat Names

Astonishingly, contemporary museums, exhibit the preserved ancient leather collars of devoted pet dogs whose names still appear clearly inscribed on them. Importantly, the names the ancient Egyptians chose for their dogs reflect the dog's personality, attributes, qualities, coloring and human comical amusement with their canine's hilarious antics, clearly expressing the love between the human animal and their companion animal.

Notably, the ancient Egyptians gave their dogs human names, recognizing their virtues shared with humans. Ancient Egyptian dogs lived with other pets in the Egyptian homes of royalty and commoners, as members of the family.

179

Ancient Egyptian dog collars provide us with a selection of dog names, some of which include "Blackie," "Good Herdsman," "North-Wind," "the Fifth," "Brave One," "Reliable" and even "Useless!" Thus, revealing that the ancient Egyptians displayed the same kind-hearted, entertaining and witty humor for which they are famed, today among their Middle Eastern neighbors.

The following name of an ancient Egyptian pet cat, preserved throughout the millennia for posterity is "Pleasant One." This graphically descriptive name provides us with a tender insight into the beloved pet friend's cherished status and relationship with its adoptive owner. Thousands of years ago, both shared their physical lives together, since then, presumably, they have also jointly enjoyed the afterlife together.

There is a belief that cats were domesticated before dogs in Egypt but it is accepted that dogs soon assumed a more elevated position. Humans and cats probably began to bond after cats were brought into the home to catch mice and rats. Dogs might have initially been brought into the home as watch dogs, offering protection. However, after assuming their dutiful roles, cats and dogs, along with monkeys and gazelles, soon became sought after companion animals for their fellow humans.

Ancient Egyptian Vegetarianism

The ancient Egyptian empire along with its pervasive culture celebrated its civilization, religious beliefs and splendor for more than thirty centuries, from the late Predynastic Period 3100-2950 BC to the end of the Roman Period in 395 AD.5 Notably, the ancient Egyptians lived in one of the most fertile valleys in the ancient world. The ever-bountiful River Nile was praised by the grateful inhabitants for its regular, benevolent floods which deposited rich fertile silt several times per year allowing the Egyptians to cultivate up to three harvests every year.

Significantly, many statues and paintings show us that many ancient Egyptians were overweight. Although the Egyptian diet may have slight variations over the millennia we are aware that, diverse types of breads, fruits, vegetables, beer and some occasional fish were their staple diet. The nourishment of these ancients also incorporated wheat, honey, dates, raisins, pomegranates, grapes, peas, beans, onions, garlic, leeks, lettuce, cabbages, turnips, salt, pepper, spices, butter, cheese, eggs and sesame seeds.

Conspicuously, most Egyptians rarely ate animal flesh, whilst certain kinds of fish were also prohibited from being eaten, due to fishes' association with the Egyptian Osiris myth. Notably, this fecund, bountiful river environment was a predominantly agricultural rather than pastoral culture, in which grazing cattle was rare. Only wealthy individuals, who are known to have drunk both wine and beer, would have possessed the means to buy animal flesh, however this practice was uncommon.

The Ancient Egyptian Vegetarian Priesthood

Typically, the ancient Egyptian priests and priestesses were appointed by the pharaoh. For a considerable period in Egyptian history, these untainted priests and priestesses were prohibited from eating animal flesh, fish was also banned. They were also forbidden to wear wool or other animal products on their body as clothing, including their feet. Further ritual and ceremonial purification involved the priesthood bathing several times each day and shaving their heads as a display of habitual purity.

Each pharaoh commissioned the priests and priestesses to represent him/her, by carrying out, on pharaoh's behalf his/her regular requisite temple duties. It was not physically possible for the pharaoh to attend to the obligatory religious ceremonies due to the ever increasing number of temples.

Pharaoh had not got the time to daily perfume and care for the gods' statues located at these holy sanctuaries. Those priests and priestesses who officiated at the temples, carrying out pharaoh's duties and wishes were frequently from a lay priesthood, simultaneously occupying other jobs in the community. Consequently, these strict vegetarians were also part of the greater community.

Traditionally, the religious role of the priesthood was passed down, generation after generation in a hereditary fashion. Evidently, priestesses usually enjoyed an equal status to their male counterparts probably as a reward for their splendid and highly respected psychic and mediumistic abilities.

Many members of the priesthood provided the public with oracles, these involved predictions of the future and contact with the deceased. These personal psychic readings which tapped into the clients' problems, including their past and future, guided and counseled the frequently distressed individual regarding the best course of action to take to solve their anxieties and concerns.

Mediumistic communications proved the clients' loved ones had survived physical death and greatly alleviated grief whilst communications, discussions and negotiations with loved ones frequently provided clients with guidance and advice assisting them to solve any particular current predicament.

The increasing hierarchies of priests and priestesses sought to maintain the harmonious status quo including their position in ancient Egyptian society, striving to maintain the religion and culture for posterity.

Ancient Egyptian Tomb and Artifact Illustrations of Pets

Illustrations of pet monkeys, cats and dogs can also be seen in ancient Egyptian tomb reliefs and as illustrative decorations on artifacts. To give one example, a pet cat has been drawn scratching the leg of a favorite wooden chair. This portrait image was obviously chosen, commissioned and paid for by a besotted pet owner who was sensitively and humorously familiar with his/her cat's droll fondness for leisurely destroying the cat's owner's chair!

Crucially, illustrations found in tombs and those depictions decorating artifacts reveal that all pets whilst physically alive were served with buffets of favorite foods in contrast with today when a pet is typically served with only one bowl at a time. They enjoyed a number of buffet bowls at any one time.

Ancient Egyptian Pet Burials ~ Tomb Evidence

The ancient Egyptians believed that the after-death regions would be populated with the diversity of all sentient beings whether two legged or four legged, including those of the land, sea and sky. They believed that a person could take all that they loved and valued during their earthly life with them to the after death domains; consequently, they had their beloved pets mummified.

These ancients firmly believed they would reunite with their loving companion animals again in the next life. Countless tomb paintings show animals sitting near to their human companion. They believed that tomb paintings clearly illustrating familiar scenes in daily life depicted would help to manifest and actualize the same earthly scenes in the afterlife.

Significantly, tomb evidence proves that pets were also gifted with plentiful supplies of food to take with them to the next life. Copious individual model figurines of pet dogs and other pets have also been discovered in tombs. Notably, pets were mummified and gifted with exceedingly expensive burials, again evidencing the fact that extremely deep, mutual bonds developed between ancient Egyptians and their adored pet companions.

The ancient Egyptian Royal Son of Chief Artificer, Tithmose of the XVIII dynasty, provides us with a glimpse of his pet's burial. He commissioned a small limestone sarcophagus to be built to house and protect the body of his treasured and much-loved, deceased cat.

The illustrations on the sarcophagus emphatically show the cat at death was gifted with an abundance of food and flowers. Notably, the hieroglyphic inscriptions are the same on both human and pet sarcophaguses ensuring both the human animal and non-human animal make their safe transitions to the regions of the afterlife. Pets, believed to have died natural deaths were placed in tombs awaiting the death of their owners so that both could travel to the after death regions together.

Pets Received Identical Mummification Process to Humans

Notably, a team of researchers from Bristol University, England, in the United Kingdom analyzed samples of tissue and wrappings from a selection of Egyptian animal and bird mummies, housed in the Liverpool Museum in England. These mummified pets included hawks, cats and an ibis ranging from 818 BC to 343 BC.

Using gas chromatography and mass spectrometry these academics were able to detect the chemicals used in the mummification process. These researchers concluded that the fats, oils, beeswax, sugar, gum, bitumen and pine tree resins which were used on human mummies were identical to that used on the animal and bird mummies and was just as carefully utilized.

It should be stressed that the ancient Egyptians accomplished an exceptional fete as these psychic and spiritually orientated people actually mummified millions of birds and animals. This research has provided us with enormous evidence that the ancient Egyptians demonstrated tremendous care and devotion towards many fellow beings who share this planet with us.

This scientific analysis answers our questions, by clearly evidencing that the millions of non-human mummies were treated with the same respect, dedication and generosity as were the human mummies. Richard Evershed notes, "… they were treated with the same sort of reverence and sophistication as human mummies. We found pretty much exactly the same materials were used on both." *6*

The scientific discovery that the ancient Egyptians took as much care in embalming and mummifying their animals, including birds and crocodiles as they did with humans, provides further evidence that the ancient Egyptians were devoted to their pets and sought to populate an otherwise frighteningly sterile, lonely and barren afterlife with them.

The dedicated and faithful mummification of companion animals with whom they sought mutually loving reunions in the afterlife, is further evidenced by abundant animal and bird paintings and engravings, graphically portraying the importance of all animals, in the life of the ancient Egyptians.

As stated, common household pets included cats, dogs, monkeys, gazelles and birds. Importantly, dogs, cats, baboons and birds including other animals have been found sharing the same sacred sarcophagus or tomb with the person with whom they shared their physical life.

With the discovery of millions of mummified animals and birds unearthed in the vast expanse of galleries, tombs and catacombs surrounding Zoser's Step Pyramid at Saqqara in Egypt including the unearthing of mummified bulls and crocodiles, we learn that it was not only beloved pets who were mummified in order to make their transition to the celestial realms.

It has been reported, pending verification that Salima Ikram, the Professor of Egyptology at the American University in Cairo, Egypt and a team of archaeologists headed by Paul Nicholson of Cardiff University, United Kingdom have unearthed practically eight million dog mummies in two dog catacombs in the Saqqara necropolis, consisting of dogs from a variety of breeds.

The dog catacombs, dedicated to the cult of Anubis are thought to have been first discovered in 1897 by the French archaeologist Jacques De Morgan. Notably, these dog catacombs are adjacent to the neighboring temple of Anubis. This extremely ancient Egyptian deity weighs an individual's heart as recorded in the Egyptian Book of the Dead, assessing whether the person's good deeds outweigh his/her bad deeds, which would allow him/her entry to the afterlife.

The ancient Egyptian cult of Anubis was extremely ancient and significantly predated the cult and role of Osiris. Anubis, known as Lord of the Hallowed Land, was the original god of the dead, who acted as guide, protector and escort of the dead. In harmony with the protective, guiding, companion-like qualities of the dog, Anubis, the dog-headed deity, friend and companion, original soul-mate and confidante of the dead, was the god of death and the afterlife.

Supervising all mummification procedures, Anubis was also the caretaker god of embalming who was painted pitch black to parallel the jet black bodies of those who have been embalmed. Notably, the embalmers wore the dog-headed mask as a symbol that they were this god of death and afterlife, during the mummification process.

The Saqqara necropolis, consisting of enormous quantities of mummified animals buried in a vast expanse of underground catacombs, is also home to many other animal cults and includes the burials of bulls, cows, baboons, ibises, hawks and cats who like dogs and other mummified canids, were believed to act as intermediaries between humans and the gods.

Notably, found in the Memphite Serapeum at Saqqara, the name of the galleries of tombs of the 'Apis Bulls,' located north-west of the Step Pyramid, were the burials of these grand animals. Throughout their lifetime of approximately twenty to twenty-five years and in death the female, males and calves were treated royally. Notably, they were embalmed in a seated pose with legs beneath them like the sphinx.

Egyptian animals and birds were preserved for posterity with great expertise, tenderness and care, many of whom can be viewed in the Cairo museum. Astonishingly, here, a person can learn about many individual, pharaoh's pets! These ancient Egyptian pet-owning pharaohs, share many experiences with today's pet-owners, extinguishing the 5000 years that apparently separated them, due to pet-owners' shared love of animals being timeless.

A person can observe cats with gilded faces enfolded in linen, formed from diamond, squares and crisscross, shrews in limestone boxes, rams enclosed in gilded and beaded coverings, a gazelle draped in papyrus, a preserved seventeen foot crocodile with babies in her mouth including linen swathed ibises, hawks, fish and scarab beetles together with their dung ball food!

In the 30th dynasty a man known as Hapi-man was buried with his small, beloved, companion dog curled besides his feet. In

2950 BC at Abydos, 1st dynasty pharaohs had dogs, lions and donkeys laid to rest in their ancient Egyptian tombs. Some animals were mummified because they were pets and others because they were living ambassadors of the gods. Animals, reptiles and birds were mummified in bandages adorned with religious incantations, typically paid for by their owners.

For thousands of years the ancient Egyptians performed these religious rituals and prayers to give their entombed mummified animals immortality together with happiness and food in the afterlife. The respect the ancient Egyptians had for the diversity of all life on earth, is strikingly evident, each of whom like us have equally struggled for survival, evolving alongside us and sharing this planet with us.

God Resides in all Animals, Human and Non-Human

The Egyptian honor and respect for our fellow, related animals is further demonstrated by the fact that the statues of many Egyptian gods possessed a combination of human animal and non-human animal features.

The god Anubis: Canine Face with a Man's Body

Anubis, the half man, half dog, god of the dead, possessing a man's body and canine head (dog or jackal), is a distinct example of the combination of half human and half animal features. Anubis was the god of the funerary cult associated with embalming, mummification and escorting the death to the landscapes of the afterlife.

Significantly, Anubis personifying the virtues of the dog which is perceived as a devoted friend during the physical life was chosen to act as the same loyal companion after death by protectively leading and escorting the dead to the landscapes beyond physical death. It cannot be overstated that an abundance of Egyptian art proves to us that dogs walked on leads side by side with humans and that these ancients were acutely aware of the extremely affectionate, emotional, intelligent, protective and leadership characteristics of dogs.

The god Sekhmet: Lion's Face with a Woman's Body

The god Sekhmet is a second example of an Egyptian god composed of human and animal features, further substantiating the fact that the ancient Egyptians had a great admiration for the many qualities of animals, personified in the Egyptian gods. Sekhmet was also known as Hathor, Bastet, Mut and the Eye of Re.

This fierce lion goddess of war typically possessed the body of a woman and the head of a lion with a serpent around it. Sekhmet sought to destroy the enemies of Re, the sun-god. She was also associated with disease, healing and medicine and was the companion to the god, Ptah. Sekhmet was the protector who destroyed wrong doers whilst she healed and protected the innocent.

The god Horus: Falcon's Face with a Man's Body

A third example of an Egyptian deity personifying animal virtues and combining the features of human and animal was Horus the falcon god. Horus had three forms he was fashioned wholly as a falcon, alternatively depicted as having the body of a man and the head of a falcon otherwise as a winged disk hovering above the head of pharaoh. Due to the belief that each pharaoh was a manifestation of the god Horus, the name Horus was incorporated into the names of the pharaohs.

Notably, the hieroglyphic symbol of a falcon represents the word 'god.' Falcons were considered to be most sacred consequently falcon cults were popular throughout ancient Egypt. It was believed that Horus' eyes were the sun and moon. This again reveals the respect and honor conveyed by the ancient Egyptians to the many qualities and virtues of the animal world.

The god Amon-Re: Ram's Head

Notably, Amon-Re is yet another god depicted expressing the qualities and characteristics of an animal either as a ram in its entirety or shown to possess a ram's head. Amon became a national god who became associated with the sun god Re producing the name Amon-Re. The enormous, labyrinthine temple of Karnak in the southern part of the kingdom was dedicated to Amon.

The god Re: Falcon Head

Solar gods such as Re, all had falcon forms. Re was assimilated into the god Horus and was represented as having a falcon head. Re was considered to be the creator god who created himself together with eight other gods from the oceans of chaos. Vanquishing evil every night, he was reborn every new day.

The god Seth: Canine Body

Seth is yet another example of an Egyptian god who had the composite form of both human and non-human personality and physical features. Seth was depicted as having a canine body, slanting eyes, square tipped ears and a tufted or forked tail. Egyptologists have suggested that his form could include features taken from a long nosed mouse, a pig, a jackal, a greyhound, a camel, an antelope or an aardvark. Seth was the patron of the eleventh province of Upper Egypt and was considered to be the murderer of the god Osiris and enemy of the god Horus.

Ancient Egyptian Animal Cemeteries

Remarkably, to date archaeologists have unearthed 130 ancient animal cemeteries throughout Egypt. The current consensus of opinion is that these animal cemeteries existed by

300 BC. Conspicuously, due to the personality qualities, mental attributes and physical beauty of animals and birds, their bodies were considered to be excellent physical homes in which a god might reside.

Consequently, the ancient Egyptians believed that the spirits of different gods dwelt peacefully within all animals at any given time. Consequently particular animals were worshipped and all creatures were treated with compassion and respect throughout the entirety of their lives, culminating in the honor of painstaking embalmment and mummification of animals and birds at death.

This ancient belief has parallels with the shared historic and contemporary belief that an aspect of the ever-present, all-pervading, creative, compassionate parent God, (God being an omnipresent, all-pervasive hologram), permanently lives within all animals, human and non-human, all creatures being loved as part of God and God part of them. As irrefutable aspects of the Divine, inevitably each and every creature has an immortal soul.

In view of the expensive and time consuming burials, gifted to ancient Egyptian land, sea and air animals, it is indisputable that throughout the earthly lives of these sentient living souls, their day to day happiness and welfare was of paramount importance.

All animals were kept safe and secure, whilst others lived inside Egyptian homes, enjoying comforts as part of the family; the quality of their lives greatly enhanced by the ancient Egyptian ethos of respect, honor and compassion for all beings, as all of whom inescapably possess an eternal soul. Ancient Egyptian doctors were frequently also surgeons who reset broken bones, stitched up wounds and utilized a wide range of herbal medicines for their clients in return for payment.

In view of the fact that animals were well fed, clothed, bejeweled and later received mummification and funeral ceremonies I believe these physicians did not limit their skills to humans, instead they were paid by adoptive families, comparable to today's veterinary surgeons, to heal all family members including all sick and injured animals.

Graves of Mummified Peruvian Pet Dogs Possessed Blankets and Food

At the outset of this chapter we discussed several examples of modern-day and historic dogs who demonstrated wonderful characteristics and virtues, we continued with an exploration of the archaeological evidence demonstrating the mutual devotion and camaraderie between ancient humans and domesticated animals.

Let us bring this survey to a close with the following later historic example which further substantiates the fact that living with dogs as members of the family, is not a modern day phenomenon but an ancient tradition. In fact the ancients went considerably further than todays' animal crematoriums the ancients buried their dogs with familiar possessions associated with their physical earthly lives to comfort them in the afterlife regions, including food, dog treats and blankets.

Many peoples of the world held dogs in high esteem including the early Peruvians who lived and prospered from 900 AD to 1350 AD before the rise of the Inca. The Chiribaya culture treated dogs as important members of the family. The early Peruvians mummified their dogs at death, evidenced by the unearthing of a human cemetery a thousand years old, south of Lima in Peru. Here, archaeologists excavated the skeletons of both dogs and humans who not only shared their lives together but also shared their graves together. Humans were indeed buried side by side with their dogs, their lifelong loyal companions.

Extraordinarily, reflecting the mutual devotion between human and companion animal, immediately next to the dogs' skeletons, were irrefutable gifts for the dogs alone, including dog treats, food and dog blankets. Undeniably, these ancient beloved dogs were lovingly gifted with comforting blankets presumably used during their physical lives.

Inevitably, these blankets were a further last token gift to tenderly keep their devoted companions warm as their highly respected bodies were initially placed in the cold graves dug into the earth. Clearly located besides the dogs, these blankets were intended to be used again along with the dog food and treats, throughout the continued existence of the dogs' souls after physical death.

Let us now look at the compassionate, highly ethically advanced, vegetarian teachings of Confucius (551-479 BC), which impacted the ancient world many centuries before the birth of Jesus.

CHAPTER 6 – VEGETARIAN CONFUCIUS AND THE CHINESE RELATIONSHIP WITH ANIMALS

Animal Brothers
When in animals our brothers we'll see,
Much cruel injustice will cease to be;
And the days on Earth will become much lighter.
As heavenly kindness will make our world brighter.

By Edgar Kupfer-Koberwitz
Poem translated from German by Ruth Mossner.

Our exploration of the globally widespread vegetarian teachings demanding compassion and respect for animals in the world before, during and several centuries after Jesus's own all-embracing compassionate vegetarian ministry now takes us to China. We will be exploring the spiritually elevated, benevolent, empathetic, sympathetic, gentle, non-violent, vegetarian philosophy of Confucius which had a commanding influence over Chinese spirituality and beyond.

In order to understand the forces that have shaped Chinese attitudes towards animals it will help us to first briefly look at some aspects of the contemporary Chinese relationship with animals followed by a brief historical background of China, China being a special case due to the number of vegetarian religious and philosophic influences that have predominated and spread within and across its borders.

Against this historical time frame the religious and philosophical influences that have sculptured, molded and fashioned Chinese attitudes, creating their subsequent level of spirituality, integrity, ethics, morality, shaping relationships with each other and fellow animals, can be better understood.

Animals in Contemporary China

As China increasingly makes its way back into the modern world, the global internet population is daily appalled when it views videoed scenes of fully conscious Chinese dogs being notoriously and pitilessly skinned alive.

China is showing itself to be home to a nation that has long lost sight of its Confucian past as it infamously, barbarically murders humankind's best and longest friend, frequently serving these thinking feeling living souls up as dinner in restaurants with alarming regularity. Aware that this brutal and heartless practice is despised by people across the globe, the Chinese government had this ruthless and shameful practice temporarily halted when they hosted the Olympics in the early part of the 21st century.

A recent news item distributed on the internet informs us that a European woman was seated in a restaurant in China, she asked the waiter if he would kindly feed and water her beloved pet dog as the two of them had been out walking and sightseeing all day. The waiter led her trusting, playful innocent 'little child' away. He returned, serving her with a plate of animal flesh, aware that her dog was nowhere to be seen, she became alarmed.

Dumbfounded, horrified and broken hearted she realized that in the few short moments she had sat comfortably, her dog had been murdered, chopped up, boiled and now served her on a dinner plate. This was an ordeal from which this bereaved woman will never emotionally recover and indeed her dog lost his life! The waiter, possessing no empathy for animals and no knowledge of Confucian teachings had tragically misunderstood her request, which seems unbelievable by western standards.

Some Psychopaths Skin Dogs Alive

Today, some Chinese people who eat animal flesh shockingly include dog flesh on their menu. These individuals have become ignorant of and oblivious to Confucius' compassionate teachings expressed wholeheartedly through vegetarianism. Dog murderers are responsible for dogs routinely suffering excruciating pain. Unbearably their four legs are tied together resulting in agonizingly distorted bodies and dislocated limbs.

They are literally pushed, by the arms and legs of their tormentors, squashing and cramming these sentient beings together into small densely packed cages. Contorted and wracked with pain, these living, flesh and blood beings are unable to move, barely surviving or functioning, they scarcely have chance to breathe or swallow, denied the natural processes we all take for granted.

If a dog tries to communicate its tortured distress by sobbing and whimpering, internet videos show the dog being brutally dragged by head or leg out of its confinement, kicked, beaten and again pushed and squashed back into the cage, packed back in, with all the others. These cages filled with the unrecognizable, twisted and suffering bodies of acutely aware, living dogs, are often thrown several feet from truck to ground, then, kicked about, causing incredible, resounding pain throughout the misshapen, deformed bodies of unbelieving dogs confined in the cages.

Many videos and photographs of this unbelievably monstrous practice detailing animal cruelty are displayed on global animal charity websites, including PETA.com and goveg.com, however there are many others. Skinned alive and thrown into nerve twitching agonized heaps with burning nerve endings, their warped, traumatized bodies and souls plead for death to end their suffering.

Death becomes a compassionate and welcome friend who finally terminates their tragic lives of inhuman abuse and suffering, gross and despicable intimidation, oppression and persecution and one of the cruelest forms of senseless brutal murder.

Arguably, those individuals who daily, routinely, carry out these barbaric, ferocious, brutal actions must surely be psychopathic, lacking any degree of empathy, sensitivity and understanding for the suffering they cause to fellow sentient beings. Unable to experience compassion for others, their vicious, callous, barbarism leaves them drenched in the flesh and blood of their victims who suffer unspeakable torture and agony.

Psychopaths are unable to sympathize, commiserate and identify with the feelings and suffering of others, whether they are an animal, husband, wife, child, brother or sister. As noted earlier, psychopaths are often intelligent, craving familial or occupational positions of power and authority facilitating and maximizing their goal which is to manipulate others.

Notably, there are many levels of psychopathy, not all are murders. Increasingly, police training programs led by psychologists, teach that many child and adolescent psychopaths begin their bullying crimes by tormenting, harming, shooting at birds and animals, typically leading to violence and murder of family or friends later in life. Psychopaths have no genuine sense of guilt as they are emotionally "not in."

A psychopath is immune to the tragedies they perpetrate on their helpless, imprisoned, traumatized, innocent victims in evil slaughterhouse dens of hell. Certainly, their savagery does devastatingly impact their grossly unhappy lives in countless ways, due to the fact that they themselves are drenched in the destructive, negative energies of adversity that they callously dole out on animals.

Those who spend their days killing in slaughterhouses in China have lost sight of the non-violent spiritually elevated vegetarian teachings of the great Chinese sage, Confucius, who taught that a person should never treat another person or animal in a manner they would rebuff themselves. Aware of the need for an ideology to reduce rising domestic and public violence and crime in China, the Chinese government is currently promoting a state supported resurgence of the humane, non-violent, vegetarian principles of Confucianism.

If a person at any point during their life is cruel enough to hurt or kill an animal, a related, feeling, flesh and blood, sentient being, likewise, they would have no guilt about hurting or killing a human animal, global police are increasingly aware of this fact. Their only self-obsessed concerned would be their fear of getting caught and punished. Consequently, the depravity of harming or killing an animal is equally intertwined with the same degeneracy as harming a human animal.

Chinese Historical Orators Perspective of Ancient Vegetarian China

A brief historical outline of China follows, helping us to understand China's historic, multicultural and religious diversity which thrived for thousands of years before Marxism became China's official ideology. Religious, spiritual philosophy and political influences have each played a role in shaping Chinese attitudes, fashioning their relationship with the countless tragically ill-fated animals born in China today.

Notably, many innately spiritual and humanitarian Chinese, born today in the non-religious society of Marxism, find the torturous murder, torment, abuse and neglect of animals totally abhorrent and certainly beneath the dignity of any decent person.

The land known today as China has an extremely ancient history which was committed to memory by ancient orators of history which was then passed down and recited by countless successive generations of orators. The following brief historical summary is provided from the salient themes given by a Chinese historical orator. These oral traditions tell us that in the most ancient of times, China, formerly known as 'Zhong Guo,' meaning 'Centre Country,' was home to a spiritual, vegetarian race, living besides the Long River and Yellow River, close to other neighboring tribes.

These orators tell us that the first Prophet-King, known as 'the Son of God,' was a vegetarian called Fu Xi who passionately encouraged an agricultural way of life.

From the earliest times these people made copious amounts of tofu to feed the population, tofu is commonly found in most supermarkets today. Tofu is an extremely versatile, low fat, high quality, vegetable protein product. As a non-animal protein it does not contain cholesterol which is found in all animal products.

Cholesterol dangerously contributes to strokes, heart disease and heart attacks and many other chronic, life-threatening diseases. Tofu was and is today chopped into variously sized cubes or strips, steamed, deep-fried or shallow fried and flavored with a wide variety of favorite sauces including lemon, orange, peanut, korma and tomato, making the textured tofu, which tastes similar to chicken flesh, taste of anything a person wishes.

Fu Xi's successors, each known as Prophet-Kings were likewise highly respected and astonishingly, each of these vegetarian rulers was called 'the Son of God.' Each in turn, continued Fu Xi's wise, spiritual leadership and with the same incredible foresight they encouraged research into the use of herbs as medicines. Progressively, in this early era, cotton was manufactured for clothing, pottery was made and both ships and houses began to be built.

When each Prophet-King approached the time of his physical death and transition to the non-physical realms of spirit, a new spiritual, vegetarian ruler had to be chosen. The most spiritually elevated vegetarian student of each Prophet-King was successively chosen to succeed his predecessor, continuing to rule the people in accord with an on-going, spiritual, vegetarian way of life known as the Way of Tao.

The core intertwined components of the Way of Tao are embodied in the virtue of 'compassion,' inevitably expressed through vegetarianism, promoting an all-embracing, non-violence, advancing the individual's ever-deepening spirituality. Cultivating vegetarianism, an expression of sincere compassion, exemplifying spiritually advanced qualities, nurtures a person's all-embracing love for the whole spectrum of related, living beings whatever their species. This spiritual way of life had inevitable, far-reaching, positive repercussions enhancing the creativity of the people, cherishing the welfare of the human animal and non-human animal as each lived in harmony with the other features of the natural world such as plants and trees treasuring the planet herself.

Today's orators of Chinese history, sadly tell us that this wonderful spiritual and creative way of life was ultimately destroyed when the Prophet-Kings were finally replaced with the hereditary succession of greedy, materialistic, non-spiritual Emperors. These emperors established the process of hereditary succession to keep the reins of power within their family, enabling their depraved, dishonest, dissolute and immoral sons' and grandsons to rule the ever growing nation.

Previously, successors were chosen as a reward for their ethically advanced virtues expressed through their vegetarianism, creating excellent leaders who led the people and animals in a non-violent, creative, prosperous and peaceful manner. Notably, the spiritually orientated Prophet-Kings were absent during the years 520-221 BC.

Chin (Qin) was the first of the hereditary, non-vegetarian emperors. This short lived dynasty 221-206 BC resulted in a turbulent and chaotic period of bloodshed and warfare in sharp contrast to the earlier reigns of the Prophet-Kings. After Chin's death, each of the famous Chinese dynasties ensued, with it a material worldly decadence replaced the innate spirituality, formerly aspired to and demonstrated by the Chinese people.

Inevitably, alongside the cultivation of technology for human slaughter and warfare was the ever increasing ethos of murdering animals and eating their flesh. When the bloodbath, carnage and butchery of animals is sanctioned, the life of any aware, thinking, feeling, flesh and blood, sentient being is perceived as expendable and not as the precious commodity it is.

Hence historically, the murder of animals, led to the murder of the human animal, because the taking of life became permissible, consequently the murder of both became intertwined, a practice that continues in modern times. These debased years were characterized by self-indulgence, acquisitiveness and a lack of compassion and respect for all living beings. Providentially, however, two spiritually elevated prophets came to the fore during the extensive period of the typically decadent and depraved, non-vegetarian dynasties, namely Laocius (604 BC) and Confucius

(551-479 BC). Due to the spiritually advanced nature of their teachings expressed through vegetarianism they became highly honored and admired.

Both prophets taught their spiritual philosophy during the long lasting Chou/Zhou Dynasty (approximately 1045/1050-256/221 BC), in an epoch within that dynasty known as the Spring and Autumn Period (8th-5th centuries BC). Laocius the vegetarian implored the people to return to the vegetarian spirituality embodied in the Way of the Tao as practiced by the ancient Prophet-Kings and their honorable people. It is believed that Laocius moved to Bharat in India.

The long line of Chinese orators, who have preserved ancient Chinese history for us today, inform us, that the Way of the Tao had a pronounced influence on the Buddha and became enshrined in his later spiritually elevated vegetarian teachings. Confucius embraced the insightful spirituality of Laocius' teachings and made it his lifetime goal to return the people to the spiritually orientated vegetarian lifestyle of their ancient past, exemplified by the Way of the Tao and practiced as the Way of the Prophet-Kings.

Confucius had a spiritually advanced, kindhearted personality and as such was a vegetarian who had a high regard for the ancient, spiritual, all-embracing, compassionate, vegetarian lifestyle of his ancestors.

Returning to the Emperor Chin, (221-206 BC), who commissioned the building of the Great Wall of China, legend has it that it was built with nothing but sorrow, blood and tears. Although vegetarianism was not encouraged or supported by the Chin/Qin Dynasty, the prevailing long term vegetarian spirituality did not die an abrupt and total death but endured in the consciousness of many, amongst the increasingly extensive populace. The Chin Dynasty came to an abrupt end with the murder of the emperor, enabling a general named Han to usurp power.

During the Han Dynasty (206 BC-220 AD), vegetarianism was again reinstated by the government, harmonizing with the long term, relentless, all-pervasive and enduring peaceful vegetarian influence of Buddhism from India and Taoism which was circulating in China around this time. Confucian vegetarianism and ideals were disseminated by this long-lasting majestic empire. This elevated vegetarian spiritual philosophy was not isolated or limited to China, it circulated overseas and across borders to other cultures, far and wide, due to the increasing development of land and sea trade routes.

Notably, state sponsored Confucian vegetarianism was taught consistently by the Han Dynasty in an uninterrupted fashion to an ever-growing populace for a further two centuries immediately prior to Jesus' own compassionate vegetarian mission and for two centuries after his death which is a considerable time: evidence for Jesus' vegetarianism will be discussed later in this serialized volume. The Han Dynasty is unquestionably the period in Chinese history most admired by the educated and ethically orientated Chinese, as being the greatest dynasty in their history.

For this reason, many Chinese proudly call themselves the Han People. They like to be associated with the Han Dynasty with its state sponsored vegetarianism, historically reinforced by the increasingly extensive vegetarian teachings, of Taoism, Confucianism and Buddhism. Inevitably, the all-embracing respect for all life forms resulted in peace, which became the catalyst for the flourishing of learning, creativity and inventions. The Han Dynasty collapsed in 220 AD with the Mongolian tribes' invasion of northern China, which led to three hundred years of warfare.

As stated, the purpose of this brief historical survey of China has been to provide the vegetarian background to the world before, during and immediately after Jesus' own all-encompassing, benevolent, vegetarian ministry. To take this historical survey further we are no longer talking about the vegetarian background to Jesus' world, however, it is valuable to finalize this historical summary bringing it to present day, helping us to understand the enduring ancient vegetarian influences that still impact that culture today.

Returning to this concise historical time frame, in 520 AD, Boddhidharma from India, (the 28th Master after the Buddha), sought to reverse the corrupting influences of the Mongolian tribes, by raising awareness amongst the Chinese of 'the Way of the Prophet,' also known as 'the Way of the Tao,' Chan or Zen in Japanese.

The Chinese progressively returned to the spiritual ethos expressed in all-inclusive compassion and non-violence towards all living souls, human and non-human, all of whom are precious, the elevated spirituality embodied in vegetarianism. A flourishing, peaceful, creative and prosperous era again ensued. Notably, Zen monks in the Shao Lin Temple were taught martial arts by Boddhidharma purely as a means of self-defense in view of earlier invasions rather than for aggressive conquest purposes.

The emperors of the Sui Dynasty, (581-618 AD), particularly supported Confucian vegetarianism, further reinforced by the popular and widespread spiritual vegetarian teachings, central to the religions of Taoism and Buddhism. In this thriving and stable era, imperative construction work joined north and south China together. Notably, the Way of Tao (Chan/Zen) was at its height during the Sui Dynasty. Conspicuously, most of the population, including the Zen monks was vegetarian at this time.

In contrast, Buddhism in India began to decline, however at this time Buddhism was actively spread to other countries and cultures where its vegetarian compassion captured the hearts and minds of increasing numbers of converts. Following the example of Laocius, the Buddhist monks, (Boddhidharma) made it their life's goal to take the Tao, encompassing compassion and vegetarianism, to the populaces of other nations.

With the assassination of the last ruler of the Sui Dynasty, the Tang Dynasty (618-907 AD) followed. The Song Dynasty (960-1279 AD) followed, offering Neo-Confucianism state sponsored authority and promotion, causing Confucianism, to again grow in popularity, in China. Significantly, Neo-Confucianism represents the synthesis of Confucianism, Buddhism and Taoism and was disseminated, in particular, by Han Yu and Li Ao during the 8-9th century AD.

Zhu Xi also known as Chu Hsi, (1130-1200 AD), the late Song Dynasty Confucian specialist, became the most influential neo-Confucian scholar in China in his role as leader of the School of Principle. As the popularity of Buddhist vegetarian teachings intertwined with pacifism and all-inclusive non-violence declined, this period became characterized by rebellions and foreign invasions.

With yet another successful Mongolian invasion the Chinese were again suppressed with the establishment of the Mongol Yen/Yuan Dynasty (1271-1368 AD). The Mongol overlords were bitterly hated by their Chinese subjects, creating an atmosphere of hatred and violence which contributed to the spiritual decline of the Chinese nation.

Notably, the Manchurians established the Qing/Ching Dynasty (1644-1911 AD), during which Confucianism was returned as the state sponsored spiritual philosophy, although backsliding waves of animal flesh eating continued. At this time China was increasingly being influenced and targeted by several religions which possessed quite different ideologies. Taoism, Confucianism, Buddhism, Islam and Christianity each vied for converts whilst foreign powers including Europe, America, Japan and Manchuria each competed for foreign domination of China. As a result of these religious and political developments rebellious reactions and warfare became common.

The Ching Dynasty had sympathies with the 'Righteousness and Harmony Boxers,' known as Yi He Quan. The Boxers sought to rid China of western influence, they equally opposed those Chinese who had converted to Christianity. A combined force of British, American, German, French, Japanese and Russians defeated the Boxers and as a consequence severely weakened the authority of the Ching Dynasty.

By 1911 the Nationalist Party established the Republic of China, simultaneously seizing Tibetan and Mongolian lands. The Nationalist Party supported Britain during the First World War, however, they later allied with Communist Russia and communism rather than a vegetarian religious ideology began to spread rapidly throughout China. The Japanese attacked China in 1931, that same year the Chinese Communist Party established the Chinese Soviet Republic. Due to the effects of Japanese aggression together with their stealing and confiscation of Chinese land in the east, the Chinese Civil War came to an end.

The Chinese Civil War had been fought between the two opposing factions, the Chinese Communist Party and the Chinese Nationalist Party. The resultant aftermath led to the Nationalist Party ruling the urban Chinese whilst the poor Chinese, living in the countryside were governed by the Communist Party.

A second civil war between the two above competitive rival parties (1945-1949) led to the victory of the Communist Party who founded the People's Republic of China. Thwarted and exiled, the Nationalist Party gained influence in Taiwan. In 1966 the leaders of the Chinese Cultural Revolution outlawed belief in all religions.

Many believe that this earth-shattering dogmatic command has had a momentous detrimental impact on the psyche, ethics, morals and spiritual consciousness of the enormous population of China. Arguably, this earlier dictate has grossly diluted the ethics of a nation, leading to a rapid and whole-scale increase in a whole spectrum of domestic and public crime including cruel, callous and barbaric behavior towards animals.

As noted earlier, violence to animals leads to violence to humans, the two being irretrievably linked, as the life of a flesh and blood being is not considered precious. Significantly, most people in the Chinese countryside either out of poverty or their desire to cling to hitherto suppressed, vegetarian spiritual philosophies, typically continue to live a vegetarian lifestyle.

In the early 21st century AD, the post reform Chinese government together with the ever-growing Chinese population appears to have accepted features of Capitalism. Indeed, wealth can be seen to be growing, however, if the Chinese consumer seeks to eat more animal flesh and forsake their former healthier vegetarian lifestyle, starvation and increased health problems will inevitably result, placing a huge burden on the already overstretched Chinese health care service.

The burgeoning future Chinese population would face starvation if they pursued an animal flesh diet which has many failings when attempting to feed a large nation apart from the obvious cruelty inherent in breeding animals to kill them.

In contrast to the animal slaughter industry, agricultural products are cheaper to produce, feeding more people per acre of cultivation and taking up far less space than pastoral farming. Agricultural cultivation is vastly more productive, economic and space efficient than the animal genocide industry which actively promotes the animal flesh diet.

The inevitable objectives of the Chinese government in the early 21st century is to reduce crime and feed a rapidly growing population, hence the government is seen to be offering a state supported resurgence of Confucianism, promoting the honorable, non-violent, compassionate, vegetarian lifestyle.

Included in Confucianism's ennobling doctrines is the command that a person should not treat any other living creature in a manner they would reject themselves. Confucianism promotes social harmony along with a profound vision of qualities that make 'a complete person.' A person becomes a Confucian 'true person' when they at first strictly follow and subsequently internalize Confucian ethics, having freewill and choices but choosing to do the right thing in accordance with the highest moral, ethical and humane behavior.

Confucius taught that his principles were incumbent on all individuals including members of the government. Each and every person was commanded to actively demonstrate the most spiritually elevated morality, a spiritually elevated humanitarianism. Confucius taught individuals to be honorable, humane, ethical, moral and righteous in all his/her activities, including mundane and practical dealings.

Significantly, Confucianism, synonymous with the highest human virtues promoting compassionate vegetarianism is in harmony with the profound spiritual and metaphysical philosophy of the Buddha after he attained spiritual enlightenment. The central tenet of Buddhism is vegetarianism, this vital first step on the spiritual journey cumulatively and progressively teaches converts to learn and demonstrate the virtues of compassion and mercy.

Significantly today, vegetarian food, delivering high quality non-animal protein is served in Chinese restaurants across the globe. These tofu dishes are typically named Buddha Delight or Buddha Vegetables in memory of the Buddha's fundamental vegetarian spiritual teachings. Buddhism, since inception is synonymous with vegetarianism and vegetarianism is identical to Buddhism.

The vegetarian religion of Buddhism was communicated to the Chinese population by the travelers who were transported long distances backwards and forwards by merchant caravans, which conducted thriving commerce on the Silk Road. The vegetarian ideologies of Confucius who died in the 5th century BC and Buddhism which spread throughout China several centuries later, during the 2nd century BC, powerfully impacted large areas of the globe prior to Jesus' birth and will be discussed in this serialized volume.

This historical summary from the perspective of Chinese orators of history has clarified the fact that vegetarianism has, from the earliest times, been deeply-rooted in the Chinese nation's culture and thinking.

Tragically, in total opposition to their rich vegetarian heritage, modern day Chinese skin animals alive, including dogs and cats and eat them, whilst neighboring Koreans brutally carve animal skins off living animals, including cats, later boiling them alive. It is cumulatively being shown that such evil cruelty to animals violates the compassionate spiritual vegetarian philosophy of Confucianism, Hinduism, Judaism, Buddhism, Christianity, Islam, and would horrify the many centuries of Greek vegetarian spiritual philosophers, each of whom taught the elevated, compassionate, pacifist, spiritual philosophy embraced by vegetarianism.

Let us now look at a summary of the life and teachings of Confucius, helping us to appreciate the rich vegetarian spiritual heritage this enlightened sage bequeathed to the Chinese nation, which at intervals throughout their long history, have deserted and again returned to this humane, principled and noble philosophy. The following brief survey of Confucianism offers another piece of the global jigsaw further illuminating just how widespread vegetarianism was amongst global populations many centuries prior to Jesus' birth.

Confucius the Vegetarian (551-479 BC)

The following extracts from the Confucian Analects highlight the overriding themes inherent in Confucius' highly ethically elevated vegetarian teachings. "Do unto others [all creatures] as you would have them do unto you." "Do not unto others [all creatures] that you would not they should do unto you." "What one does not wish for oneself, one ought not to do to any [other creature]; what one recognizes as desirable for oneself, one ought to be willing to grant to [all creatures].

Confucius is important to our understanding of the ancient nature of Chinese vegetarianism as his life and teachings embody the highest virtues of the Han peoples outlined in the historical summary. Notably, the honorable Chinese moral vegetarian philosopher, Confucius, was born in the 6th century BC, several centuries before the birth of Jesus.

Confucius' honorable and principled code of conduct including his ethical vegetarian teachings became increasingly widespread and entrenched in the nation's consciousness during his own lifetime and his ethical vegetarian legacy has enjoyed repeated revivals for more than two thousand years after his death.

Confucius' ancient and enduring historically recurrent vegetarian philosophy is yet again experiencing a contemporary resurgence in China due to the state supported merciful revival of Confucianism in the 21st century AD. Incredibly, the vegetarian spiritual philosophy of Confucianism spread far and wide, impacting the world five hundred years before Jesus was born. This summary will help to show that Jesus' vegetarianism which will be proven later was not isolated or in a vacuum but part of a global continuum reflecting humankind's compassionate spirituality embodied in vegetarianism.

Confucius's upright, decent, proper and admirable philosophy taught others that they would find emotional and spiritual fulfillment if they lived compassionate, moral, respectable and praiseworthy lives. His teachings were personified in his own gentle, kind and benevolent lifestyle as a vegetarian.

"For more than 2,000 years the Chinese people have been guided by the ideals of Confucianism. Its founder and greatest teacher was Confucius, whose humane philosophy also influenced the civilization of all of eastern Asia. [Confucius was] China's most famous teacher, philosopher, and political theorist…" *1*

Although Confucius is thought to have been born to poor parents in 551 BC, it is believed he came from an aristocratic family lineage. He was born in Qufu in the Chinese feudal state of Lu, known today as Shandong Province. Fittingly, Confucius passed away in Lu at the age of seventy-three in the 5th century BC at this time it is believed he had more than three thousand followers.

Today, in the 21st century AD the enormous populations living in East Asia, annually celebrate Confucius' birthday on September 28.th The Taiwanese mark the event as a national holiday known as "Teacher's Day," honoring this wise sage who spent his life teaching and opening up ethical education for all.

The online Encyclopedia Britannica clarifies the resounding importance of Confucius who shaped Chinese ethics and the Chinese attitude towards fellow animals: "It has been said that to be Chinese is to be Confucian no matter what the temporary political or religious fashion may be. It is difficult to think of any other society where the influence of one person's writings and thought has been so great and dominated for so long as that of Confucius of China. Perhaps only the influence of Moses in Judaism is comparable." *2*

Kongfuzi known as Confucius

At birth Confucius was named Qiu whilst his family name was Kong. The Chinese address him as Master Kong, hence the Chinese know him as Kongzi or Kongfuzi. Notably, Confucius was not the sage's authentic name, this name together with the term Confucianism, describing his philosophy, is an 18th century AD European, construct. Significantly, over the millennia, temples and monasteries have been constructed throughout China and East Asia with the goal of commemorating and perpetuating the life and works of this eminent teacher.

"Confucius taught that right conduct was a means of acquiring ideal harmony with the Way (Tao) of Heaven and that the "holy rulers of primal times" were representative examples of such ideal conduct. In the oldest known Chinese historical work, the Shu Ching (Classic of History), such a ruler, King T'ang (11th century BC), is described as one who 'possessed the highest degree of virtue, and so it came to be that he acquired the bright authority of Heaven.'

Thus, in Confucianism, the saintliness of its holy men lay in ethical perfection, and through the practice of ethical ideals a contact with heaven (T'ien) was established. Confucius himself serves as an example of a man who was first regarded as a saint because of his deep wisdom and conscientious observance of ethical precepts and was even considered to be 'more than human.'" *3*

Since childhood Kongfuzi demonstrated that he had a superior intellect, possessing an insatiable appetite for learning, mastering many subjects including 'the six arts,' consisting of ritual, music, archery, charioteering, calligraphy and arithmetic. He was also accomplished in poetry and history. Equipped with this knowledge he created an excellent role for himself as the first teacher in China.

His goal was to democratize learning, making education available as a lifetime pursuit for all, embracing the poor as well as the rich. In the 5th can 6th centuries BC it was customary for education to be limited to the sons of wealthy families, who exclusively received instruction from paid private tutors, specializing in one or more subjects. Kongfuzi "… was the first person to devote his whole life to learning and teaching for the purpose of transforming and improving society. He believed that all human beings could benefit from self-cultivation. He inaugurated a humanities program for potential leaders, opened the doors to all, and defined learning not merely as the acquisition of knowledge but also as character building." *4*

The central, fundamental and most important tenet of Kongfuzi's teachings is his command:

"Do not unto [all creatures] that you would not they should do unto you."

His decree requires all people to treat all other beings, human and non-human, in a manner they themselves would find acceptable. Sadly, at historical intervals Confucius' doctrine has been distorted as a result of humanity's frequently predominant cruel nature. Kongfuzi preached all-embracing non-violence, treating all creatures with dignity, compassion and respect, demonstrated by his own admirable, honorable, principled, vegetarian lifestyle.

Historical accounts are emphatic that Kongfuzi always requested chopsticks at the dinner table in preference to knives, as a permanent reminder of his compassion for all beings reflected in his non-violent, vegetarian lifestyle.

Knives reminded Kongfuzi of the monstrous brutality that animals suffer in slaughterhouses at the hands of ethically inferior, dishonorable individuals. Celebrating and honoring Kongfuzi's spiritual wisdom, embracing his all-inclusive kind-hearted compassion and empathy with all beings, human and non-human, chopsticks continue to be used instead of knives to this day in China, Vietnam, Korea and Japan.

Kongfuzi required every individual to work on themselves to improve the many strands of their character. He wished individuals to internalize and demonstrate the finest ethical and moral attributes, becoming the finest examples of humanity. He was acutely aware that in order to become a fine, praiseworthy, upright, respectable, compassionate man and woman, it is essential that individuals receive a high standard of well-rounded education.

Kongfuzi believed that; "...the primary function of education was to provide the proper way of training exemplary persons (junzi), a process that involved constant self-improvement and continuous social interaction. Although he emphatically noted that learning was for...self-knowledge and self-realization...he found public service integral to true education....learned hermits...challenged the validity of his desire to serve the world; he resisted the temptation to...live apart from the human community, and opted to try to transform the world from within."
5

Kongfuzi's singular reason for entering the world of politics was to create Chinese laws which would embody and endorse his spiritually superior non-violent vegetarian philosophy. He strove to make the Chinese legal system reflect the highest righteous humanitarian virtues including compassion for all creatures, a principle he taught to all of his students. He worked tirelessly to create a world order that demonstrated and upheld the highest human merits and qualities. He was continually thwarted by the powerful Ji families and those who monopolized the king with sensual pursuits.

The writer of the Analects 3:24, informs us Kongfuzi's; "…reputation as a man of vision and mission spread. A guardian of a border post once characterized him as the "wooden tongue for a bell" of the age, sounding heaven's prophetic note to awaken the people. The Encyclopedia Britannica adds: "Indeed, Confucius was perceived as the heroic conscience who knew realistically that he might not succeed but, fired by righteous passion, continuously did the best he could." *6*

The Analects and the Classic of Documents

The term, the Analects or Lun Yu, is applied to the most important Confucian texts, translated from the Chinese these terms mean 'conversations.' All academic schools of thought have confirmed that the Analects are a reliable and authentic text, providing future generations with the original teachings and sayings of this remarkable, ancient spiritual teacher. Kongfuzi's sayings and teachings were originally faithfully committed to memory by his immediate followers.

This original oral tradition was meticulously safeguarded in the writings of the Analects for future generations. It is believed that the second generation of Kongfuzi's followers faithfully and painstakingly assembled this written text using direct, authentic oral traditions, preserving and immortalizing this sage's teachings for posterity.

Interestingly, Kongfuzi's teachings continue to be recited, passing them down through countless successive generations, perpetuated by oral and written traditions. Chu His was an early 12th century AD Neo-Confucian philosopher famed for having these writings, along with three other Confucian texts, compiled together and published, forming the 'four books' known as the Chinese classic, Ssu Shu.

It is believed that Kongfuzi himself, in the 5th century BC, assembled many more ancient documents that spanned one thousand seven hundred years until the year 630 BC. This vast collection of fifty eight chapters is known as Shu Ching, translated the term means, 'Classic of Documents' or 'Classic History.'

Incredibly, five chapters from Kongfuzi's enormous ancient volume which preserves teachings from antiquity for posterity are believed to have their origins in 2,400 and 2,300 BC. Notably, the Emperors Yao and Shun reigned within this period in history. Kongfuzi taught his followers that these emperors were spiritually exemplary vegetarian rulers who had set ethically high standards for the populace and future governments to follow.

Kongfuzi's Teachings

Despite the fact that during Kongfuzi's lifetime, China was composed of a number of warring kingdoms, he developed a system of elevated moral ethics to create and guide morally elevated societies. His inspired teachings gave people insights into nature, the world and human behavior. Notably, Kongfuzi exemplified his teachings by his own personal conduct throughout his life.

His teachings were composed of four central tenets, requiring people to demonstrate the correct conduct in all their dealings, to support culture, to be honest and loyal in all their affairs and to show respect to those in government. In return, he demanded that all government members act in a kindly, ethical and honorable manner undertaking their role as the nation's principled and upright parents ruling by good example in contrast to violence. Kongfuzi believed that:

"If the ruler is virtuous then the people will be virtuous."

Essentially, Kongfuzi taught a peaceful doctrine to rulers and their populace, instructing rulers in methods of good practice associated with their responsibilities as leaders, which in turn would earn respect and loyalty from the people. Kongfuzi did not seem to credit himself with his achievement of practically founding a new religion however he certainly did believe that life continues after physical death, though his teachings do not elaborate on the nature of the afterlife. Kongfuzi believed his mission was to restore and reaffirm the vegetarian spirituality of the extremely ancient Zhou/Chou Dynasty.

Notably, Kongfuzi taught his followers how essential it is to live by the highest moral code of conduct hence his teachings have much in common with the spirituality of many ancient and on-going, vegetarian world religions. His ethical doctrines taught the importance of loving others, honoring our parents and taking the correct, honest, righteous course of action in all our dealings in contrast to unfair dealings which disadvantage a person or animal.

People were taught to show kindness and respect to all beings, human and non-human as 'a golden rule,' doing no misdeed or neglectful omission to any living soul. Kongfuzi left the world an extremely ancient and morally rich legacy consisting of an exhaustive list of incredibly wise and honorable quotations and theories about good practice in life, law and government. Importantly, Kongfuzi taught that if a person harmed an animal then he/she is cruel and despicable and he/she has debased, dishonored and disrespected his/herself resulting in spiritually irrevocable consequences.

Central to Kongfuzi's spiritual philosophy was his teaching of the fundamental importance of 'Jen;' translated, this term signifies all-embracing compassion to all creatures, kindness, altruism and benevolence. Kongfuzi's teachings inspired people to cultivate and demonstrate the finest qualities and characteristics of human nature.

The term Jen has much in common with Christian teachings about the necessity to be charitable, loving, kind, compassionate, benevolent, just, respectful and generous in all a person's dealings with all life forms. When Jen is exhibited in human relationships it is translated as 'Te' which means 'virtue.'

In ancient Confucianism yi and li are terms that are closely associated with one another, translated Yi means righteousness. A person is emphatically encouraged to demonstrate the most superior ethical behavior in any given situation with all living creatures, including all life forms. This term represents the opposite of doing something for self-interested or unjust reasons. People are encouraged to work for the greater good for all by demonstrating Yi; Yi is based upon reciprocity, carrying out right action for the right reasons.

Significantly, Kongfuzi taught his ever growing number of converts to make their own moral decisions relating to all creatures based upon the demonstration of compassion, empathy, understanding and superior spiritual ethics. In view of this, all Confucians were and are vegetarian, following the principled compassionate example of their master.

Kongfuzi demonstrated great insight into human nature, he was aware that at a future date after his own death, humanity would inevitably distort his commands, molding them to permit all manner of wrongs, such as allowing them to pursue selfish preferences including the preference to eat animal flesh. Notably, the Buddha foretold of the day when his future followers would wrongly eat animal flesh and wrongly still call themselves his followers!

Consequently, Kongfuzi demanded compassion, empathy, ethical, righteous and honorable behavior to be used as an internalized moral yardstick in all dealings with human and non-human animals. He considered this internal spiritual barometer superior to teaching people to mindlessly follow rules that over time would be diluted and polluted with the rules of others, all of which would inevitably lead to all manner of ethical blunders. Kongfuzi preferred each person to rely on his/her own schooled and internalized spiritual code based on Kongfuzi's teachings; no-one could therefore harm an animal or person, eat animal flesh or act in a disreputable manner and still call themselves a Confucian!

Kongfuzi knew that mistakes regarding ethical codes of conduct would certainly occur if the rules of future rulers were not as profoundly righteous and ethical as those taught by and ingrained in the character of Kongfuzi. Errors in just, honest and righteous conduct would also occur if future rulers did not ensure that the population received adequate, well-rounded educational and spiritual instruction. Wisely, he knew that people throughout history and the globe need to awaken, nourish and nurture, a mature, deeply cultivated, internalized, ethically advanced, moral code of conduct.

Kongfuzi used the term 'ren' meaning to carry out 'right action.' He expected righteous deeds to ultimately become spontaneous, having freewill to choose but always choosing right action, demonstrating that spiritually ethical conduct had indeed become internalized and integrated into 'the self' rather than merely a set of rules to follow. For an individual to nurture his/her 'ren,' each person was told to judge it in accordance with whether they would like to be the recipients of that action or not - would they like that deed or omission done to them or not? The Confucian Analects tell us:

"What one does not wish for oneself, one ought not to do to anyone else; [Confucian vegetarian principles referred to all creatures] what one recognizes as desirable for oneself, one ought to be willing to grant to [all creatures].

Notably, 'right action' had to be demonstrated to all life forms and in all situations, if not, the perpetrator was classed as someone who had degraded him/herself, as an immoral debased degenerate. Kongfuzi taught that virtue is demonstrated when a person uses intuitive compassionate empathy in order to become sensitively aware of the plight, needs and interests of others, they were also discouraged from preoccupation with self-interests.

A familiar, spiritually advanced theme runs throughout the entirety of Kongfuzi's teachings; encouraging all who come after him, to tirelessly and relentlessly work towards internalizing perfect virtue in all their thoughts, words and actions towards all creatures. The following sample of Kongfuzi's teachings help each of us to understand the spirituality, profundity and innate wisdom of this divinely inspired vegetarian sage's teachings:

"Do unto others as you would have them do unto you. ~ Men's natures are alike; it is their habits that separate them. ~ To see what is right and not to do it, is want of courage. ~ Have no friends, not equal to yourself. ~ It is only the wisest and the very stupidest who cannot change.

~ When you know a thing, to hold that you know it and when you do not know a thing, to allow that you do not know it: this is knowledge. ~ The superior man is distressed by his want of ability. ~ What one does not wish for oneself, one ought not to do to anyone else; what one recognizes as desirable for oneself, one ought to be willing to grant to others.

~ If you govern people legalistically and control them by punishment, they will avoid crime, but have no personal sense of shame. If you govern them by means of virtue and control them with propriety, they will gain their own sense of shame, and thus correct themselves. ~ If you govern with the power of your virtue, you will be like the Northern Star. It just stays in its place while all the other stars position themselves around it."

Kongfuzi emphasized that every person should be encouraged and assisted in the attainment of the highest levels of education, continuing to study; gaining knowledge throughout their lives. He believed this type of society would empower all people to aspire to the highest good and enable them to think profoundly on all topics.

Notably, he wanted people to live in peace and prosperity and for individual's to rise to positions of authority based on their virtuous character and abilities rather than as the result of their formidable, influential, wealthy family background. He saw the abject danger and utter folly inherent in the policy of giving authoritative and well-paid leadership positions to individuals, rewarding them because they had been born into powerful wealthy families.

Confucianism ~ A Way of Life or Religion

As has become clear, Confucianism is the product of the ancient compassionate vegetarian teachings collected and promoted by Kongfuzi, which in turn after his death, were gathered together by Kongfuzi's earliest followers. These were set out in writings known as the Analects, Mencius, Xunzi and lesser known Confucian classics, compiled between his death in 479 BC and 221 BC when the first Chinese empire was established. Neo-Confucianism was formulated by Zhu Xi (1130-1200 AD) and dominated thinking and daily life in China and Vietnam until the 1800's.

For over two thousand years, including the present-day, many people follow Confucian doctrines, considering Confucianism to be an ethically advanced vegetarian religion founded in exceedingly ancient times. Incredibly, for over twenty centuries this spiritually elevated code of conduct has been repeatedly held in high esteem and even today, converts visit the numerous temples built to honor and perpetuate the spiritually lofty vegetarian teachings of this wise and deeply spiritual, vegetarian sage.

Commencing during Kongfuzi's lifetime and continuing for some considerable time after his death, his noble vegetarian teachings became the official state ideology, practiced by members of government. Confucian doctrines were considered of such importance, government ministers demanded all civil servants pass examinations based on Kongfuzi's teachings before gaining employment.

Importantly, through extensive study of his writings, civil servants had to show themselves to have cultivated and internalized the highest of virtues. Notably, to pass these examinations civil servants also had to demonstrate the most elevated moral caliber in all of their actions, making China a unique and extraordinary place to live. What a world the Chinese would have lived in, perhaps beyond our present day comprehension!

Kongfuzi, a practical man, sought to teach people how to become true gentle-men and gentle-women, exhibiting proper conduct in all their dealings. Proper conduct meant they followed Kongfuzi's ethical directions, which taught people to conduct themselves humanely, fairly, righteously, compassionately and respectfully with all living beings.

Notably, kind, honorable, honest people were deemed to be 'true men and women,' or 'true gentle-men and gentle-women.' All true gentlemen and women demonstrated the highest qualities including compassion to all beings, human and non-human, altruism, goodness, gentility, righteousness, integrity and loyalty.

He was aware that this was the most elevated way of living in this earthly world for a range of profoundly thought out reasons. In many ways, he had created a new and enduring ethical vegetarian religion. To show his respect and admiration for any poor follower who demonstrated ethically elevated actions towards a person or animal, Kongfuzi deliberately addressed his follower with the term 'Chun tze,' meaning 'the son of a ruler or aristocrat.'

Obviously this term honors the follower, no matter how lowly their background, demonstrating Kongfuzi's approval and high regard for their righteous actions. Kongfuzi's statement recorded in the Analects 13:23-24 illustrates his teachings very clearly. When asked by Tzu-Kung: "What would you feel about a man who was loved by all his fellow-villagers?

The Master said: "That is not good enough…Best of all would be that the good people in his village loved him and the bad hated him."

Kongfuzi taught his followers, the importance of demonstrating kindness, love and respect for all creatures, promoting happiness amongst all beings, human and non-human, thereby living in harmony and balance. Those who violated these virtuous directives were considered to have dishonored, disgraced and defiled themselves. The Encyclopedia Britannica clarifies how pervasive Confucian values are: "Confucianism serves as a way of life, a source of values, as well as a social code for its followers." 7

The Vegetarianism of Confucianism, Taoism and Buddhism Shaped Jesus' World

The excellent literary work known as Tao-te Ching meaning 'Classic of the Way of Power' is not included in the Confucian classics due to the belief that Lao-tzu, the founder of the Taoist religion, was the author. Interestingly, scholars have noted many parallel teachings in Confucianism with the Taoist writings found in the Classic of the Way of Power. Notably, Lao-tzu, the famous, spiritual vegetarian teacher was an older contemporary of Confucius.

These writings offer highly elevated spiritual philosophy and are revered as one of the most holy scriptures of the Taoist religion. Indeed, there is a spiritual kinship between the advanced ethical philosophies of these two great vegetarian spiritual teachers.

Both Confucius and Taoist monks endorsed and fostered compassion, morals and humane behavior towards all creatures amongst their converts. However, in addition, Taoist followers were taught to also strive to attain a non-emotional union with the Divine. Historically, the ethical vegetarian teachings of Confucianism, Taoism and Buddhism have had an enormous impact molding the Chinese culture and civilization shaping a predominantly vegetarian world before the birth of Jesus.

Confucianism Shaped Vegetarianism in China, Korea, Japan, Taiwan and Vietnam

At the age of twenty two Kongfuzi founded his own school of vegetarian spiritual philosophy and taught his students about the world and nature including his exemplary vegetarian spiritual philosophy which was spread by thousands of his disciples throughout China, Korea, Japan, Taiwan, Vietnam and beyond.

Notably, Confucian vegetarian, ethical and social values have been inherent in Chinese society for more than two thousand five hundred years and have, since ancient times, been passed down through the generations. It is important to point out that the spiritually elevated Confucian teachings, demonstrating morality and compassion to all creatures, embodied by vegetarianism, were an integral part of a far more ancient Chinese society than that of Kongfuzi.

Since Kongfuzi's restoration and revitalization of these incredibly ancient compassionate vegetarian beliefs during his own lifetime in the 5th century BC, ethical vegetarian conduct distinctly and repeatedly guided countless generations of Chinese people. The practice of vegetarianism promoting peace and creativity in society had been integral to the earliest spiritual philosophy in this region, surviving for countless centuries.

In the 5th century BC, Kongfuzi reinstated and reaffirmed the most ancient and long forgotten vegetarian spiritual teachings of these lands. To his credit, Kongfuzi made an enormous impact on the spiritual vegetarianism of the people born in the lands known today as China, Korea, Japan, Taiwan and Vietnam.

State Supported Confucian Vegetarian Revival

Having discussed the ancient Chinese vegetarian traditions including those of Confucius which impacted enormous areas of the vegetarian world in which Jesus lived, it is informative to conclude this historical survey with a comment on the contemporary Confucian vegetarian resurgence in China, where it is experiencing a state supported 21st century AD revival.

In 2007 the Chinese Beijing government officially announced their support for Confucius by broadcasting Confucius' birthday celebrations on Chinese television. Importantly, the flickering lights of a Confucian, peace generating, spiritual, vegetarian, resurgence is being witnessed in parts of China today.

Conspicuously, Chinese book shops are again displaying large stocks of Confucian texts, including the Analects, Mencius, Xunzi and lesser known Confucian classics. No longer is Confucianism criticized for encompassing aspects of feudal ideology. The Chinese government is recognizing the fact that compassionate, pacifist, vegetarian teachings, heralded by Kongfuzi, have a core cultural value, cultivating the highest virtues in the individual, in turn promoting a creative and harmonious society.

Although this revival has been initiated by the government it is giving a stronger sense of cultural identity to the Chinese people. Confucianism is replacing aspects of Marxist ideology and during these days of an ideology vacuum, these honorable vegetarian teachings support peaceful social stability, together with the promotion of non-violence, honest, ethical, moral, fair, compassionate and principled behavior towards all creatures.

Notably, Confucianism is acceptable to the Chinese government as it is perceived to uphold a principled society without providing the Chinese people with religious beliefs in a God and the continuation of life after death. Governments sometimes oppose religious beliefs as typically spiritual philosophies empower people, encouraging independent thought, providing them with tremendous spiritual strength and amazing courage, in the face of adversity, when questioning the present social order.

Today, Confucian state approved schools, offering similar syllabi have opened in China. Two examples are the Sihai Confucius School and the Xiangtang Confucius School both of which are located near to Beijing. Children start these private boarding schools at the age of three. Initially they are taught to recite the Confucian classics, after which they learn the English language, the philosophy of Plato and many of Shakespeare's literary works.

Wisely, demonstrating great foresight, the Chinese government encourages the students in the proliferating Confucian schools to be daily given an organic vegetarian diet. As noted earlier, a vegetarian diet rather than a flesh eating diet is better equipped to prevent starvation, feeding both China's and the world's rapidly increasing population. Astutely, the government rules that the children carry out organic arable farming activities in the afternoon, in order to learn about environmental conservation.

Obviously Confucianism is being revitalized and reinterpreted to accommodate the mental, physical, emotional and spiritual needs of the modern era in post-reform China. Confucianism is being used to fulfill the innate human spiritual hunger for spirituality and need for moral instruction. There is an obvious religious vacuum in China which was historically a multi-religious country, home to Confucianism, Taoism, Buddhism, Christianity and Islam.

Kongfuzi's teachings helped to mold an ancient and on-going ethical vegetarian Chinese society, guiding decisions on practical day to day matters. However, the depth of his all-embracing compassion for all creatures illustrates his elevated spirituality, clearly indicating that he was a spiritually inspired teacher. Emperors of the Han Dynasty, ranging from 206 BC to 220 AD, revered Confucius erecting and dedicating temples in his honor.

Today there is a re-emergence and ongoing celebration of his life and teachings. Emperors, including Emperor Wu, established Kongfuzi's humane philosophy as the state sanctioned ideology of China. Praised as 'the perfect sage,' Kongfuzi was also known as a 'duke' and a 'king.' Significantly, in 1906, Kongfuzi was hailed as 'equal to the Lord of Heaven.' As noted, historically, Confucianism spread to Korea, Japan, Taiwan and Vietnam and has again become a central feature in contemporary Chinese culture. The Encyclopedia Britannica adds:

"Confucius's life, in contrast to his tremendous importance, seems starkly undramatic, or as a Chinese expression has it, it seems, 'plain and real.' The plainness and reality of Confucius' life, however, underlines that his humanity was....an expression of self-cultivation...[Reflecting his faith]...in the possibility of ordinary beings [becoming] awe-inspiring sages and worthies is deeply rooted in the Confucian heritage, and the insistence that human beings are teachable, improvable and perfectable through personal and communal endeavor is typically Confucian." *8*

China is presently unearthing its spiritual roots and in turn seeking to advance both the individual and society. Hopefully, the state sponsorship of Confucian vegetarian ethics will nurture honorable, compassionate Chinese citizens who will again follow in the footsteps of their ancestors and treat all animals, human and non-human with dignity, kindness, mercy and respect.

At this juncture a person should be reminded of the profound insights of the Italian genius, Leonardo da Vinci (1452-1519 AD) who warns us:

"The day will come when a civilization will be judged by the way it treats its animals."

222

Da Vinci proved his genius in countless disciplines including sculpting, painting, science, architecture, engineering inventions and mathematics. Notably, da Vinci possessed the profound spiritual insight that truly civilized people will become aware that the prohibition of all murder to human and non-human animals will literally result in world peace.

Prohibiting the suffering and murder of all animals, human and non-human, sets humanity on the spiritual path, igniting and nurturing our ability to feel compassion for all interrelated and interdependent life forms, thereby activating pacifism expressed through vegetarianism.

Let us now look at the philosophical lineages of ancient Greek vegetarian spiritual philosophers, whose teachings impacted the ancient world many centuries before the birth of Jesus and for several centuries after his death. Generation after generation of vegetarian spiritual philosophers promoted vegetarianism and the highest qualities of humankind, teachings which spread far and wide until they were suppressed by the powerful orthodox religious leaders of Judaism, Christianity and Islam.

CHAPTER 7 – THE ANCIENT GREEK SPIRITUAL PHILOSOPHERS WERE VEGETARIAN

If men with fleshly mortals must be fed,
And chew with bleeding teeth the breathing bread;
What else is this but to devour our guests?
And barbarously renew Cyclopean feasts?
While Earth not only can your needs supply,
But, lavish of her store, provides for luxury;
A guiltless feast administer with ease,
And without blood is prodigal to please.

Pythagoras, (6th-5th century BC)

Let us now look at the Greek spiritual philosophers' gargantuan vegetarian impact on the world many centuries before and after the life of Jesus. This discussion will again show that Jesus' and his first converts' vegetarianism which will be proven later was by no means unique or isolated but was in harmony with other ethically elevated vegetarian spiritual philosophies. This serialized volume is progressively proving that the Chinese and now the Greeks living in Jesus' ancient world were not alone in their vegetarianism.

Notably, ancient Greece is heralded as one of the greatest civilizations that ever existed. Resulting from the teachings of its philosophers, this remarkable culture taught the importance of the individual. It highlighted the tremendous value of the attainment of physical excellence and high levels of well-rounded education, so individuals could reach their highest potential. Philosophy was invented by the ancient Greeks, for them philosophy is truly religion, enquiring into and expressing the meaning and mysteries of life. Undeniably, many of these spiritual philosophers were also brilliant scientists and polymaths.

The ancient Greek philosophers saw themselves as 'seekers and lovers of wisdom,' examining, experiencing and understanding the world around them, utilizing a wide range of skills including logic, reason and mystical and ecstatic union with God through meditation and contemplation.

The distinguished ancient Greek spiritual philosophers had a colossal vegetarian influence in the ancient world that encompassed mainland Greece and its islands shaping vegetarian thought far beyond Greek borders. Ranging from approximately the 6th century BC, continuing for many centuries, ancient Greece produced countless generations of vegetarian polymaths inspired by the vegetarian philosophical convictions of many such as Pythagoras, Empedocles, Socrates, Plato and Plutarch. These famous spiritual philosophers acted as inspired ethically elevated role models for countless generations of vegetarian students.

Truth seekers of all ages and backgrounds came from far and wide to study with such spiritual sages typically attending the centers of learning and excellence they founded. The scientific, philosophical, metaphysical and spiritual discussions that took place amongst students and teachers in turn molded the well-established, renowned vegetarian core of Greek philosophical society. Due to the perpetuation of successive vegetarian philosophical masters' spiritual philosophy long after their deaths, which demanded vegetarianism, for many the non-flesh eating lifestyle became the accepted norm.

The ancient Greek philosophical geniuses who lived from approximately the 6th century BC possessed remarkable multi-disciplinary intellects. These intellectuals founded many academic subjects, all of whom were profound thinkers and leading innovators. Revealing the exceptionally high caliber of these eminent ancient scholars, these remarkable geniuses are revered by academics today for their incredible intellectual and spiritual insights, original ideas and wealth of knowledge.

The outstanding caliber and enduring legacy of the ancient Greek vegetarian philosophers, to be discussed in this chapter, is ironically largely forgotten by the global populace today. Yet the advanced spiritual vegetarian philosophy to which they were passionately committed, produced by these great intellects who also excelled in a variety of academic disciplines, is certainly worthy of great respect and consideration today.

Their deductions led them to the conviction that the soul transmigrates at death into new bodies, incarnating as animals and as humans. It is the goal of this chapter to briefly introduce these individuals and summarize their vegetarianism which was a product of their sophisticated and high-minded spiritual philosophy which will be followed in chapter 7 with a brief survey into their belief in the transmigration of the soul (reincarnation).

Many of these exceptional geniuses wrote volumes regarding their brilliant deductions on all manner of subjects. Possessing remarkable intellects they have contributed a vast amount of knowledge to the human civilization, yet they are typically overlooked today by the vast majority of people. Giving the reader the flavor of the excellence that gushed out of ancient Greece for many centuries, the following examples illustrate some of the subjects the ancient Greek masters founded, excelled in and reformatted: mathematics, ethics, medicine, surgery, biology, logic, observational science, astronomy, metaphysics, philosophy and religion.

These leading innovators made pivotal discoveries and major advances in a vast array of subjects including the science of geometry and mathematics providing the foundational laws which we continue to use today. Their genius included their remarkably accurate models of the earth and universe. The research results of these modernizing visionaries revealed to the ancient Greeks that the world was curved, not flat, far in advance of other civilizations.

Incredibly, as early as the 6th century BC Pythagoras taught that the earth was spherical in shape. Extraordinarily, Democritus, the originator of the world's first atomic theory also deduced that the lights within the Milky Way were stars comparable to our own sun. Democritus reasoned that the moon was a planetary body characterized by deserts and mountain ranges analogous to the earth.

It should be emphasized that these stupendous ancient geniuses had no scientific technology, observatories or telescopes to support their remarkably accurate astronomical theories, mathematical calculations and natural science making their outstanding achievements all the more incredible. Astonishingly, the ancient Greek known as Eratosthenes, calculated the size of the earth with remarkable accuracy by utilizing mathematics and measuring the angles of the sun's rays in two Egyptian cities, Aswan (Syene) and Alexandria at the time of the summer solstice.

Introducing Pythagoras of Samos (6th-5th century BC)

Pythagoras was an ancient Greek vegetarian philosopher and mathematician who founded European science and philosophy. Indeed, he was one of the most legendary and illustrious philosophers of the ancient world. The wisdom and spirituality of Pythagoras's philosophical teachings was highly regarded and perpetuated by a long line of later celebrated philosophers including Socrates, Plato, Plutarch and Porphyry.

This scientist and a pre-Socratic spiritual vegetarian philosopher is perhaps most known today for his discovery of the foundationally important Pythagorean Theorem which is still used in much of geometry to find the lengths of the sides of triangles.

Pythagoras deduced that everything can be reduced to the harmony of mathematics hence the world for him was based on mathematics. Notably, this far-sighted and novel concept is accepted and utilized by the contemporary leading global mathematical and medical researchers who use mathematics to simulate the human body resulting in the most accurate medical research and dependable medical cures. This is in sharp contrast to the typically grossly flawed results obtained from experimentation on animals which is unethical and needless.

Pythagoras's goal was to harmonize religious belief with reason, being both a mystic and a rationalist. He accepted that the cosmos consists of spheres and that the infinite was of the utmost importance and that air/ether underlies everything. As an ascetic, believing in simple vegetarian living, Pythagoras upheld ethics and the belief in reincarnation (metempsychosis, the transmigration of the soul).

Vegetarianism for Pythagoras, in harmony with other eminent vegetarian spiritual teachers of humankind, meant the attainment of inner peace, spiritual enlightenment and compassion. His dramatic impact on the widespread nature of vegetarianism in the ancient world was outstanding.

His vegetarianism was associated with his conviction that humanity should aspire to becoming and expressing the highest ethical convictions towards each other and fellow animals. His beliefs in reincarnation which he may have learned from the ancient Indian Brahmins will be discussed in the following chapter.

Background to Pythagoras

Born in Samos, Greece in 580 BC, Pythagoras demonstrated a remarkably deep, innate wisdom, an insatiable appetite for learning and a profound depth of compassion for all animals. He was acutely aware that the violent and insensitive way humanity treat animals has a direct bearing on the violence and insensitivity with which they treat each other. Most of Pythagoras' writings were destroyed in a fire however many generations of his fervent disciples, becoming renowned in their own right, kept Pythagoreanism, synonymous with vegetarianism alive.

Plato, who was acquainted with the works of many philosophers, considered Pythagoras' teachings of such tremendous importance he sold all of his possessions, to buy a single remaining piece of Pythagoras's outstanding writings which had not been destroyed by fire. We know of Pythagoras' teachings primarily from the writings of Philolaus (470 BC - 385 BC), Plato

(427-347 BC), Iamblichus (250 AD - 330 AD), the Roman poet Ovid (43 BC - 17/18 AD) and Plutarch (46 AD - 120 AD).

Pythagoras Student of Pherekydes, Anaximander and Thales of Miletus

Pythagoras spent his youth as a disciple of eminently wise ancient Greek spiritual philosophers who like him were also polymaths accomplished in many subjects. These mentors included Pherekydes, Anaximander and Thales. Pherekydes appears to be the earliest Greek to teach the concept of the transmigration of the soul at death and vegetarianism. These intertwined spiritual beliefs which promoted the highest compassionate virtues among humanity will be discussed in chapter six.

The following brief account of the earliest ancient Greek intellectual deductions of Thales of Miletus and Anaximander, promoted together with their vegetarian religious philosophy provides us with an insight into the depths and profundity of the astonishing intellectual and philosophical accomplishment that burst forth from ancient Greece commencing six centuries before the birth of Jesus.

Aristotle who lived many centuries later, hailed the first philosopher to be Thales who believed all things are engendered by water. Many scholars today agree that he was the first man of science because he offered a naturalistic description and clarification of the cosmos supporting it with reasons. Thales gave rise to the Milesian school of philosophy.

His ideas were furthered by Anaximander who posited that underlying existence was something 'unlimited' and 'indefinite,' denoting a fluidity such as air, meaning 'transparent mist' or 'ether.' He suggested ether as he sought out a natural substance that would remain unchanged despite appearing in different forms in the natural world, this was indeed the beginnings of present day atomic theory.

Although we know very little about Thales himself, we do know that as a result of his astronomical and geometric research he predicted the eclipse of 28 May 585 BC and was able to measure the pyramids. It is believed that he contributed to European culture through his research which sought to offer rational explanations for physical phenomena. Notably underlying the phenomena was not a list of gods but one single first principle.

Thales thought this first principle was water, interestingly, in many ways he was on the right path of enquiry, as we now know all life forms did have their mysterious origins in the oceans of the world whilst many people believe the first cause to be a creative parental God. Notably his preoccupation with deeper causes gave birth to both philosophy and science. Pythagoras, similar to Thales, Anaximander, Heraclitus, Parmenides and Democritus likewise searched for the answer to the enigmatic questions of the first cause for the diversity of nature and existence and what underlies all phenomena.

Pythagoras and the Cross-Cultural Exchange of Beliefs

Whilst in his early thirties, Pythagoras was honored with the opportunity to be mentored by the ancient Egyptian priesthood. This privilege was enhanced by his knowledge of the Egyptian language. Remarkably, he spent twenty two years being tutored by the wise ancient Egyptian spiritual vegetarian teachers who finally honored him by initiating him into the Egyptian Mysteries. Later, Pythagoras was captured and taken prisoner to Babylon in 525 BC.

Characteristically, he used this eventuality as an opportunity to continue his lifelong quest searching for answers through education. Noted for his remarkable intellect, he was soon studying with the Babylonian Magi, remaining in Babylon for twelve years. It is believed that Pythagoras also travelled to Persia to study with the Zoroastrian magi where he learned about the Zoroastrian good god Ahura Mazda and his evil adversary, the god named, Angra Mainyu.

However, some scholars believe he met the Zoroastrian magi in Babylon where they mentored him and a long-standing cross-cultural exchange took place. The philosophy detailing a good god with an evil, devilish adversary became a founding principle, fundamental to the teachings of Christianity, instituted more than five centuries later.

This fact reveals that once spiritual philosophical concepts are born they remain established in the human consciousness, ultimately spreading across borders, becoming absorbed and amalgamated into the beliefs of different cultures. Cumulatively it is being shown how pervasive the vegetarian lifestyle was in the ancient world and how it spread throughout cultures impacting many peoples throughout the globe.

Regarding the concept of good fighting evil found in the ancient religion of Zoroastrianism and later absorbed into the teachings of Christianity, although this concept is not typically found in the biblical Old Testament, with the exception of the story of Job, it is indeed found in the much later biblical New Testament. Notably, scholars agree that the story of Job was absorbed into Christianity from ancient foreign myths that were not original to Judaism. This again substantiates the fact of the cross-cultural exchange of vegetarian and other religious beliefs and practices among different cultures in the ancient world.

Undoubtedly, Jesus would have come into contact with the vegetarian teachings of others in the ancient world. These discussions of the widespread global impact of ancient, eminent, vegetarian spiritual teachers from different cultures is providing an essential background, enhancing understanding of later pages which prove Jesus' vegetarianism.

It will be shown later in this serialized research how Jesus' and his first followers' vegetarianism and the vegetarianism of several centuries of their descendants, had much in common with the spiritually advanced, compassionate, vegetarian teachings of others which were inescapable, persistent, pervasive and enduring.

Pythagoras's Vegetarian Lifestyle

Liberated from Babylon, where he had studied with the Babylonian magi, Pythagoras continued to travel seeking truth through knowledge, exchanging spiritual philosophy with some of the greatest minds of his day. At the age of fifty six, he returned to Samos. Pythagoras was a highly educated genius; this student now became the teacher of an advanced spirituality through his philosophy and as such was a passionately committed vegetarian.

Over the course of his lifetime he became accomplished in mathematics, philosophy, astronomy, geometry, herbal medicine, music, spiritual philosophy and esoteric knowledge. Replete with knowledge, Pythagoras founded his enormously successful institute of learning at Crotona, in which spiritual philosophy, vegetarianism and the doctrine of the transmigration of the soul were emphatically taught. The institute, sponsored by senators of Crotona, resembled a small city and included his school of philosophy, school of moral training and a school of science.

Due to his profound and ethically advanced vegetarian spiritual beliefs Pythagoras taught that a singular God was the light of heaven, Father of all creation, an animating intelligence and the all-encompassing soul of the universe. He had an immense compassion for all animals who he quite naturally viewed as family and friends due to his conviction in the transmigration of the soul, namely reincarnation. Pythagoras the vegetarian would have certainly continued his vegetarianism during the twenty two years in which he lived and studied with the elite ancient Egyptian vegetarian priesthood.

Notably, his vegetarian convictions were so strong he also abstained from eating beans and from wearing wool again typically in harmony with the ancient Egyptian vegetarian teachings. Crucially, although the Hebrews had been released from Babylonian captivity by the time Pythagoras was taken to Babylon, the Jews still had a presence in Babylon and many Jewish teachers could still be found there. Inevitably, a philosophic vegetarian cultural exchange took place not only between Pythagoras and the Babylonian magi but also between Pythagoras and the remaining Jewish exiles who had established their homes and livelihood there.

Although most Jews returned home when liberated from Babylonian captivity, all nationalities remaining in Babylon would have been aware of Jewish spiritual beliefs, in effect they

232

left behind their own legacy of cultural influence and exchange. Importantly, families would travel backwards and forwards to visit each other whilst other Jews left Babylon at a later date. Upheaval, travel and living amongst other cultures acted as a catalyst for the transmission and exchange of pervasive Greek, Jewish and Babylonian philosophy and vegetarian spiritual vegetarian.

In Babylon, Pythagoras would certainly have learned of the highly revered 7th and 8th century BC Jewish prophets including Jeremiah, Ezekiel, Isaiah, Amos, Hosea and Micah. He would have known that in recent centuries they had dynamically condemned animal sacrifice, a practice which was characteristically associated with eating animal flesh. Believing they were God's mouth pieces they had vigorously informed the Jewish populace that God hated and loathed their sickeningly misguided cruelty and murder of vulnerable, defenseless, innocent and terrified animals.

These trusting childlike animals were typically eaten afterwards hence the Jewish prophets' condemnation of animal sacrifice was closely intertwined with compassionate vegetarianism. Animal sacrifice had become a relentless, horrific and pervasive Jewish custom. The errant Jewish populace were cajoled and manipulated by the authorities into believing the murder of animals would absolve their sins.

Typically, those in authority sold each of the populace an animal, they killed it on their behalf and the authorities ate the animal afterwards. This deeply flawed murderous practice, forsaking the prohibition of murder found in the Ten Commandments, was obviously a very lucrative business that perpetuated cruelty and slaughter.

Vegetarian Pythagoras Known as the 'Man' ~ Jesus Known as the 'Son of Man'

As a life-long, entrenched spiritual vegetarian student turned teacher, it was Pythagoras who actually invented the term 'philosopher' to represent a person who has the ardent desire to relentlessly seek truth in order to acquire wisdom. Pythagoras used this term to describe himself in preference to the term 'sage,' which he believed suggested he had finished learning. Pythagoras was indeed an exceptionally intelligent, talented polymath who demonstrated the highest expertise in a wide range of subjects. Pythagoras' students and followers cumulatively took his teachings far and wide.

Notably, Pythagoras shared the Jewish prophets' condemnation of animal sacrifice, intertwined with eating animal flesh. He also prohibited the eating of animals, the wearing of wool, drinking wine, adultery, slavery, revenge, the use of public baths, the egocentric desire to acquire earthly power and wealth for its own sake and the use of oaths to prove that a person is speaking the truth.

Significantly, Pythagoras and his followers wore their hair long and wore simple white clothing, advocating simple, communal living. His missionary disciples who travelled extensively to share Pythagorean teachings with others also typically generously shared their simple resources with each other. Pythagoras and his disciples also propagated the concept of the transmigration of the soul between human and non-human animals wherein the soul would be afforded opportunities for spiritual advancement.

Importantly, through the belief in the transmigration of the soul, reincarnating as human and animal, Pythagoreans were convinced that all beings human and non-human were interrelated, belonging to one single earth family.

It will be shown later that Jesus and his first followers, known and honored by the term the 'the poor,' likewise shared their simple resources, often lived in ascetic communes, wore their hair long, wore white linen clothes and ate a vegetarian diet and therefore had astonishingly much in common with Pythagorean spiritual principles and teachings, as set out above. Again, specifically, following Pythagorean doctrines, Jesus was emphatic that people should not use oaths. Instead he believed individuals should be believed for their truthfulness and integrity, making the use of swearing oaths of truthfulness, superfluous.

Importantly, Jesus and his disciples taught core Pythagorean concepts. As will be clarified later, many of the above spiritual beliefs and practices were carried out by Jesus and his first loyal converts who were faithful to Jesus' original, undistorted teachings.

Significantly, much of Pythagoras' vegetarian spiritual philosophy can be found at the heart of the remarkably similar vegetarian teachings of the Egyptian Therapeute and the vegetarian sects amongst the Palestinian Jewish Essenes, Essenes being an umbrella term. Notably, Jesus and his family belonged to the latter, which will be elaborated upon later.

Iamblichus (250-330 AD) wrote a detailed biography of Pythagoras' life, informing us that this spiritual genius was so revered he was never addressed by his name. Instead he was called 'The Divine' and after Pythagoras' death, he was popularly called, 'Man' and 'The Man.' Significantly, as we shall see later, when clarifying Jesus' distorted and suppressed teachings regarding Jesus' vegetarianism, Jesus described himself throughout his own ministry as 'the Son of Man' and 'the Son of the Man.'

Jesus' self-appointed name, 'the Son of Man,' emphatically illustrates Jesus' support and perpetuation of the famous compassionate vegetarian teachings of this highly esteemed spiritual master. Both Pythagoras and Jesus, in turn, breathed life back into God's first and foremost vegetarian commands to humanity notably found in Genesis, the first book of the bible, fulfilling the teachings of the 7th and 8th century Jewish prophets. In his Sermon on the Mount, Jesus stated that the purpose of his earthly mission was both to restore and fulfill his prophetic ancestors' condemnations of animal sacrifice associated with the eating of animal flesh.

Due to the fact that Pythagoras' teachings had spread extensively through cultural exchange in the ancient world, certainly Jesus would have known that many Jewish Essene sects advocated remarkably similar spiritual vegetarian teachings to those of Pythagoras and his disciples. These vegetarian teachings were in harmony with God's first vegetarian commands and fulfilled the teachings of the Jewish prophets.

235

As stated at the outset, evidence proves that Jesus' brother James, known as James the Just, was a vegetarian since birth. Putting the fragments of the jigsaw puzzle together, James would not have been born a vegetarian unless he was born into a vegetarian family who taught him this spiritual vegetarian practice from birth. The family of Jesus and Jesus himself were inevitably members of a vegetarian Essene cult whose teachings were in harmony with the Pythagoreans, which will be proven later in this series.

Pythagoras preached the concept of reincarnation, namely the transmigration of the soul between human and non-human animals. He taught that all animals are as family and friends and therefore should be treated with kindness and compassion. Notably, he was aware that humanity should deal with all beings in a manner befitting humanity's highest compassionate virtues. Vegetarianism, all-embracing compassion for all living beings, human and non-human, pacifism and a simple, communal lifestyle were integral to both Pythagoras' and Jesus' teachings.

Pythagoras emphatically instructed his disciples to avoid the type of person, capable of murdering animals and equally to shun the type of person, capable of butchering animals after their deaths. Pythagoras taught: "For as long as man continues to be the ruthless destroyer of lower living beings he will never know health or peace. For as long as men massacre animals, they will kill each other. Indeed he who sows the seeds of murder and pain cannot reap joy and love." *1* Socrates and Plato were two of Pythagoras' most famous distinguished followers who helped perpetuate his teachings for posterity.

Pythagoras Follows the Buddha

After his liberation from Babylonian captivity, it is believed that Pythagoras travelled to Persia to study with the Persian magi, then on to India, where many believe he was mentored by the Indian Brahmins who at this early date, taught him pure, undiluted, uncorrupted vegetarian Buddhism as the Buddha himself had not long passed away.

236

Viewed by the vegetarian Indian Buddhists as a remarkable individual, they honored Pythagoras with the name, the Ionian teacher, 'Yavanacharya.' The Buddhists were aware that throughout Pythagoras' life and travels, he sought truth, transmitting his wealth of knowledge to others, living as an eternal student and teacher, thriving on intellectual, spiritual and philosophical exchange.

Pythagoras' Vegetarianism Impacted the Ancient World

Pythagoras was both an advanced intellect and a spiritually elevated philosopher and as such was a confirmed vegetarian. Iamblichus tells us that Pythagoras told his disciples: "We should never do anything with a view to pleasure as an end. We should perform what is right, because it is right to do so."

Every night at bedtime Pythagoras asked his followers to evaluate their daily good and bad thoughts, their deeds and their omissions. He told them to be critical of themselves for their wrongdoing and to be pleased with themselves for their good deeds. Significantly, Pythagorean principles are remarkably similar to those of uncorrupted vegetarian Buddhism as are the teachings of Jesus.

Students of the Pythagorean esoteric school, following the spiritual example set by their eminent teacher, abstained from eating animal flesh and beans, wore linen instead of wool, condemned animal sacrifice, prevalent in Greece and Judaism at that time, lived in pacifist communes, avoided luxurious living and wore their hair long. Pythagoras taught compassion and friendship towards all living creatures.

Pythagoras' influence on the widespread perpetuation of the non-animal flesh diet became gargantuan. Due to his strict vegetarian lifestyle, his name became synonymous with vegetarianism for more than two and a half thousand years until the recent mid-19th century AD. Consequently, historically many vegetarians have been called Pythagoreans or followers of the Pythagorean System.

Pythagoras passionately condemned animal sacrifice, prohibited as abhorrent, the murder of any living creature and vehemently forbade the eating of animal flesh. Notably, Pythagoras' vegetarian diet equipped him with amazingly good health. The myriad health benefits of the vegetarian diet are proven today by countless medical studies that evaluate the health over many years of vegetarians contrasted with that of animal flesh eaters. Recent proof of the health promoting vegetarian diet has been substantiated by Harvard University, USA in 2012.

As evidence of his good health, Pythagoras died at the age of ninety nine, a considerable feat in ancient times. Typically, historically, people died much younger than they do today due to the lack of our contemporary, state of the art, health care. As the natural and inevitable result of Pythagoras' pure vegetarian living, we are told by Iamblichus that;

"...his sleep was brief, his soul vigilant and pure and his body confirmed in a state of perfect and invariable health. As for his diet;

"...he was satisfied [says Porphyry] with honey or the honeycomb or with bread only and he did not taste wine from morning to night [and] his principal dish was often kitchen herbs, cooked or uncooked. Fish he ate rarely." *2*

Pythagoras's vegetarianism was intended to spread to governments. He emphatically taught that all members of governments should set a good example to the populace by abstaining from animal flesh, proving that they too upheld the sanctity of all life. Importantly, he expected good governments to demonstrate their awareness and sensitivity to the fact that all creatures feel pain and suffering, especially fellow flesh and blood animals.

These flesh and blood relatives share the same nervous systems as humans which certainly transmits, physical pain to the brain, making all animals sensitive to and deeply aware of discomfort, pain and agony which in turn causes them mental and emotional despair, distress and anguish.

"Amongst other reasons, Pythagoras" (says Iamblichus) "enjoined abstinence from the flesh of animals because it is conducive to peace; for those who are accustomed to abominate

238

the slaughter of other animals, as iniquitous and unnatural, will think it still more unjust and unlawful to kill a man or to engage in war…Specially, he exhorted those politicians who are legislators to abstain [from eating animals].

For, if they were willing to act justly in the highest degree, it was indubitably incumbent upon them not to injure any of the lower animals. Since how could they persuade others to act justly, if they themselves were proved to be indulging an insatiable avidity by devouring these animals that are allied to us? For through the communion of life and the same elements, and the sympathy thus existing, they are, as it were, conjoined to us by a fraternal alliance." *3*

Ovid Endorses the Pythagoreans

We know much of Pythagoras' advanced spiritual philosophy, expressed through his vegetarianism, through later writers including Publius Ovidius Naso, known as Ovid, (43 BC-17 AD). Living many centuries later, in a country beyond Greece, his works perpetuating Pythagorean vegetarianism evidence the extensive impact of Pythagorean vegetarianism in the ancient world.

This acclaimed Roman poet was born in Sulmo, Italy, (known today as Sulmona), ninety miles east of Rome. Significantly, Ovid would have been a Roman contemporary of Jesus. Profoundly influenced by the widespread Pythagorean vegetarian spiritual philosophy of Jesus' day, which had long since burst out of Greece, Ovid was a staunch advocate of compassionate vegetarianism.

One of Ovid's finest achievements is his twelve thousand word poem consisting of more than fifteen books, known as Metamorphoses. Preserving Pythagoras' compassionate vegetarian teachings for future generations Ovid writes:

"Human beings, stop desecrating your bodies with impious foodstuffs. There are crops, there are apples weighing down the branches and ripening grapes on the vines; there are flavorsome herbs and those that can be rendered mild and gentle over the flames and you do not lack flowing milk, or honey fragrant from the flowering thyme. The earth prodigal of its wealth supplies you with gentle sustenance and offers you food without, killing or shedding blood." *4*

Expressing the compassionate vegetarian sentiments of Pythagoras, Ovid writes:

"Alas, what wickedness to swallow flesh into our own flesh, to fatten our greedy bodies by cramming in other bodies, to have one living creature fed by the death of another! In the midst of such wealth as Earth, the best of mothers provides nothing forsooth satisfies you, but to behave like the Cyclopes, inflicting sorry wounds with cruel teeth! You cannot appease the hungry cravings of your wicked, gluttonous stomachs except by destroying some other life." *5*

Explaining Pythagoras' spiritual and philosophic insights into the significance of the human relationship with animals Ovid tells us: "As long as man continues to be the ruthless destroyer of lower beings he will never know health or peace. For as long as men massacre animals, they will kill each other. Indeed, he who sows the seed of murder and pain cannot reap joy and love….Animals share with us privilege of having a soul…"

Ovid adds:

If men with fleshy mortals must be fed,
And chew with bleeding teeth the breathing bread;
What else is this but to devour our guests?
And barbarously renew Cyclopean feasts?
While Earth not only can your needs supply,
But, lavish of her store, provides for luxury;
A guiltless feast administers with ease,
And without blood is prodigal to please." *6*

Ancient Greek Sensitivity to Animals' Facial, Bodily and Acoustic Vocabulary

Aware that all animals live in a world dominated by humans and are therefore tragically disadvantaged by their lack of human vocal chords, preventing them from communicating in human languages, Pythagoras demanded his followers develop qualities of empathy, sympathy, compassion, responsiveness and identification with animals.

Pythagoras taught his fellow Greek scholars and spiritual philosophy students alike, that animals clearly demonstrate intelligence and reasoning abilities and a wide-range of emotions including, contentment, happiness, excitement, hunger, thirst, fear, anxiety, sorrow, loneliness, curiosity, anger, love, loyalty, compassion, insecurity and self-sacrificing protection of their animal companions and adoptive human families.

Notably, Pythagoras was aware that animals use face and body language and acoustic vocabulary, making different sounds to indicate a wide range of emotions, communicating with each other and with those humans sensitive enough to notice. The following is an extract from a passage in the Doxographists concerning Pythagoras and the Pythagoreans:

"The souls of animals called unreasoning are reasonable, [their pleas are misunderstood and ignored]...because they do not have the power of speech, [for example]... apes and dogs...have intelligence but not the power of speech." *11*

Animals Possess the Highest Attributes

Obviously Pythagoras' powers of observation, sensitivity and reasoning led him to the full knowledge that animals possess intelligence, emotions and many components and characteristics that make up individual personalities, all of which are shared by the fellow human animal. Countless examples of animals from all species demonstrating their noble, courageous and valiant willingness to sacrifice themselves to protect others can be given.

Typically, parents from all species are known for their gallant protection of their young, for example a female wilder beast, driven by her love and commitment to protect her young will defy all odds and attack a lion in the hope of rescuing her offspring. Videos show countless, courageous, tragic female foxes running as decoy from their dens in the vein attempt to protect their terrorized infant cubs, instead of following the all-powerful instinct to hide and save their own lives.

Acting as a decoy, males and females of all animal species typically tragically attempt to take the hunters away from their infant young with the desperate hope that hunters will leave their vulnerable, playful and trusting young babies in safety. Videos show countless female foxes being torn apart by dogs severely disciplined and trained by hunters.

These foxes readily lay down their lives for others, giving their lives so bravely and heroically with alarming regularity against a background, a few feet away, of hunters' outdoor celebration parties. These mothers die clinging to the desperate hope that their defenseless, innocent babies will not be robbed of joyful play in sunshine and fields by successfully hiding from the hunters.

Dog and cat owners in particular, who sleep with their pets in the bedroom, are aware that animals talk in their sleep, softly barking and mewing, legs running and tails wagging, proving they dream in the same way as fellow human animals. Rescued dogs and cats in particular, clearly have nightmares, visibly remembering cruelty and abuse, fearfully crying in their sleep. Animals know a wide range of emotions, including fear, loneliness, anxiety, excitement, love, protectiveness and even insecurity.

They experience depression and insecurity in a wide range of circumstances including when a new, additional pet is brought into the home and given extra attention, when a human family or animal family member dies and when their human family is absent for a period of time or have rejected them, throwing them out like a discarded piece of inanimate rubbish.

The animal videos discussed earlier, clearly demonstrate the highest forms of gallantry, heroism, self-sacrifice, bravery, love and devotion. These are rare qualities, highly praised when found amongst humanity. Many internet videos prove that the highest attributes are common amongst fellow animals, witnessed accounts and photographs such as these, abound throughout the millennia and globe.

Pythagoras Broken-Hearted by Sight of Beaten Dog

Notably, Pythagoras condemned those who ate animal flesh and those who sacrificed animals to the gods. Significantly, he also opposed drinking wine due to the excesses and abuses it caused when alcohol was in the wrong hands. Pythagoras warned that humans would learn from their cruelty when it was their turn to reincarnate as an abused, heartbroken, victimized animal.

As the result of non-human animal incarnations, they would personally experience the cruelty inflicted on animals themselves, awakening their dormant and undeveloped sensitivity, empathy and compassion for the degradation and suffering of all animals, human and non-human, qualities to be used in further, more spiritually advanced incarnations.

Ancient texts inform us that Pythagoras was horrified and deeply distraught when quite by chance he saw a tragic dog being violently and cruelly assaulted. Filled with compassion for this innocent, trusting and faithful infant who had had the misfortune to become a vulnerable victim of humankind, he said:

"Stop beating him, [the dog] for I recognized a friend's soul when I heard his voice." *8*

Human Brother's Face Photographed inside Vivisected Mouse

Pythagoras' comments remind me of a memorable event photographed by a man who was busily working alone, dissecting a mouse, when suddenly there appeared on the mouse's body, a clear, practically perfect image of his deceased brother's face. He sent the photograph for analysis which was vindicated by the team of scientists working in Il Laboratorio, based in Bologna, Italy. The enigmatic photograph was presented by Dr. Michele Dinicastro during his power-point presentation, describing the outstanding research carried out at Il Laboratorio.

Dinicastro gave his lecture to members of the Scottish Society for Psychical Research in the Theosophical Centre in Glasgow, Scotland, in July 2008. Dinicastro is one of six scientists who established this non-profit making organization, carrying out bio-psychocybernetic research as outlined below. "Through scientific methods and instruments the Laboratory is interested in researching and studying anomalous, unusual or non-conventional phenomena of 'psychic interaction,' phenomena, depending on particular 'biopsychic conditions' and on bio-resonance phenomena in which man has always been directly or indirectly involved." *9*

Incredibly important issues are raised here. The deceased brother having survived physical death was clearly attempting to communicate with his physically alive, vivisectionist brother. Crucially, was the mouse literally his reincarnated 'deceased,' brother. Indeed was the deceased brother telling the vivisectionist that he had reincarnated as the very mouse the vivisectionist brother was dissecting?

Alternatively, was the deceased brother teaching the vivisectionist a further profound message? Namely, harming this tiny, defenseless, innocent, traumatized flesh and blood mouse, a representative member of the entire interdependent, interrelated earth family, also harms the deceased brother now a soul living in the spirit realms and the vivisectionist?

Indeed by harming one being the vivisectionist is harming all brothers and sisters of creation? Importantly, the spirit brother appears to be symbolically showing his physically alive, vivisectionist brother that the mouse is equally his brother, due to the interrelatedness of all creatures, harming one creature, harms us all, including the spirit brother and vivisectionist brother, on levels which we are unaware, as all species are members of the single family of creation.

A Mouse is 125 Million Year Old Shared Relative

Let us continue this clarifying digression a moment longer before we return to the ancient Greek vegetarian philosophers who believed in reincarnation, namely the transmigration of the soul at death, amongst the single earth family, between non-human animal to the human animal. I believe it is of profound importance

244

that the vivisectionist objectively saw a remarkably clear image of his brother's face which he photographed inside a mouse's body rather than in any other animal.

I believe there are two reasons for this, the first being surely he learnt that no matter how small and apparently insignificant any creature is, each and every creature is important, as all feel pain and many like humanity possess emotions, feeling distress, fear and horror.

At this juncture a person is reminded of Jesus' claim that God is aware of the suffering and sorrows of the smallest sparrow. Secondly, notably ancient mice are a shared ancestor of humankind (who are classified as animals, primates and mammals) and of many other mammals.

Importantly an international team of scientists found a 125 million year old fossil of an extinct mouse-like creature, five inches long and weighing 25 grams, that resembled present day tree shrews of Asia. This fossil was found in a quarry in Liaoning Province in China, famous for the earlier discovery of feathered dinosaur remains.

This mouse-like creature is called Eomaia scansoria which is a placental mammal, with a name derived from both Greek and Latin origins. Importantly, all mammals today are placental mammals proving that Eomaia Scansoria is the most ancient shared ancestor of mice and humans and all other present day mammals.

Astonishingly, this fossil represents the remains of a creature who is the most ancient shared ancestor found to date of contemporary mammals, some examples of which include humans, cows, horses, sheep, pigs, primates, dogs, cats, whales and so forth.

Approximately 6 million years ago the related genus Mus was established and was very similar in appearance to Eomaia Scansoria. This creature was renamed in Latin from the Sanskrit word meaning 'to steal.' This species began after the last ice age approximately 8,000 years ago. Significantly, revealing the close relatedness of both humans and mice, mice possess approximately 30,000 genes, incredibly 99% of which are exactly the same as each other!

However, the mouse genome is shorter than that of humans, who have 2.9 billion letters whilst mice have 2.5 billion letters. Significantly mice are humans with tails! Remarkably, human embryos exhibit a tail, some human babies are born with tails and humans still possess the gene that can make a tail!

Crucially, however, with regard to medical experimentation purposes there are too many minute differences between mice and humans for the results to be accurate or have meaning. Having so much in common with humans, along with other mammals, arguably ethically it is wrong to experiment on such closely related fellow mammals as indeed it would be wrong to experiment on any other living creature.

Unable to speak as we do, they communicate in different and often subtle ways to us, as mentioned earlier, only those who are sensitively aware perceive this. Animals' lack of overt human language has been conveniently used to suppress awareness amongst the public that they do indeed feel pain as acutely as you and I, due to their possession of flesh, blood, nerve endings and the same organs.

Professor Charles R. Magel points out: "Ask the experimenters why they experiment on animals, and the answer is: "Because the animals are like us." Ask the experimenters why it is morally okay to experiment on animals and the answer is: "Because the animals are not like us." Animal experimentation rests on a logical contradiction." *10*

The renowned Anglican priest, Humphrey Primatt expresses the same compassion as those we are discussing in the ancient world: "Pain is pain, whether it is inflicted on man or on beast; and the creature that suffers it, whether man or beast, being sensible of the misery of it whilst it lasts, suffers Evil. *11*

Charles Mayo PhD agrees: "I abhor vivisection…it should be abolished. I know of no achievement through vivisection, no scientific discovery that could not have been obtained without such barbarism and cruelty. The whole thing is evil." *12*

Chief Seattle (1786-1866) expresses the same compassionate vegetarian philosophy as the ancient Egyptians, Chinese and Greeks; "…the deer, the horse, the great eagle, these are our brothers. The rocky crests, the juices in the meadows, the body heat of the pony and man—all belong to the same family...the White Man must treat the beasts of this land as his brothers." *13*

Friedrich Nietzsche (1844-1900) the late 19th century AD, German born philosopher who challenged the foundations of distorted Orthodox Christianity, explains the importance of vegetarianism and compassion for all creatures:

"All ancient philosophy was orientated toward the simplicity of life and taught a certain kind of modesty in one's need. In light of this, the few philosophic vegetarians have done more for mankind than all new philosophers and as long as philosophers do not take courage to seek out a totally changed way of life and to demonstrate it by their example, they are worth nothing." *14*

Pythagoras Enhances Modern-Day Research

Pythagoras' highly ethically advanced compassionate vegetarian spiritual philosophy has been endorsed by great minds throughout the ages, as shown above. Remarkably, Pythagoras deduced that everything, including all life forms, can be reduced to being illustrated by numbers.

Proving the correctness of Pythagoras' deductions, sciences such as physics, chemistry and computer modeling are based on mathematics and can indeed most accurately illustrate life forms through mathematical equations. Demonstrating the wisdom of Pythagoras' insights, increasingly computer modeling is replacing outworn inaccurate inhumane animal testing, known for incredible inaccuracies and errors due to the subtle and profound differences between all related animal species.

Computer modeling is progressively providing much more accurate results than animal testing ever did. Using mathematics and computer modeling instead of brutal animal testing obviously demonstrates respect and compassion for all related animals, in turn creating a non-violent society for all.

By illustrating all life forms as the numbers of their composition as Pythagoras instructed, research into diseases can become increasingly accurate and in harmony with his far-sighted, compassionate vegetarian spiritual philosophy.

Socrates (469/470-399 BC) and Athens in the 5th century BC

Illustrating the extraordinary ancient Greek culture which has been influential in shaping modern day western society, let us briefly look at a further number of eminent ancient Greeks many of whom studied in Athens. Socrates, born in Athens in the 5th century BC, is a famed classical Greek philosopher. He is acclaimed for being the founder of Western political and ethical philosophy.

Cicero tells us that Socrates should be admired for beginning the process of bringing philosophy down to earth from the heavens to the streets, delivering it to common men, women and families. He enabled common folk to understand philosophical concepts from which they learnt morals, vegetarianism and the differences between good and evil.

Socrates believed that no individual wants what is bad hence he/she who acts in a bad way must have done so against his/her wishes or out of ignorance, Consequently, Socrates taught that virtue was based on knowledge hence his key phrase was:

"Know thyself to be true" or "Be true to yourself." Prompting his fellows to heighten their moral standards, teaching them the overt and subtle differences between good and evil, Socrates also founded political philosophy revealing the true nature of their society and how it should best be organized.

Regularly in the agoras, the market places of Athens, he initiated dialogues with the public, frequently exposing Athenian ignorance, hypocrisy and conceit, no doubt creating many enemies particularly amongst the rich and powerful.

Socrates believed that a person would never knowingly do a bad thing hence he taught his pupils ethics and questioned their understanding of true courage, love and friendship, in the belief, if they understood the meanings of these terms they would act accordingly. Some advised they also needed strength of character like Socrates and the resolve to always pursue the good and honest path in all their dealings, hence they pursued physical training and abstained from a luxurious lifestyle.

Socrates spoke about the voices he heard presumably in the manner historically and today of a clairaudient medium. He suggested to his students that the voices gave him advice and guidance from the gods. Notably, he created the Socratic Method, a process of analyzing subjects utilizing a question and answer system. Notably the term the Athenian School is applied to Socrates, Plato and Aristotle.

The Athens Socrates knew in the 5th century BC was a center of excellence and learning, teeming with students of all ages and backgrounds each seeking knowledge. Students travelled for many weeks in order to study in Athens whilst scholars of a wide range of subjects including rhetoric, astronomy, geometry and cosmology, likewise converged on this hub of civilization.

Contravening this focus on knowledge at intervals the ruling Athenian nobility demonstrated a jealous, conservative reaction to the highly respected philosophers by curtailing and condemning their research into the objects above the heavens and below the earth.

Their insecure and reactionary stance forced those philosophers who came under their spotlight to flee the Athenian nucleus of activity. Socrates fell out of favor with the authorities due to his forthrightness, the activities of some of his students and the weight of the obstructive, backward-looking aristocratic dictates to which he did not comply.

Nobly, rather than flee the city, Socrates faced their intransigent intolerance. Sentenced to death, he drank poisonous hemlock as his means of execution. Socrates oration in his defense, at his trial, recorded by Plato, informs us that the ruling classes had become resentful and envious of the increasing popularity and influence of the philosophers.

Plato the Vegetarian (428-348/347 BC)

Born in Athens, in 428 BC, Plato's philosophy is a brilliant synthesis, interpretation and elaboration of the philosophy of a number of his esteemed Greek vegetarian predecessors. The most memorable of whom include Pythagoras (570/580 - 495/500 BC), Empedocles (490-430 BC), Socrates (469/470 BC - 399 BC) and several Orphic prophets.

Most importantly, it is useful to be reminded that when Pythagoras' writings were all but destroyed in a fire, Plato sold everything he had to raise the money to buy Pythagoras' surviving writings. At the age of twenty, Plato became the student of the famous Socrates who perpetuated many Pythagorean principles including strict vegetarianism. Plato, born to one of the noblest families in Athens, became a renowned philosopher himself, recording for posterity much of Pythagoras' and Socrates' teachings.

In later years, Plato founded his own famous school of philosophy in Athens named, the Academy. Incredibly, this institution flourished and endured for approximately one thousand years. Here formal classes on specific subjects did not take place instead a person would ask a question and others would offer answers initiating challenging on-going lengthy and profound debates, which in turn gave rise to new questions and discussions.

In 529 AD, Justinian a Christian Emperor, tragically suppressed the Academy and other Greek schools of academic excellence. Importantly, when Plato reached the age of sixty, Aristotle asked Plato to do him the honor of tutoring him. In later years, Aristotle himself became a famous philosopher. Aristotle became the teacher of Alexander the Great, later famed for travelling extensively with his mighty armies across the globe, seeking to conquer and govern the world.

Continuing the Pythagorean vegetarian tradition, fundamentally intertwined with the concept of the transmigration of the soul at physical death, Plato continued the spiritual philosophy of his venerable predecessors, teaching us that the soul migrates at death to a new body to live out successive physical incarnations, seeking to attain spiritual advancement, revealing, the extremely close familial relationship between human and animal. Inevitably, this centuries-old, vegetarian spiritual philosophy inevitably had a deeply profound and enduring impact on the way people perceived animals.

Plato, who died at the age of eighty, had a high level of knowledge regarding the philosophy of his predecessors and was fully versed in science and mathematics. Distraught by the corruption of the ruling Athenian classes that led to Socrates' execution, Plato did not enter politics.

Instead, he concluded that humankind's destiny was doomed unless he could instigate a profound change amongst humankind's education including those who intended to govern others. Plato believed that 'philosophy' which meant 'friendship and wisdom' could make them suitable and acceptable for the task of governing. In his VII Letter, 326 a-b Plato writes: "Mankind will not get rid of its evils until either the class of those who philosophize in truth and rectitude reach political power or those most powerful in cities, under some divine dispensation, really get to philosophizing."

Plato is famed for his writings known as dialogues in which his eminent teacher, Socrates is a foremost personality. From his most notable work known as The Republic we learn about the importance of vegetarianism for both the animals and the public good, how rulers should best govern the people and the nature of true justice. Revealing the extraordinary significance of this work, still scrutinized by scholars today, Plato's beliefs have historically shaped philosophy and political theory.

Plato believed that no individual deserved to live an opulent life-style to the detriment of others and that only philosopher-kings should govern the people as they alone would possess the correct wise and moral attributes necessary for proper ruler-ship. Obviously it was this belief that philosophers would make the best rulers that antagonized members of the Athenian ruling classes.

Notably, Plato believed the world of phenomena to be a meager shadow of the real world of ideas. For example according to Plato's theories when we look at a horse, we know what it is because our soul recalls the idea of a horse from the time before we were physically born. Platonic philosophy surmises that all souls lived previously in a superior place before their incarnation into this fallen world.

Consequently Plato's speculations were easily blended with Christianity, making Platonism popular in Late Antiquity. The following dialogue between Socrates and Glaucon taken from Plato's writings known as the Republic reveals both Plato's revulsion at the thought of eating animal flesh and the base folly of this practice:

Socrates: Would this habit of eating animals not require that we slaughter animals that we knew as individuals, and in whose eyes we could gaze and see ourselves reflected, only a few hours before our meal?

Glaucon: This habit would require that of us.

Socrates: Wouldn't this [knowledge of our role in turning a flesh and blood emotional reasoning and feeling being into a thing] hinder us in achieving happiness?

Glaucon: It could so hinder us in our quest for happiness.

Socrates: And, if we pursue this way of living, will we not heave need to visit the doctor more often?

Glaucon: We would have such need.

Socrates: If we pursue our habit of eating animals, and if our neighbor follows a similar path, will we not have need to go to war against our neighbor to secure greater pasturage, because ours will not be enough to sustain us, and our neighbor will have a similar need to wage war on us for this same reason?

Glaucon: We would be so compelled.

Socrates: Would not these facts prevent us from achieving happiness, and therefore the conditions necessary to the building of a just society, if we pursue a desire to eat animals?

Glaucon: Yes, they would so prevent us.

Plato clearly reveals in the above extract that Socrates' teachings parallel those of Pythagoras, both of which were perpetuated by Plato. Interestingly, the teachings of these three scholars have much in common with great minds throughout the ages including the insights of Leo Tolstoy who stated:
"As long as there are slaughterhouses there will be battlefields."
Tolstoy adds:
"A man can live and be healthy without killing animals for food; therefore, if he eats meat, he participates in taking animal life merely for the sake of his appetite. And to act so is immoral."
Indeed, Plato wanted vegetarianism to be practiced as a lifestyle in keeping with his concept of an ideal and exemplary society for all to follow. Remarkably, echoing ancient Jewish beliefs regarding God's first commands to the first of humankind in the Garden of Eden, recorded in the Book of Genesis, speaking of a vegetarian diet Plato stated: "The Gods created certain kinds of [nutrition] to replenish our bodies; they are the trees and the plants and the seeds."

Plato's Beliefs, Health and Longevity

Plato believed the soul to be immortal, transmigrating at death to other living creatures, during the practically relentless wheel of rebirth. Consequently, in harmony with Pythagoras and Socrates, he believed all individuals should receive a balanced, thorough education in order to support each soul's spiritual and intellectual advancement. Inherent within Plato's advanced spiritual philosophy, is the belief that there is another world experienced after physical death, consisting of unchanging, eternal forms.

This after-death region was considered to be beyond our material world which consists of changeable, destructible forms. Plato likened the human condition with its limited understanding of the mysteries of life to a person sitting in a cave facing the wall, watching only the shadows of reality, which are only dim reflections of the unseen reality behind him. Using this analogy, Plato claimed that humanity can only perceive the limited, dim reflections of the shadows of true reality.

The following demonstrates something of Plato's wisdom and practical insights into the nature of democratic governments, providing lessons for us today. As a result of his discernment and vision, he believed that 'the public' will always consist of a vast majority of people who possess no political education, plans or solutions, making the global populace ill-equipped to vote others into power.

Similarly, Plato believed that most individuals voted into positions of power, lack intellectual and political acumen and ethical integrity, being ill-equipped to lead the people by providing political solutions. He believed their primary concern to be the acquisition of power, wealth and personal prestige, sadly, nothing more than their own self-aggrandizement. Plato's ideal rulers were ethical vegetarian philosophers, who were proven spiritual intellectuals who would rule the populace in accordance with the nature of benevolent parental guardians.

Revealing Plato's extraordinary wisdom and foresight, writing in the book known as Laws, (Book 10), Plato admonished his followers, warning them that the ethical and compassionate quality of each person's lifetime would have a direct bearing on his/her next lifetime:

"Recognize, if you become baser you will go to baser souls and if higher, to the higher and in every course of life and death you will do and suffer what like may appropriately suffer at the hands of like." Plato taught that every soul would experience life as a terrestrial, marine and aerial creature and when the soul came to dwell in a human, over time it would sample life from the perspective of different hierarchical human professions.

Unsurprisingly, as one of Pythagoras' leading proponents, Plato's vegetarian teachings have remarkable similarities with the all-embracing, compassionate vegetarian Hindu teachings expressed in their holy book known as the Upanishads, the all-inclusive, merciful and respectful vegetarian teachings of the Buddha and Confucius and were later demonstrated by the all-encompassing, kind-hearted vegetarian teachings of Jesus.

In Plato's books known as the Republic, Books II and III, proving he was a man ahead of his time, he cleverly appeals to those individuals who do not spontaneously feel compassion for animals, by making them aware of the innumerable personal health benefits of the non-animal flesh diet. Plato is here emphatically elaborating on Pythagoras' and Socrates' vegetarian teachings. In the Republic Book II, Plato again uses dialogues between Socrates and Glaucon who asks questions, revealing the multifarious health and social benefits of a non-animal flesh diet.

Socrates states; "…people will live…on barley and wheat, baking cakes of the meal and kneading loves of the flour. …they will be merry, themselves and their children …We shall also set before them a desert…of figs, peas and beans; they may roast myrtle berries and beech nuts at the fire, taking wine with their fruit in great moderation. And thus passing their days in tranquility and sound health, they will, in all probability, live to a very advanced age and dying, bequeath to their children a life in which their own will be reproduced." *15*

Again, using Socrates as his mouth piece, Plato unites his old teacher with their shared philosophy. He warns humanity that when societies greedily demand more than the necessities of life, changing to an animal flesh diet, social decay and injustice will inevitably follow. Notably, he uses Socrates to point out that the flesh eating diet would necessitate the importation of; "…great quantities of all kinds of cattle for those who may wish to eat them. Then decline and decay." *16*

Remarkably, 2,500 years ago in Plato's series of books named the Republic, Plato provides Socrates with dialogue clarifying the negative health consequences and spiritual and political disadvantages of eating the flesh of an animal. He also points out that the flesh inevitably belongs to a person who has newly reincarnated as an animal. Echoing those teachings of his celebrated predecessors, the following summarized extract reiterates their shared, profound and far-sighted wisdom noting the global, spiritual, economic, and health benefits of a non-animal flesh diet.

Socrates asks: "Would this habit of eating animals not require that we slaughter animals that we knew as individuals, and in whose eyes we could gaze and see ourselves reflected, only a few hours before our meal?...[this would] hinder us in achieving happiness...if we pursue this way of living [we will] have need to visit the doctor more...

If we pursue our habit of eating animals, and if our neighbor follows a similar path, we will... have need to go to war against our neighbor to secure greater pasturage, because ours will not be enough to sustain us, and our neighbor will have a similar need to wage war on us for the same reason...Would not these facts prevent us from achieving happiness and therefore the conditions necessary to the building of a just society, if we pursue a desire to eat animals?" *17*

Plato made his transition to spirit at the age of approximately eighty. His robust health and longevity was comparable to that of Pythagoras and was inevitably supported by his non- animal flesh diet.

Following the guidance of his predecessors his diet included fruits, berries, herbs, vegetables, nuts and grains. Significantly, the teachings of these great vegetarian spiritual philosophers, Pythagoras, Socrates and Plato are as relevant today as they were historically.

Exchange and Integration of Greek and Jewish Beliefs

Notably, the exchange, incorporation and merging of Greek and Jewish spiritual philosophy was greatly facilitated by Plato's fluency with ancient Hebrew philosophy. Ancient Jewish and Greek religious authorities were enthusiastically drawn to both listen to and provide lectures in Athens followed by intense lengthy debates on profound spiritual matters. Progressively the philosophies of each became blended as they absorbed and harmonized religious concepts with each other. Summaries, insights and conclusions were later shared with the populace.

Crucially, Plato's teachings and writings amalgamated, integrated and synthesized ancient Hebrew spiritual philosophy with his own which was profoundly shaped by the vegetarianism of Pythagoras and Socrates.

Consequently, Plato's philosophy offers us a clear insight into the ancient Hebrew spiritual teachings with which Jesus would have been familiar. Plato's teachings are particularly valuable because they reveal original elements of early Hebrew teachings which were diluted and distorted by the later orthodox Christian church.

Aristotle is the most significant secondary source providing us with a reliable biography of Plato. It is believed that Plato's writings, much of which is in the form of dialogues, have survived intact. His teachings can be found in a plethora of works including: The Apology, Laws, Phaedo, Symposium and the series of books known as The Republic. Plato's enquiring mind and his philosophical teachings probed and dealt with diverse issues such as spiritual philosophy, ethics, metaphysics, education, natural science, mathematics and epistemology.

For practically ten centuries, the Academy's tutors perpetuated the vegetarian spiritual illumination and profound educational insights of Plato and his venerable predecessors, including the works of Pythagoras. Inevitably, the honorable reputation of the flourishing Academy as an excellent center of learning spread throughout the ancient world. Tragically, Plato's valuable impact, shining enlightenment on the globe, was all but extinguished in the early 6th century AD by the closure of his glorious Academy, by the sadly misguided Christian Emperor Justinian.

Aristotle of Stagira (384-322 BC)

Pythagoras, Socrates and Plato are the most celebrated and legendary philosophers due to their gargantuan contributions to civilization. However, the most well-known student of Plato is the aristocratic son of a doctor Aristotle of Stagira, famed for his role as teacher of Alexander the Great. This aristocratic Macedonian philosopher and scientist continued the tradition of studying spiritual philosophy together with science, unlike today where the two subjects have been falsely divorced.

Notably, Aristotle's works, in contrast to Plato's, were never revered for their literary expertise. After Aristotle's death his library, notes and lecture notes were bequeathed to Theophrastus, Aristotle's friend, student and vegetarian philosophical successor.

Upon death, Theophrastus bestowed these works to his own beneficiary. Sometime after, Aristotle's labors were deposited for many decades in a damp basement for their safety and protection. Interestingly, they were unearthed in 100 BC and bought by a book collector who travelled to Athens. Here they were seized and sent to Rome around 86 BC. By this time, Aristotle's literary output was in a muddled and dilapidated state.

Roman librarians and scholars who were obviously not vegetarians, living in the blood lust society of Rome, edited and in-filled countless missing segments of Aristotle's writings, with their own opinions, attitudes, views and judgments, in an unsystematic manner. An erroneous, plagiarized version of Aristotle's writings was disseminated which was later followed around 70 BC with a more professional version.

Interestingly, Aristotle's Lyceum did not possess any decisive accounts of his teachings. It has been said that Aristotle wrote several hundred books and treatises of a wide range of subjects however around two hundred only are known today, many of which are duplications, others are not authentic and others appear to be written by his successors at the Lyceum.

Importantly, the works known as Aristotelian today are the resultant adaptations that were carved into the muddled documents that arrived in Rome in 86 BC. These renderings have been severely edited with the opinions of Roman librarians, consisting of forty seven long and short treatises, around twenty of which are indeed bogus and excerpts or references found in the works of other ancient scholars. Consequently, when I refer to Aristotle's works which have influenced historic and contemporary civilization, the above facts, expressing Roman anti-vegetarian views, should be born in mind.

Aristotle was particularly interested in the study of biology, physics, metaphysics, ethics, logic, zoology politics and the physical world including the more practical aspects of philosophy. Although he studied and worked for twenty years at Plato's academy, he criticized and veered away from Socrates' and Plato's core vegetarian teachings including much of their philosophy.

This may have been the result of his wealthy less spiritually orientated aristocratic upbringing. Socrates had been particularly disdainful of the ruling aristocratic classes for their intellectual and spiritual inferiority which he believed gave rise to their jealousy and opposition to philosophers.

Startlingly, unlike his passionately committed eminent vegetarian forefathers, Aristotle's writings demonstrate typically inconsistent, conflicting, contradictory and ill-thought out statements regarding animals. Tragically, a number of Aristotle's ill-informed, negative views on animals, which are in sharp contrast to the beliefs of the long line of his illustrious predecessors, have been deliberately chosen and focused upon by medieval Christian scholastic philosophers including Muslim philosophers, influencing and shaping erroneous, callously indifferent attitudes towards animals to this day.

His variable attitudes towards Pythagoras,' Socrates' and Plato's far-sighted vegetarian philosophy is tragic in the sense that it was Aristotle's egocentric and non-vegetarian statements that medieval Christendom and Islam chose to consult fashioning and permitting horrendous, barbaric cruelty, slaughter and insensitivity towards animals to this day. Sadly, it is the negative aspect rather than the perceptive, accurate and positive aspects of Aristotle's statements regarding animals on which contemporary views on animals are based.

Notably, Pythagoras, Socrates and Plato and their generations of disciples perceived a beautiful immortal soul in all animals, human and non-human and in all other life forms. Aristotle was a sad shadow of his renowned predecessors due to his changeable and contradictory views on animals and vegetarianism which was in sharp contrast to the erudite spiritual philosophy of his illustrious ancestors.

Aristotle's careless, inferior and self-obsessed view expresses his preference that both plants and animals live only for human use in the manner of Greek slaves. He erroneously stated that animals do not think, they merely experience sensation and appetite and need humankind to help them survive. Amazingly, his substandard comments, fail to appreciate that animals free from human exploitation, both survive and thrive.

To give one example of Aristotle's contradictory and inconsistent attitudes towards animals and vegetarianism, when flouting Pythagoras,' Socrates' and Plato's compassionate vegetarian doctrines, he changes and in full agreement with them he states; "we should approach the inquiry about each animal without aversion, knowing that in all of them there is something natural and beautiful." Importantly, it should be noted that Aristotle is also supportive of Orphic beliefs typically expressed through poetry which claim that the soul is born by the winds and from the air the soul enters animals when they take their breath.

Aristotle's inconsistency is again shown when he writes in his book named Politics that humans are the only animal able to reason then in complete contradiction he writes in the first chapter of his book named Metaphysics that animals demonstrate perception, reasoning abilities and intelligence!

It is the former erroneous idea that the medieval Christian church and Islam concentrated upon and adopted. Notably, Aristotle believed animals can learn, that they possess memory, that they not only perceive immediate sensations but can make connections regarding sensations, they know passion and relationships and they demonstrate voluntary motion hence they are not propelled by mere spontaneous impulses.

Before leaving Aristotle it is valuable to be aware how influenced we are today by the insensitive and inaccurate aspects of his philosophy towards animals. Predominantly a scientist and a down to earth philosopher, many believe Aristotle to be the founder of modern science. He founded his own school known as the Lyceum. Today many people who have not lived or worked with animals, having little or nothing to do with them believe they are inanimate machines, responding with mindless reactions caused by instinctive forces to environmental stimuli.

This belief was born of the philosophical school known as the Stoics (336-264 BC) founded by Zeno. Their gross reduction and even negation of animal emotions, characteristics, reasoning and intellect has conveniently distanced human animals from their fellow animals, resulting in today's multibillion dollar animal slaughter industry.

This is carried out on behalf of 'good' people who choose to eat fellow animal flesh as a food preference. They not only permit this sorrowful bloody carnage but typically don't give animal misery and slaughter a thought. Most people feel they owe no justice, compassion, sensitivity, mercy or moral consideration to fellow flesh and blood animals who are indeed feeling, emotional and reasoning beings.

Aristotle's beliefs and the Stoic beliefs rather than the compassionate spiritual vegetarian beliefs of Pythagoras, Socrates and Plato were absorbed into Christian theorizing by Augustine and have historically shaped beliefs till today. Pythagoras, Socrates and Plato unlike Aristotle did not waiver toing and froing, changing their minds this way and that, about animal characteristics, instead they were passionately dedicated vegetarians perceiving beautiful souls dwelling in all animals human and non-human.

Tragically, many of the complete works written by a number of Aristotle's celebrated vegetarian predecessors have not survived for posterity which in part has reduced their vegetarian influence on today's society abetted by the fact that killing animals has globally, throughout time, equated with a highly profitable business. Such historic and contemporary business men and women who seek to brainwash the public to eat animal flesh look for endorsements for their murder of animals from historic figures, suppressing and silencing the voices of those who have condemned it throughout history.

As alluded to earlier humans themselves are biologically classified as "animals, mammals and primates." Typically, humans avoid the use of these terms when referring to themselves, separating, distancing and detaching themselves from the rest of their animal family. Notably, attempting to divorce and isolate themselves from the rest of animal kind, they like to call themselves human beings or humankind, discarding all others with the man-made name 'creatures!' Through this dissociation they delude themselves giving themselves perceived permission to cruelly exploit and murder their fellow flesh and blood relatives.

The author and Professor Carl Sagan (1934-1996) sums-up human attitudes well:

"Humans – who enslave, castrate, experiment on, and fillet other animals - have had an understandable penchant for pretending animals do not feel pain. A sharp distinction between humans and "animals" is essential if we are to bend them to our will, make them work for us, wear them, eat them - without any disquieting tinges of guilt or regret.

It is unseemly of us, who often behave so unfeelingly toward other animals, to contend that only humans can suffer. The behavior of other animals renders such pretensions specious. They are just too much like us."

Aristotle's Vegetarian Student and Successor: Theophrastus (372-287 BC)

Aristotle's student, Theophrastus, born in Lesbos, was indeed a devout vegetarian. Interestingly, it is startlingly unusual for a student to differ so drastically from his teacher. Perhaps this difference actually reveals that Aristotle's true sentiments were supportive of animals and vegetarianism. Pursuing his studies in Athens, regularly travelling with Aristotle the two became friends.

Notably, Theophrastus was emphatic that animals did not exist to serve humans. Unlike Aristotle, he passionately opposed any form of exploitation, cruelty and murder of animals. He surmised that the tradition of eating animals was born at times of war when agricultural food, through destruction, was scarce or non-existent. If other means of food are available Theophrastus believed no one should ever eat animal flesh. He was the leader of the Peripatos and Platonists, arguing that the gap between human animal psychology and non-human animal psychology is not wide.

Plutarch the Vegetarian (45 AD-125 AD)

Notably, living only decades after Jesus' death, during the period when Jesus' followers remained faithful to vegetarianism, Plutarch's honorable reputation and passionately held vegetarian teachings spread extensively in the ancient world. This Greek who became a Roman citizen, took up the reins of his ancient spiritual vegetarian heritage, continuing the work of his highly acclaimed vegetarian Greek predecessors. Plutarch was a Greek historian, biographer, essayist and vegetarian philosopher. Plutarch's writings; "strongly influenced the evolution of the essay, the biography and historical writing in Europe from the 16th to 19th century CE." *18*

Plutarch studied mathematics and spiritual philosophy at Plato's Academy in Athens which was still flourishing at this time. He later became a magistrate, ambassador and Delphian oracle priest. He was extremely popular due to his ability to clarify the resulting conclusions of philosophical debates to the public. Plutarch wrote 227 works.

He wrote a number of moral treatises encouraging people to resist anger, how to become virtuous and the importance of listening carefully to others. In his writings known as Parallel Lives, which are his best known works he describes the biographies, noble deeds and personalities of a number of famous Romans and Greeks, setting a high moral standard for others to follow. One example of Plutarch's double biographies is his comparison of the morally exemplary characteristics of both the Greek, Alexander the Great and the Roman, Julius Caesar, for others to use as role models.

As was the case with his eminent Greek vegetarian mentors, his students travelled extensively, to learn from him. He taught that all animals feel pain, fear suffering and death and therefore should be treated with compassion and respect. The best way to summarize Plutarch's highly elevated vegetarian spiritual philosophy, following in the footsteps of Pythagoras, Socrates and Plato, is to provide a series of highly illustrative extracts from his profound and voluminous writings on ethics, vegetarianism and compassion to animals.

Few individuals can express Plutarch's sentiments as well as he does, as will be shown below. This sensitive, compassionate, highly spiritual intellectual's teachings regarding the preciousness of all animals and the need for humans to demonstrate the highest virtues, morality, ethics and kindness when dealing with them, is most passionately, eloquently and clearly demonstrated in his following statements:

From the section on Morals, called "Whether it be Lawful to Eat Flesh or No," Plutarch wrote;

"...to the Dolphin alone, beyond all other, nature has granted what the best philosophers seek: friendship for no advantage." *19*

In his writings known as the Moralia or Ethica, consisting of 60 essays, Plutarch primarily wrote about ethics, religion and politics. Writing in the Moralia about Pythagoras' reasons for not eating animal flesh, Plutarch turns the discussion around, condemning humanity for thinking about eating the corpses of flesh and blood bodies, in the first place. The following are extracts from The Extended circle by Jon Wynne-Tyson shown at www.ivu.org/history/greece_rome/plutarch.html.

"Can you really ask what reason Pythagoras had for abstaining from flesh? For my part I rather wonder both by what accident and in what state of soul or mind the first man did so, touched his mouth to gore and brought his lips to the flesh of a dead creature, he who set forth tables of dead, stale bodies and ventured to call food and nourishment the parts that had a little before bellowed and cried, moved and lived.

How could his eyes endure the slaughter when throats were slit and hides flayed and limbs torn from limb? How could his nose endure the stench? How was it that the pollution did not turn away his taste, which made contact with the sores of others and sucked juices and serums, from mortal wounds?"

"The obligations of law and equity reach only to mankind, but kindness and benevolence should be extended to the creatures of every species, and these will flow from the breast of a true man, in streams that issue from the living fountain.

Man makes use of flesh not out of want and necessity, seeing that he has the liberty to make his choice of herbs and fruits, the plenty of which is inexhaustible; but out of luxury, and being cloyed with necessaries, he seeks after impure and inconvenient diet, purchased by the slaughter of living beasts; by showing himself more cruel than the most savage of wild beasts...were it only to learn benevolence to humankind, we should be merciful to other creatures."

"...we eat not lions and wolves by way of revenge, but we let those go and catch the harmless and tame sort, such as have neither stings nor teeth to bite with, and slay them....But if you will contend that yourself were born to an inclination to such food as you have now a mind to eat, do you then yourself kill what you would eat.

But do it yourself, without the help of a chopping-knife, mallet, or axe – as wolves, bears, and lions do, who kill and eat at once. Rend an ox with thy teeth, worry a hog with thy mouth, tear a lamb or a hare to pieces, and fall on it and eat it alive as they do. But if thou hadst rather stay until what thou eatest is to become dead, and if thou art loath to force a soul out of its body, why then dost thou against Nature eat an animate thing?"

"Why do you belie the earth, as if it were unable to feed and nourish you? Does it not shame you to mingle murder and blood with her beneficent fruits? Other carnivora you call savage and ferocious – lions and tigers and serpents – while yourselves come behind them [as a species of more] barbarity. And yet for them murder is the only means of sustenance! Whereas to you it is superfluous luxury and crime!"

"But for the sake of some little mouthful of flesh we deprive a soul of the sun and light, and of that proportion of life and time it had been born into the world to enjoy."

The following further extracts of Plutarch's compassionate vegetarian teachings have been taken from the 1957 IVU Congress souvenir book also shown at www.ivu.org/history/greee_rome/plutarch.html.

"For the wretches who first applied to flesh-eating may justly be alleged in excuse their utter resourcefulness and destitution, inasmuch as it was not to indulge in lawless desires, or amidst the superfluities of necessaries, for the pleasure of wanton indulgence in unnatural luxuries that they (the primeval people) betook themselves to carnivorous habits…"

"Nothing puts us out of countenance, not the charming beauty of their form, not the plaintive sweetness of their voice or cry, not their mental intelligence, not the purity of their diet, not superiority of understanding. For the sake of a part of their flesh only, we deprive them of the glorious light of the sun – or the life, for which they were born.

The plaintive cries they utter we affect to take to be meaningless; whereas, in fact, they are entreaties and supplications and prayers addressed to us by each which say, "It is not the satisfaction of your real necessities we deprecate, but the wanton indulgence of your appetites. Kill to eat, if you must or will, but do not slay me that you may feed luxuriously!"

"Alas for our savage inhumanity! It is a terrible thing to see the table of rich men decked out by those layers-out of corpses: the butchers and coos; a still more terrible sight is the same table after the feast – for the wasted relics are even more than the consumption. These victims, then, have given us their lives uselessly. As other times, from mere niggardliness, the host will grudge to distribute his dishes, and yet he grudged not to deprive innocent beings of their existence!"

"Well I have taken away the excuse of those who allege that they have the authority and sanction of Nature. For that man is not, by nature, carnivorous is proved, in the first place, by the external frame of his body – seeing that to none of the animal designed for living on flesh has the human body any resemblance.

He has no curved beak, no sharp talons and claws, no pointed teeth, no intense power of stomach or heat of blood which might help him to masticate and digest the gross and tough flesh-substance. On the contrary, by the smoothness of his teeth, the small capacity of his mouth, the softness of his tongue, and the sluggishness of his digestive apparatus, Nature sternly forbids him to feed on flesh."

"If, in spite of all this, you still affirm that you were, to begin with, kill yourself what you wish to eat – but do it yourself with your own natural weapons, without the use of butcher's knife, or axe, or club. No; as the wolves and lions and bears themselves slay all they feed on, so in like manner, do you kill the cow or ox with a grip of your jaw, or the pig with your teeth, or a hare or a lamb by falling upon and rending them there and then.

Having gone through all these preliminaries then sit down to your repast. If, however, you wait until the living and intelligent existence be deprived of life, and if it would disgust you to have to rend out the heart and shed the life-blood of your victim, why, I ask, in the very fact of Nature, and in despite of her, do you feed on beings endowed with sentient life?"

"But more than this – not even, after your victims have been killed, will you eat them just as they are from the slaughter-house. You boil, roast, and altogether metamorphose them by fire and condiments. You entirely alter and disguise the murdered animal by use of ten thousand sweet herbs and spices that your

267

natural taste may be deceived and be prepared to take the unnatural food. A proper and witty rebuke was that of the Spartan who bought a fish and gave it to his cook to dress. When the latter asked for butter, and olive oil, and vinegar, he replied, "Why, if I had all these things I should not have bought the fish!"

"To such a degree do we make luxuries of bloodshed that we call flesh a 'delicacy,' and forthwith require delicate sauces for this same flesh-meat, and mix together oil and wine and pickle and vinegar with all the spices of Syria and Arabia – for all the world as though we were embalming a human corpse.

After all these heterogenous matters have been mixed and dissolved and, in a manner, corrupted, it is for the stomach, forsooth, to masticate and assimilate them – if it can.

And though this may be, for the time, accomplished, the natural sequence is a variety of diseases produced by imperfect digestion and repletion. Flesh-eating is not unnatural to our physical constitution only. The mind and intellect are made gross by gorging and repletion; for flesh meat and wine may possibly tend to robustness of the body, but it gives only feebleness to the mind...

It is hard to argue with stomachs since they have no ears; and the inebriating potion of custom has been drunk like Circe's, with all its deceptions and witcheries. Now that men are saturated and penetrated, as it were, with love of pleasure, it is not an easy task to attempt to luck out from their bodies the flesh-baited hook.

Well would it be if, as the people of Egypt turning their back to the pure light of day disemboweled their dead and cast away the offal as the very source and origin of their sins, we too, in like manner, were to eradicate bloodshed and gluttony from ourselves and purify the remainder of our lives.

If the irreproachable diet be impossible to any by reason of inveterate habit, at least let them devour their flesh as driven to it by hunger, not in luxurious wantonness, but with feelings of shame. Slay your victim, but at least do so with feelings of pity and pain, not with callous heedlessness wand with torture. And yet that is what is done in a variety of ways."

"Ill-digestion is most to be feared after flesh-eating, for it very soon clogs us and leaves ill consequences behind it. It would be best to accustom ourselves to eat no flesh at all, for the earth affords plenty enough of things fit not only for nourishment, but for delight and enjoyment...

But you, pursuing the pleasures of eating and drinking beyond the satisfaction of nature are punished with many and lingering diseases, which arising from the single fountain of superfluous gormandizing, fill your bodies with all manner of wind and vapors, not easy by purgation to expel. In the first place, all species of the lower animals, according to their kind, feed upon one sort of food which is proper to their natures- some upon grass, some upon roots, and others upon fruits.

Neither do they rob the weaker of their nourishment. But man, such is his voracity, falls upon all to satisfy the pleasures of his appetite, tries all things, tastes all things; and, as if he were yet to see what were the most proper diet and most agreeable to his nature, amongst all animals is the only all-devourous (omnivorous).

He makes us of flesh not out of want and necessity, but out of luxury and being clogged with necessaries, he seeks after an impure and inconvenient diet, purchased by the slaughter of living beings; for this, showing himself more cruel than the most savage of wild beasts.

The lower animals abstain from most of other kinds and are at enmity with only a few, and that only compelled by necessities of hunger: but neither fish nor fowl nor anything that lives upon the land, escapes your tables, though they bear the name of humane and hospitable."

Plutarch's observations are quite true, if a person considers the prey of lions for example when in herds they do not run away once the lion has struck one of their number, aware that the lion struck out of hunger and the necessity to feed its family, they know it will not kill a second time that day. Plutarch teaches humankind to care for animals in sickness and old age:

"For my own part, I would not sell even an old ox that has labored for me."

Plutarch Clarifies Pythagoras' Vegetarianism

Providing the reader with a fuller understanding of the eloquence and passion inherent in Plutarch's ethically advanced vegetarian spirituality, a different translation of a longer extract follows commencing with Plutarch's answer when asked exactly why Pythagoras demanded a vegetarian lifestyle for humanity.

"You ask me upon what ground Pythagoras abstained from feeding on the flesh of animals. I, for my part, marvel of what sort of feeling, mind, or reason, that man possessed who was the first to pollute his mouth with gore, and to allow his lips to touch the flesh of a murdered being; who spread his table with the mangled forms of dead bodies, and claimed as his daily food what were but now beings endowed with movement, with perception, and with voice.

How could his eyes endure the spectacle of the flayed and dismembered limbs? How could his sense of smell endure the horrid effluvium? How, I ask, was his taste not sickened by contact with festering wounds, with the pollution of corrupted blood and juices?...the first man who set the example of this savagery is the person to arraign; not, assuredly, that great mind [Pythagoras] which, in a later age, determined to have nothing to do with such horrors....

Does it not shame you to mingle murder and blood with her beneficent fruits? Other carnivores you call savage and ferocious – lions and tigers and serpents- while yourselves come...in...barbarity. And yet for them murder is the only means of sustenance; whereas to you it is a superfluous luxury and crime.

For in point of fact, we do not kill and eat lions and wolves, as we might do in self-defense - on the contrary, we leave them unmolested; and yet the innocent and the domesticated and helpless and unprovided with weapons of offence – these we hunt and kill, whom nature seems to have brought into existence for their beauty and gracefulness.

Nothing puts us out of countenance, not the charming beauty of their form, not the plaintive sweetness of their voice or cry, not their mental intelligence, not the purity of their diet, not superiority of understanding. For the sake of a part of their flesh only, we deprive them of the glorious light of the sun – of the life, for which they were born.

The plaintive cries they utter, we affect to take to be meaningless; whereas, in fact, they are entreaties and supplications and prayers addressed to us... Alas for our savage inhumanity! It is a terrible thing to see the table of rich men decked out by those layers - out of corpses: the butchers and cooks; a still more terrible sight is the same table after the feast – for the wasted relics are even more than the consumption. These victims, then, have given us their lives uselessly....

Well I have taken away the excuse of those who allege that they have the authority and sanction of Nature. For that man is not, by nature, carnivorous is proved, in the first place, by the external frame of his body - seeing that to none of the animals designed for living on flesh has the human body any resemblance.

He has no curved beak, no sharp talons and claws...no pointed teeth, no intense powers of stomach...On the contrary, by the smoothness of his teeth, the small capacity of his mouth, the softness of his tongue, and the sluggishness of his digestive apparatus, Nature sternly forbids him to feed on flesh.

...If, in spite of all this...kill yourself what you wish to eat...without the use of butcher's knife, or axe, or club. No; as the wolves and lions and bears themselves slay all they feed on, so, in like manner, do you kill the cow or ox with a grip of your jaw, or the pig with your teeth, or a hare or lamb by falling upon and rending them there and then....then sit down to your repast.

If, however, you wait until the living and intelligent existence be deprived of life, and if it would disgust you to have to rend out the heart and shed the life-blood of your victim, why, I ask, in the very fact of nature, and in despite of her, do you feed on beings endowed with sentient life? But more than this – not even, after your victims have been killed, will you eat them just as they are from the slaughter-house. You boil roast and altogether metamorphoses them by fire and condiments. You entirely alter

271

and disguise the murdered animal by use of ten thousand sweet herbs and spices, that your natural taste be deceived and be prepared to take the unnatural food." *20*

From Morals, the section named That Brute Beasts Have Use of Reason Plutarch states:

"That the soule of brute beasts is by nature more kinde, more perfect and better disposed to yield virtue, considering that without compulsion, without commandement or any teaching...Nay what virtue are they not capable of? Yea and more than the wisest man that is." *21*

Platonic Vegetarians: Plotinus (204/5-270 AD) and Porphyry (234-305 AD): Rome 250 AD

Of the cross-cultural, indeed global impact of the ancient Greek vegetarian spiritual philosophy, which endured for many centuries, let us briefly consider Plotinus, who lived in 3rd century AD Rome. He is of interest to our discussions as this Roman vegetarian follower of Plato lived approximately seven centuries after the death of the patriarchal Pythagoras and two and a half centuries after the death of Jesus.

Furthermore, Plotinus lived in Rome, proving the widespread nature of ancient Greek vegetarian spiritual philosophy. Notably, the Romans cumulatively received Paul's distorted and suppressed version of Jesus' original vegetarian teachings. Plotinus is known as a Neo-Platonist due to the profound influence of Platonic vegetarian teachings, integral to his philosophy, which he developed and modified.

Plotinus studied in Alexandria, Egypt and Rome, again proving that even in these ancient times people travelled and with them religious ideas spread vast distances circulating amongst many countries. Importantly, extensive travel led to the philosophical exchange of religious ideas, beliefs and practices, spreading Pythagorean vegetarianism far and wide. Plotinus' most well-known student Porphyry was neither, Roman or Greek.

He was born in Tyre in Phoenicia, now known as the Lebanon. However, living as a Greek, he had an extensive Greek upbringing and education, again corroborating the fact that individuals travelled extensively in the ancient world. Porphyry became Plotinus' biographer and the collector of Plotinus' writings. The various treatises written by Plotinus, particularly during the last twenty years of his life, were collected and systematized by his devotee, Porphyry in 301 AD and are known as the Enneads.

Porphyry's major work is highly praised revealing this compiler's meticulous attention to detail, accurately conveying the rich legacy of his teacher's vegetarian Neo-Platonic spiritual philosophy for posterity. Crucially, Porphyry informs us that Plotinus his master, in harmony with a long line of revered and distinguished predecessors, condemned those who ate animal flesh and those who accepted medicines containing any part of an animal.

Porphyry also tells us of Plotinus' ability during meditation to reach ecstatic union with and enlightenment from the Supreme God. Porphyry became a renowned Greek philosopher in his own right.

The following extracts from the 1957 IVU Congress Souvenir Book (further quoted at www.ivu.org/history/greece_rome/porphyry.html) graphically illustrate Porphyry's committed vegetarianism, continuing a long line of vegetarian spiritual philosophers since the days of Pythagoras:

"It is not from those who have lived on innocent foods that murderers, tyrants, robbers, and sycophants have come, but from eaters of flesh. The necessaries of life are few and easily procured, without violation of justice, liberty, or peace of mind; whereas luxury obliges these ordinary souls who take delight in it to covet riches, to give up their liberty, to sell justice, to misspend their time, to ruin their health, and to renounce the satisfaction of an upright conscience."

"Since, then, justice is due to rational beings, as our opponents allow, how is it possible to evade the admission also that we are bound to act justly towards the races of beings below us? We do not extend the obligations of justice to plants, because there appears in them no indication of reason: although, even in the case of these, while we eat the fruits we do not, with the fruits, cut away the trunks. We use corn and leguminous vegetables when they have fallen on the earth and are dead. But no one uses for food the flesh of dead animals, unless they have been killed by violence, so that there is in these things a radical injustice."

"Wilt thou draw near to [Divinity]? Draw near [Divinity] in being merciful. True mercy is nobility's true badge. ... If we depend on the argument of utility, we cannot avoid admitting by implication that we, ourselves, were created only for the sake of certain destructive animals, such as crocodiles and snakes and other monsters, who seize and destroy men whom they meet – in so doing acting not at all more cruelly than we ... those who first perpetrated these iniquities fatally blunted the most important part of the human mind. Therefore, it is that Pythagoras considers kindness and gentleness to the lower animals to be an exercise of gentleness and philanthropy. ... He who does not restrict harmless conduct to man, but extends it to other animals, most closely approaches Divinity. ... According to Xenocrates ... injure no animals."

The following extracts have been taken from Porphyry's book On Abstinence from Animal Food quoted in the Extended Circle by Jon Wynne-Tyson:

"But to deliver animals to be slaughtered and cooked, and thus be filled with murder, not for the sake of nutriment and satisfying the wants of nature, but making pleasure and gluttony the end of such conduct, is transcendently iniquitous and dire."

274

"He who abstains from anything animate ... will be much more careful not to injure those of his own species. For he who loves the genus will not hate any species of animals."

"And is it not absurd, sine we see that many of our own species live from sense alone, but do not possess intellect and reason; and since we also see that many of them surpass the most terrible of wild beasts in cruelty, anger, and rapine, being murderous of their children and their parents, and also being tyrants and the tools of kings [is it not, I say, absurd] to fancy that we ought to act justly towards these, but that no justice is due from us to the ox that ploughs, the dog that is fed with us, and the animals that nourish us with their milk and adorn our bodies with their wool? Is not such an opinion most irrational and absurd?

Vegetarianism under Attack

From the second half of the 5th century BC the Golden Age of Athens burgeoned. This was an age of unparalleled cultural activity during which the famous Parthenon was built and the public progressively listened to the teachings of Socrates, Plato and Aristotle.

Artistic and intellectual excellence flourished setting ancient Greece as an example for other cultures to follow. Alexander the Great, (356-323 BC) the son of the ruler Philip of Macedon, expanded the Greek Empire through military conquests stretching as far as the Indus River in the east and embracing ancient Egypt in the south.

The blossoming period that ensued after Alexander's death is known as the Hellenistic Age during which Greek culture, philosophy and learning spread extensively across the globe reaching the western world. In 27 BC, years close to the date of Jesus' birth, Greece became the Roman province named Achaea however Greece's cultural excellence continued to be revered and perpetuated by like-minded scholars and their students alike.

Graphically portraying the fierce Roman opposition to vegetarianism that imperiled the Pythagoreans, the Platonists and indeed endangered the first vegetarian followers of Jesus, we learn that:

"Pythagorean ideals found very limited sympathy within the brutality of Ancient Rome, where many wild animals were murdered at the hands of gladiators in the name of sport and spectacle. Pythagoreans were despised as subversives, with many keeping their vegetarianism to themselves for fear of persecution. However, vegetarianism was to spread throughout the Roman Empire from the 3rd to 6th centuries among those influenced by Neo-Platonist philosophy, a progression from the teachings of Plato." *22*

Significantly, the aggressive weight and might of Rome gripped the infant vegetarian Christian Church and vegetarian Pythagoreans and Platonists alike. The violent and hostile Roman anti-vegetarian culture prevailed in this animal eating, blood lust society. Ultimately through the passage of the centuries, flesh eating became the dominant unquestioned norm, historically passed down to unsuspecting Christians to this day. Proof of Jesus' vegetarianism and the suppression of his vegetarian teachings will be discussed later in this serialized research.

The greedy fingers of the Roman flesh-eating society progressively stretched out across the lands. Harnessing, controlling and dominating an empire that mirrored Rome, which increasingly became the absolute antithesis of the cultured, intellectual, ethically advanced vegetarianism of Pythagoreanism. Pythagoreanism was perpetuated by many generations of eminent like-minded philosophers. The newly instated Roman rule of the lands of Jesus' birth heralded the direct opposite of Jesus', 'the Son of the Man's,' authentic and undistorted brand of vegetarian Jewish-Christianity.

The all-inclusive, compassionate vegetarian Jesus, taught his followers and their descendants to use him as a role model and to offer kindness to all those who were hitherto shunned, disadvantaged, down-trodden, exploited and neglected by society, human and animal alike.

This included showing kindness to the socially alienated, isolated and ostracized, the untouchables, the lepers, the prostitutes, the Samaritans, the tax collectors and the burdened, innocent, vulnerable animals so often mentioned in Jesus' teachings. Jesus' all-embracing, compassionate, vegetarian teachings by their very nature were extended to our fellow animal relatives.

Jesus' vegetarian teachings were loyally perpetuated by Jesus' disciples. However, even as they became his apostles they faced the same persecution and underlying opposition from religio-political authorities as Jesus during his lifetime. Later their vegetarian voice was also suppressed by Paul, who was known long term by the apostles as 'the enemy.'

Paul, the former murderer of Christians turned self-appointed apostle sought to make Jesus' vegetarian Jewish-Christianity, as practiced by the first followers of Jesus, more palatable to foreign animal flesh eating converts. Consequently, vegetarianism was unimportant to Paul who watered it down and finally suppressed it, to the utter dismay of Jesus' apostles. Paul had never known Jesus, in sharp contrast to the true apostles who had lived with Jesus' tutelage for years. In terms of Paul's negation of Jesus and his family's vegetarianism, Paul became the direct opposite of Jesus' mission.

Plato's famous Academy that had perpetuated the highest virtues of humanity inevitably expressed through vegetarianism for one thousand years was closed in 529 AD by a Christian emperor known as Justinian and the medieval Christian philosophers deliberately looked amongst Aristotle's contradictory views on animals to search out those that opposed vegetarianism and put paid to his long line of legendary vegetarian predecessors.

The following is taken from an extract from a review of Animal Minds and Human Morals – The Origins of the Western Debate by Richard Sorabji: Review by Stephen Salkever. Shown at www.ivu.org/history/greece_rome/plutarch.html:

"For Sorabji, the pro-animal side of the ancient debate, the side arguing that the gap between human and animal psychology is not so large, is best represented by various Aristotelians (especially Theophrastus, Aristotle's successor as leader of the Peripatos) and Platonists (especially Plutarch and Porphyry). A key figure in Sorabji's history of the fading away of this alternative is Iamblichus, who turned Neoplatonism away from its earlier assertions of a significant kinship between humans and other animals and so sets the stage for the nearly complete triumph of the anti-animal view."

Surely, it is ridiculous to suggest that Jesus, famed for his all-inclusive compassion, did not possess as much all-embracing compassion as the Greek vegetarian spiritual philosophers whose vegetarian spiritual philosophy flourished, spreading far and wide across the globe, many centuries before Jesus' birth and many centuries after Jesus' death?

Demonstrated by his parables, Jesus embraced and intertwined the suffering of animals and humans alike and for this he was aptly named the Good Shepherd, whose teachings initiated a religion surviving twenty centuries after his death but not without distortion and suppression of his original vegetarian teachings.

Let us now consider the ancient religious concept, touched upon in this chapter, of the transmigration of the soul. This religious conviction, typically intertwined with vegetarianism, arose independently amongst the earliest peoples, joint spiritual principles that have enveloped, historically to present day, a large proportion of our planet.

CHAPTER 8 – GLOBAL BELIEFS IN THE TRANSMIGRATION OF THE SOUL

Stop beating him, [the dog] for I recognized a friend's
soul when I heard his voice.
Pythagoras

Animals share with us the privilege of having a soul.
Pythagoras

The soul is the same in all living creatures, although
the body of each is different.
Hippocrates

In the last chapter of this volume let us briefly look at the ancient, on-going and world-wide belief in the transmigration of the soul which was mentioned in the last chapter in terms of the ancient Greeks who were major proponents of this spiritual belief which is typically accompanied by vegetarianism. Whilst the Greeks arrived at these spiritual concepts from a blend of intuition, mystical experiences and profoundly wise, far-sighted intellectual deductions many other peoples across the globe from the most primitive times also held parallel beliefs in the transmigration of the soul.

Importantly, it will be shown that this belief was born in humankind's earliest spiritual consciousness as a form of instinctive, inborn knowingness and continues today to be integral to the beliefs and practices of a large proportion of the planet. Consequently, the transmigration of the soul characteristically accompanied by vegetarianism is certainly worth great respect and consideration.

Let us commence this summary account of humankind's shared belief in the transmigration of the soul with a brief overview of some of the ancient Greek contributions to civilization. Proving the foundational contributions to present-day academia of many acclaimed ancient Greeks should help us gain a profound respect for their spiritually elevated practice of vegetarianism together with their deductive belief in the transmigration of the soul as these highly accomplished intellectual fathers of academia may well have discovered the answer to yet another of life's mysteries.

Indeed, as these astounding ancient Greek geniuses teach us, almost certainly an individual's soul does transmigrate at death from one animal body to another, both human and non-human, for yet another incarnation.

Herodotus, Hippocrates, Euclid, Aeschylus, Aristophanes, Sophocles, Homer, Pindar, Sappho, Parmenides and Aesop

Herodotus (484-425 BC) is celebrated today as being the Father of History; his extensive writings detail many ancient historical events, including the Persian Wars. Hippocrates (460-377 BC) is hailed today as the Father of Western Medicine; he was a brilliant pioneering medical scientist. Still today, newly trained doctors take the Hippocratic Oath, swearing to do their best to heal the sick.

Notably, Hippocrates is famed for his all-inclusive compassionate statement: "The soul is the same in all living creatures, although the body of each is different." Euclid, the brilliant mathematician is applauded today as the Father of

Geometry, his book, Elements, is recognized by scholars as being the most famous book on mathematics ever. This ancient Greek studied in Plato's Academy in Athens but also emigrated to Alexandria, Egypt, during the reign of Ptolemy I (323-283 BC).

Ancient Greece also produced many renowned playwrights including examples such as Aeschylus (525-456 BC), honored today as the Father of Tragedy whilst Aristophanes (450-388 BC), the Athenian playwright is venerated today as the Father of Comedy due to him being the best writer of comedy in literary history.

The extremely popular Sophocles, (496-406/405 BC), born in Colonus, now part of Athens, won many ancient competitions for his works; it is believed he wrote more than one hundred plays. Famous, ancient Greek poets include Homer, (9th-7th centuries BC), celebrated for his two epic poems, making him the most supreme poet of classical antiquity.

Living in such ancient days we know little about Homer except clues gained from the Iliad set in the ancient Greek city of Troy and the Odyssey, in which the characters return from Troy to the island of Ithaca. Due to the fact that 'homros' meant 'blind man,' there may have been two brilliant Homers, who wrote the above two epic poems, namely blind old men who wandered entertaining the populace reciting heroic legends in return for money.

Pindar, (522-443 BC), famous for his odes, is believed to be the best of Greece's nine lyric poets. The incredible female poet, Sappho (600 BC) whose voice tells us most distinctly about herself and others, is famed for her extremely popular romantic lyric poems. Sappho was born in Lesbos a large island in the Aegean which is now Turkey, in exile she later lived in Sicily, revealing yet again that travel in these ancient times was common.

The diligent genius of Parmenides is demonstrated by his brilliant deductions after observing an eclipse of the Moon in approximately 470 BC. Paying attention to detail, he noticed the eclipse resulted in the earth having a curved shadow. Consequently, this ancient assiduous intellectual construed that the Earth must be round, a fact that was not accepted in Europe until many centuries later!

Living in approximately 550 BC, Aesop, famed for Aesop's fables, told countless stories using a wide-range of talking animals. Each of his remarkable and fascinating fables, teach his readers a vital message of wisdom and morals. It is a mystery whether Aesop was indeed a fable himself and whether the stories were historically composed by an unknown author. Accounts tell us that Aesop was a Greek slave living in Rome, freed by his Roman master as a reward for delighting him with his enthralling, thought-provoking stories of talking animals.

It is believed that Aesop's fables were written down and recorded for posterity after his death. Aesop's fine accomplishment is confirmed by the fact that his ethically orientated stories, which were first told 2,500 years ago, entertaining and enlightening the ancient Greeks, have cumulatively been translated into most languages, remaining incredibly popular in the 21st century AD. Aesop's tales are in harmony with the teachings of Socrates who believed virtue was born of knowledge.

Introducing the Ancient Greek Belief in the Transmigration of the Soul

In order to gain a deeper insight into the Greek all-inclusive, non-violent, benevolent vegetarian teachings, deeply ingrained into the Greek spiritual consciousness, it will be helpful to provide the reader with a brief survey of the Greek belief in the transmigration of the soul alternatively known as reincarnation or metempsychosis.

The ancient Greek spiritual philosophy regarding the human animal's correct relationship with fellow animals is an encyclopedic topic, due to the limitations of time and space, the fascinating, astute, perceptive and intuitive belief in the transmigration of the soul will be summarized, presenting the salient points.

Employing their impeccable intellectual scholarly insights and unassailable problem solving abilities, the ancient Greek philosophers gained understanding of a whole range of spiritual mysteries. To do this they employed their wisdom, logic, intuition and profound mystical experiences of the Divine.

The results of this array of research into life's perplexing mysteries led to conclusions, giving rise to their vegetarian spiritual philosophy, to ultimately end violence on our planet and instigate healthier, more spiritually advanced lives and their certainty that the soul transmigrates at death from the human animal to the non-human animal and vice versa. They came to believe in the supreme God and advanced knowledge into the true nature of reality.

For example, apart from the transmigration of the soul and vegetarianism, Plato taught creation was brought into being by a Divine Craftsman whilst the material world including the body is perishable and the world of forms of true piety including perfect justice and the soul is everlasting and immortal. Whilst Aristotle believed in a great chain of being, at the bottom end was unknowable pure matter - mere potentiality – which ranged to the highest end consisting of pure form which is God – namely perfect actuality.

Significantly, among the most notable of these ancient, incontestable geniuses, were Pythagoras, Socrates and Plato who each arrived at deeply profound conclusions deducing that the soul as a natural law of the universe transmigrates to a new human or animal, physical body at death. They upheld the necessity for humanity to act in accordance with its higher nature, living healthy, non-violent, compassionate, vegetarian lives whilst vegetarianism was also fundamentally intertwined with the belief in the transmigration of the soul.

Remarkably, these invincible academics' endless debates resulted in, philosophic and spiritual analyses which were far in advance of the fiercely endorsed, simplistic, systematized dogmas, invented and policed by later rivals, such as the council members of the powerful Christian Orthodoxy. Although these spiritual philosophers, who were indeed veritable polymaths, came to the fore from approximately the 6th BC, their contributions to human knowledge has had a far reaching influence on global cultures.

In sharp contrast to that, ironically, many people today are not aware of their spiritual philosophy, integral to which were the concepts of reincarnation and vegetarianism, which were fundamental to many of humankind's religious beliefs, yet have become lost to us today due to Jewish, Christian, and Islamic Orthodoxy's suppression of them!

Accepted for their genius, it is paradoxical that an average person today is unaware of their vegetarianism and conviction that the soul transmigrates at death. Many people today would be astounded by their immense intellect which gave rise to many academic subjects and the enormous range and depth of knowledge of these eminent minds components of which have been deliberately silenced by the powerful, adversarial members of religious Orthodoxy.

Orphism at the Heart of Ancient Greek Religious Beliefs

Orphism, the ancient Greek mystery cult was an extremely influential vegetarian religious movement that flourished in ancient Greece in the early 5th century BC and had its origins in the 6th century BC. This Dionysian cult had its origins in Thrace. Converts were taught to use ascetic practices including meditation, prayer and vegetarianism to free themselves from bodily entanglement, which would ultimately lead to the reward of immortality.

The concept of the transmigration of the soul from one life form to another, human and animal, was fundamental to Orphic beliefs. Significantly, devotees were to dedicate their lives to the attainment of life in the next world. These ancients possessed great reverence and admiration for fellow animals, encouraging exceedingly compassionate relationships with them.

Notably, due to the concept of the Orphic belief in the transmigration of the soul there is not a "them" and "us," the destinies of the two are irrevocably and eternally interweaved.

At death they believed their soul would be temporarily liberated only to be imprisoned again in the next physical body, human and animal. They trusted that through experiencing the world from the perspective of different creatures, an individual's soul would gain the opportunity to develop spiritually. Each successive incarnation was dependent upon the ethical, compassionate quality of their previous incarnation. This burgeoning religious cult taught that the soul had become polluted by a primordial error and being no longer pure it had become trapped in a physical body.

Significantly, by rejecting animal flesh both for food and clothing, they released themselves from humanity's shared responsibility for animal suffering and murder. Through their vegetarianism, no animal was slain on their behalf. As a consequence, fewer animals were slaughtered and if everyone joined their ranks, no-one would choose to eat animals and no animal would suffer cruel exploitation, victimization and massacre. Importantly, great store was set in vegetarianism, meditative practices and prayer to promote and enhance the spiritual quality of Greek souls.

Pythagoras (530 BC) the religious teacher and philosopher absorbed many ascetic Orphic spiritual concepts including the transmigration of the soul and vegetarianism into his spiritual doctrines and thus demanded ethically elevated vegetarian behavior from his followers. Notably Pythagoras taught his followers that all human animals, all non-human animals and all plants possess souls.

Orphic beliefs were transmitted from Pythagoras to Socrates and later to Plato (427-347 BC), who each taught the need for highly ethical behavior, vegetarianism and the concept of the transmigration of the beautiful, immortal soul. In particular, Plato discusses the immortal soul in his writings known as Phaedo.

Ancient Greece: The Transmigration of the Soul and Vegetarianism

Due to the predominant staunch, ancient Greek conviction that at physical death, souls as a fact of nature reincarnate in an almost relentless cycle of rebirth, into animal bodies, both human and non-human, they confidently regarded human and animal life as interchangeable. During the practically unremitting cycle of rebirth, the ancient Greeks believed that all beings make a transition at death and reincarnate and all are beings are governed by this continuous life process.

They believed that the beautiful immortal soul dwells for an infinite number of life times in human and animal bodies, gaining experience from the perspective of each life time, cumulatively learning wisdom and virtues. This age-old theory expresses humankind's intuitive spiritual belief in the unity and kinship of all living creatures and the need to have more than one lifetime to experience and learn, thereby evolving and advancing each and every souls level of spirituality.

Inevitably, the ancient Greek followers of these entrenched beliefs, fostered tender care, empathy, kindness and respect for fellow animals and in so doing nurtured and developed their own level of spirituality. Acting with confidant certainty they were educated not to harm our extended animal family instead to show our reincarnated flesh and blood fathers, mothers, brothers, sisters and children, the utmost humanitarian charity.

Apart from encompassing all beings with the creed of kindness and compassion, as members of our single earth family, mutually sharing our planetary home, there was indeed the most elevated spirituality, logic and wisdom inherent in their benevolent vegetarianism.

The Greeks were certain of the fact that inevitably all future human incarnations would intermittently take the form of a non-human animal. They hoped that their many anticipated future animal lifetimes would not be characterized by human cruelty, exploitation, suffering and slaughter. They held the conviction that those individuals who do eat animal flesh are to be held responsible for the suffering and murder of all animals, any of whom could be a beloved relative who has newly reincarnated as a non-human animal.

The transmigration of the soul was integral to Greek thought, demonstrated by the ancient spiritual, vegetarian philosophy of Pherecydes of Syros during the 6th century BC. Pherecydes was the teacher of the brilliant student Pythagoras who became a famous teacher himself. This concept with its inevitable vegetarian consequences was further elaborated by the eminent philosopher Plato and later by the esteemed Plotinus (205-270 AD).

Illustrious teachers such as Pythagoras, Plato, Empedocles and Plotinus were indeed legendary during their lifetimes. Their vegetarian spiritual philosophy impacted the globe, gaining many students who travelled far and wide to gain the honor of being mentored by them so they could follow their insightful, enlightened and far-sighted vegetarian spiritual philosophy.

The famous, highly regarded vegetarian philosophers such as Pythagoras, Empedocles, Plato and Plotinus and their philosophical lineages, namely successive generations of students who spread their masters' vegetarian teachings, continued to teach that the soul migrates at physical death, reincarnating as animals, human and non-human. Empedocles' (490-430 BC) writings reflect Pythagorean thought as he was significantly influenced by this celebrated, earlier mentor.

Amazingly, Empedocles who lived in such ancient times taught that nothing in the universe is ever created or destroyed, it simply changes, transmuting in form. His deductions relate to the soul; when the physical body dies, the non-physical soul, spirit or consciousness, leaves the body, continuing to live, having transmuted in form.

Significantly, modern day physicists have indeed verified Empedocles' ancient deductions, proving that energy cannot be destroyed but does indeed transmute in form! Perhaps we should also take note of Empedocles' findings when he stated that it would take thirty thousand years and an infinite number of incarnations for a soul to achieve liberation from the physical condition. For Empedocles, the route to freedom from endless rebirths was to carry out a purification process, the most important aspect of which was to totally abstain from eating animal flesh as animals incarnate as humans and humans incarnate as animals, the two being irrevocably intertwined. This compassionate spiritual philosophy held that it is totally wrong to take the life of any living creature, warning that any soul may find itself mercilessly victimized and murdered on behalf of the food preferences of an animal flesh eater.

Plato makes his religious beliefs in the reality of the non-physical realms contrasted with the physical life known in his writings known as the Republic. Here he tells us about a man called Er who at death made his transition from the physical to the non-physical realms. Er then returned to the physical life to describe the scenes he witnessed in the after-death landscapes. Significantly, Er described his experience in the celestial regions, of watching souls choosing animal bodies human and non-human for the lessons they would learn in these bodies for their next incarnation on earth.

"After death, he said he went with others to the place of Judgment and saw the souls returning from heaven, and proceeded with them to a place where they chose new lives, human and animal. He saw the soul of Orpheus changing into a swan, Thamyras becoming a nightingale, musical birds choosing to be men, the soul of Atlanta choosing the honors of an athlete.

Men were seen passing into animals and wild and tame animals changing into each other. After their choice the souls drank of Lethe and then shot away like stars to their birth. There are myths and theories to the same effect in other dialogues, the Phaedrus, Meno, Phaedo, Timaeus and Laws." *1*

In his writings of 360 BC, known as Timaeus, Plato writes in the form of questions and answers known as a Socratic dialogue. These conversations reflect the results of Plato's experiences, insights, research and beliefs as he discusses the nature of the physical world, the creatures that live on it and the purpose and properties of the universe. Remarkably, gaining the following profound insight from Pythagoras, Plato tells us that the world too, is a living organism that possesses intelligence.

The present day theory of Gaia, suggesting that the earth is a living organism is therefore not a modern discovery. Instead, this highly perceptive insight has been derived from the ancient teachings of Pythagoras and Plato.

Reincarnation an Ancient, Global Belief

Believing life to be a continuous process without end, the ancient Greeks deemed the process of transmigration to be inevitable. This endless wheel of life afforded every living soul the opportunity to evolve spiritually as a result of the experiences gained and choices made in each successive life time. The belief in the transmigration of the soul and vegetarianism impacted the world before, during and after Jesus lived.

Due to the fact that these spiritual concepts impacted Jesus' world, it is beneficial to provide the following brief overview, proving that the beliefs in the transmigration of the soul and vegetarianism were not exclusive to Greek thought but will be shown to be inherent in the belief systems of many human cultures, indeed being historically and globally pervasive.

These spiritual concepts emerged independently across the globe in ancient preliterate tribal communities. Notably, the spiritual and intellectual discovery of this innate wisdom was indeed born independently on many continents across the globe revealing powerful evidence that the belief in the transmigration of the soul at physical death was a product of human spiritual intuition and mystical experiences supported later, by intellectual reasoning.

The eminent Greek spiritual philosophers dating from the 6th century BC found the belief in successive rebirths in different incarnations to be a perfectly natural, reasonable and understandable method for the progressive education, maturation and spiritualization of the soul of all living creatures.

It will remain a mystery whether the ancient Greeks originally received the spiritual concepts of the transmigration of the soul and vegetarianism from ancient Egypt, India or from other early cultures, or whether these beliefs were inherent in their own early beginnings.

Consequently, the ancient Greek belief in the transmigration of the soul and vegetarianism is old as humankind itself. These beliefs are fundamental to many world-wide spiritual philosophies, dominating the historic and contemporary beliefs of a large proportion of our planet. The later rise of the Orthodox

Christian Church led to the suppression of pervasive beliefs in reincarnation and vegetarianism amongst Christians.

The concept of the transmigration of the soul was/is central to the spiritual philosophies of many human cultures from the earliest times to present day. While most of these religious traditions hold that an individual's soul, (spirit, life force, consciousness, disembodied personality) successively reincarnates at physical death into a series of human and animal bodies, some cultures believe this includes the bodies of insects and plants.

The belief in the transmigration of the soul is found worldwide in the earliest tribal religions of non-literate cultures, including those in central Australia and West Africa. This concept, typically intertwined with vegetarianism, is also the central doctrine and norm for the countless millions of followers of many ancient yet on-going world religions practiced in the 21st century AD, including Hinduism, Buddhism and Jainism.

Of these vegetarian religions there are approximately 376 million Buddhists, 851 million Hindus and over 15 million Jains found worldwide today. In particular, this ancient religious belief matured and flourished both in ancient India and ancient Greece spilling out across borders frequently along multiple and labyrinthine, far reaching, land and sea trade routes.

Notably, belief in the transmigration of the soul was also integral to the teachings of Manichaeism in Persia during the 3rd century AD and in the later religion of Sikhism which commenced during the life of its founder Guru Nanak (1469-1539AD). Guru Nanak's core teachings were cumulatively developed into a religion by a number of successor Gurus.

This line ended with the death of Guru Gobind Singh in 1708. As indicated earlier Judaism, Christianity and Islam lost touch with these spiritual beliefs due to the increasingly powerful Orthodox opinion amongst Judaism, Christianity and Islam which chose to divorce these religions from the extensive and enduring doctrines of the transmigration of the soul which is frequently intertwined with vegetarianism.

Transmigration: On-Going Stone Age Arunta Tribe, Australia

The fascinating Arunta (Arunda) tribe of central Australia has been designated in modern times as an on-going Stone Age society. Astonishingly, this tribe continues to live as Stone Age men and women in the 21st century AD, due to their isolation from the modern world. Uniquely, their beliefs and practices have been frozen in time comparable to a preserved yet living fossil.

Notably, the members of the Arunta tribe continue to teach the concept of the transmigration of the soul and pre-existence offering further excellent proof that this principle originated with the intuitive spiritual consciousness of the first members of humankind. Indeed, this ancient belief was confirmed by the perceptive, intuitive, mystical and logical deductions of the ancient Greek scholarly spiritual philosophers.

Transmigration: The Aborigines of Australia

The Australian Aborigines are a further ancient and on-going tribal society whose members are certain of their conviction that the soul transmigrates, changing bodies at death. Contemporary Aborigines are as assured today as they were historically that repeatedly newly reincarnated souls animate a wide range of life forms including insects and animals, human and non-human. Due to the belief that our ancestors return to live physical lives on the earth, inhabiting the bodies of an assortment of living creatures, the belief in the transmigration of the soul is sometimes associated with ancestor worship.

Transmigration: Yoruba, Edo and Zulu Tribes of Africa

Interestingly, each and every male baby born among the Yoruba and Edo tribes of Africa is called, 'father has returned' and all female babies are called, 'mother has returned.' The belief in the transmigration of the soul is also integral to Zulu religious beliefs which assert that a soul's countless succeeding incarnations range from the soul dwelling in the smallest insect to the most enormous elephant.

Transmigration: Ancient Egyptian Vegetarianism

Herodotus, the ancient Greek historian, informs us that the ancient Egyptians were among the first civilizations to hold the joint convictions that the soul transmigrates at death and vegetarianism. These religious concepts were taught to the public by the royal cultus of the ancient Egyptian pharaohs.

Astonishingly, the Egyptian principles of vegetarianism and the transmigration of the soul are incredibly ancient as the Vegetarian Society clarifies: "A vegetarian ideology was practiced among religious groups in Egypt around 3200 BC, with abstinence from flesh based upon karmic beliefs in reincarnation."*2*

Interestingly, Herodotus tells us that the ancient Egyptians believed that for three thousand years, repeatedly at death, the soul is subject to a succession of rebirths experiencing life as a terrestrial, marine and aerial animal before incarnating as a human animal again. They too believed that each incarnation allowed the soul to learn and evolve. Experiencing life from the perspective of a diverse range of life forms, each soul increasingly accrues a vast wealth of experience.

Successive life times, progressively offer each individual soul, the opportunity to nurture and heighten its level of spirituality through the attainment of empathy, compassion, understanding, sympathy, responsiveness, fellow-feeling, respect and identification with all our related fellow sentient beings and all other creatures.

Transmigration: Hindu Vegetarians

Kindness, admiration and reverence for all life forms who are relentlessly bound together by the perfectly just principle of karma and the transmigration of the soul, is a conviction inseparable from vegetarianism. Consequently, vast numbers of ancient peoples and civilizations who believed in these doctrines ate a vegetarian diet, notably millions of vegetarians live around the world today.

"Abstention from meat was central to such early philosophies as Hinduism, Brahmanism, Zoroastrianism and Jainism. Vegetarianism was encouraged in the ancient verses of the Upanishads and also mentioned in the Rig Veda—the most sacred of ancient Hindu texts. Pivotal to such religions were doctrines of non-violence and respect for all life forms." *3*

Notably, the ancient metaphysical religion of Hinduism teaches the concept of the transmigration of the soul, through which Hindus aspire to evolve spiritually throughout the course of many lifetimes. Hindus strive to accomplish the ultimate mystical goal which is to finally end the cycle of rebirth. To do this Hindus strive to transform, advance, uplift and spiritualize their consciousness through meditative practices attempting to attain a spiritual union with the eternal, universal spirit known as Brahman (God).

The hierarchical status of each lifetime, bestows upon the soul, advantages and disadvantages, which are considered to be directly deserved by the soul as a reward or punishment for its former good or bad thoughts and actions. This perfect form of justice is known as karma. All souls, those of animals, human and non-human, find they have progressed and regressed, the latter is due to their own failings.

The Creator's perfect form of divine justice is perceived to take the form of God working through natural events and these laws of nature determine the nature and form of each rebirth. Each lifetime is viewed as offering new opportunities for the soul to progress and enhance its level of spirituality, no lifetime should be wasted, as all life forms are precious and have much to teach each soul.

The unremitting wheel of individuality is believed to finally cease when the soul ultimately attains union with God, known as the transcendent consciousness. Unification with God is believed to be the true spiritual destiny for all living creatures. Notably, all life forms, all of which have immortal souls, experience incarnations as animals, human and non-human, therefore all souls/all life forms are fundamentally and intrinsically bound together.

All life forms are essentially linked on a soul level. They are interrelated and interdependent on a physical level too having evolved side by side over countless millennia from a shared common ancestor. Vegetarianism and the belief in the transmigration of the soul are doctrines fundamental to Hinduism. In modern times, there are approximately 851 million Hindus alive today.

Transmigration: Buddhist Vegetarians

Authentic Buddhists are vegetarian as vegetarianism is known to progressively teach an individual, ever growing heights of compassion. The attainment of compassion is the first step for all truth seekers on the spiritual journey. Buddhists also believe in the transmigration of the soul, confirming that birth and death are mere interruptions in the infinite, on-going process of life.

Typically, they believe the nature of the life and body in which the soul reincarnates is dependent on the level of spirituality achieved during the souls' previous lifetime or the lessons the soul newly seeks to learn. They also believe that the soul may receive an extremely challenging incarnation as it is aspiring to gain ethically advanced qualities in its next incarnation. Notably, many souls dwelling in animals show souls dwelling in human bodies astonishing levels of forgiveness, love and loyalty indicating that these apparent, so-called 'animal souls,' are indeed, highly ethically advanced souls.

Buddhists possess some minor differences in their belief system. Some believe that a soul at death is reincarnated in each of the following bodies; as a god, an animal, a ghost and as a creature of hell. Some Buddhists believe reincarnation to be the rebirth of character but not a transmigration of the self, indicating that a person's thought forms reappear but no ego entity travels from body to body. The following famous Buddhist saying graphically illustrates the Buddhist belief that all life forms are precious:

"One hundred thousand universes conspire in the creation of the iridescent eye that graces the feather in the peacock's tail."

Tibetan Buddhists carefully observe their children as they grow up in order to discover which child is the newly reincarnated lama, their holy leader.

"Vegetarianism has always been central to Buddhism, which enshrines compassion to all living creatures. The Indian king Asoka [who reigned between 264-232 BC] converted to Buddhism, shocked by the horrors of battle. Animal sacrifices were ended as his kingdom became vegetarian." *4* Vegetarianism and the belief in the transmigration of the soul are core doctrines essential to Buddhism. In contemporary times, there are approximately 376 million practicing Buddhists in the 21st century AD.

Transmigration: Jain Vegetarians

The Indian prophet, Mahavira (599-527 BC) also known as Vardhamana, founded the religion of Jainism. Central to Jain teachings is the conviction that the soul transmigrates at physical death to human and animal bodies, practically endlessly from one life time to another, in order to advance the soul's spirituality ultimately gaining spiritual enlightenment. Integral to the ancient and on-going Jain belief in the transmigration of the soul and karma, is the compassionate prohibition of eating animal flesh.

Consequently, vegetarianism associated with beliefs, in the transmigration of the soul has a diverse, extensive and ancient history. Vegetarianism and the belief in the transmigration of the soul are creeds central to the religion of Jainism. In present day times, there are approximately 15 million Jains in the 21st century AD.

Judaism and Vegetarianism

Vegetarianism was not exclusive to the civilizations and peoples mentioned above. There were many ancient Jewish sects living as communities who were strict vegetarians. By the 2nd century BC., some of these vegetarian Jewish settlements were called Essenes, which is best understood as an umbrella term. In keeping with their respect and compassion for animals as co-creations of God, these Jews and their forebears condemned animal sacrifices, with just as much fervor as they upheld their vegetarianism. The denunciation of animal sacrifice was integral to their vegetarianism, as these two compassionate concepts were frequently intertwined.

They adhered to the 7th and 8th century BC prophets' compassionate condemnation of animal sacrifice which was typically carried out in order for the animal flesh to be eaten afterwards. Notably, ancient Jewish sects, obeying the first commandment not to kill, who will be discussed later in this serialized volume, associated with the proof of Jesus' vegetarianism, shared their vegetarianism with many other historical peoples, whose pervasive vegetarianism and belief in the transmigration of the soul impacted enormous areas of the globe. Let us now turn to the Conclusion, which draws the first installment of the Animal Souls serialization to a close.

CONCLUSION

"At the moment our human world is based on the suffering and destruction of millions of non-humans. To perceive this and to do something to change it in personal and public ways is to undergo a change of perception akin to a religious conversion. Nothing can ever be seen in quite the same way again because once you have admitted the terror and pain of other species you will, unless you resist conversion, be always aware of the endless permutations of suffering that support our society."

Sir Arthur Conan Doyle (1859-1930)

My Animal Souls serialization, offers a window into the past, delivering a clearer understanding of the vegetarian ways of the ancient world, molded by a wide variety of ethically advanced vegetarian religious traditions, prevalent many centuries before and after the spiritual ministry of Jesus. Advancing our understanding, this series provides valuable, insightful, background information revealing how the world in which Jesus lived was chiefly shaped by spiritually elevated vegetarian teachings.

This serialized research progressively transports the reader on a fascinating journey of discovery into a bygone age, astonishingly, laying bare the predominantly vegetarian ancient world, very different to the animal-flesh eating lifestyle that dominated later. Due to the expansive network in the ancient world of tirelessly travelled land and sea, trade routes, religious teachings were transported and exchanged along with people and merchandise from continent to continent. No culture was an isolated island instead each was bathed in the beliefs and traditions of other cultures.

This survey increasingly reveals that the major powerful and pervasive cultures of the distant past had spiritual vegetarian roots. Shockingly, to the materialist, factory farming, industrialized animal genocide world of today, most historic animals lived in a very different, predominantly vegetarian world, proving that vegetarianism is not a peculiar idiosyncratic modern-day fad, but a return to the spiritual norm of billions of people who lived during the days of antiquity!

We pride ourselves today for being technologically advanced however technology underlies the construction of weapons of war. Consequently, the peace-loving vegetarian ministries of ancient prophetic teachers and the civilizations that followed their doctrines were in many ways our spiritual superiors.

As disclosed in the introduction to this serialized research, these pages are progressively exploring and assessing the many different historical vegetarian cultures, each demonstrating the most elevated spiritual ideals. The vegetarian spiritual philosophies that have been evaluated in this installment include the vegetarianism of the ancient Egyptians, that of Confucius, spread through Confucianism and the many generations of vegetarian, Greek, spiritual philosophers.

The highly ethically advanced spiritual teachings fundamental to vegetarianism traversed many cultures and spanned innumerable centuries. You are now invited to again be taken back in time to the ancient realities of vegetarianism in the next installments of this serialized research. Together, we will experience the vegetarianism of the ancient authentic Hindus and Buddhists, the early Jewish sects known as the Essenes/Nazareans and of course the evidence for Jesus' vegetarianism.

The original, unadulterated teachings of each spiritual philosophy demanded converts demonstrate the utmost respect, fellow-feeling, empathy and compassion for all life forms, promoting creativity not destruction. These vegetarian religious teachings were nurtured and fuelled by the ethos of peace, harmony and non-violence to all animals, human and non-human alike.

These spiritually advanced doctrines, historically shaped and continue today to influence how a person lives his/her life, condemning the exploitation, abuse and murder of all 'living souls,' human and non-human animals, most of whom are sentient, conscious, feeling, flesh and blood beings like ourselves.

The earlier pages in this serialized volume prepare the ground for the later examination of the original, authentic teachings of Jesus, lost throughout the centuries and formerly concealed from us today. Accounts of Jesus' teachings were hidden by their guardians to protect them from the all-consuming avalanche of suppression and distortion directed by the man-made whims of religio-political authorities.

As revealed in the introduction to the Animal Souls research, archaeological discoveries of irreplaceable, precious scriptures, hidden from those who sought to destroy them, shine a clear torch light on the persecution and oppression that took place after Jesus' death, whilst Christianity was evolving as a religion. Raised awareness of this state of affairs, progressively provides the reader with a deeper understanding of the religio-political oppression that subjugated and distorted Jesus' true and original vegetarian teachings which continued to be thwarted after his death by opposition to Jesus' faithful vegetarian disciples.

The on-going harassment, censorship and containment faced by Jesus throughout his spiritual ministry continued after his death to impede his loyal disciples. Honoring their dedication to him, they were committed to the preservation, dissemination and immortalization of Jesus' entire and authentic teachings, including his vegetarianism.

However, their perpetuating vegetarian ministries were opposed, falsified and later silenced by the decisions and accretions of the self-appointed apostle Paul, who had never met the man, Jesus and by the religio-political council members of later Orthodox Christianity.

Tragically, Jesus' vegetarian teachings demanding all-inclusive compassion for all flesh and blood animals, human and non-human, had become all but lost to us today as the highly profitable man-made opposition to vegetarianism, indoctrinating children with animal cookery shows, resulting in ignorant or indulgent human food preferences has created an animal flesh eating society.

Vegetarianism is a way of life which epitomizes, exemplifies and demonstrates some of the most spiritually elevated divine and/or humanitarian commands. It will become increasingly apparent that human intervention curtailed and distorted Jesus' original vegetarian teachings, deciding which beings would reap the benefits of compassionate treatment and which tragic beings would not.

As will become clear throughout the course of this research, opposition to Jesus' vegetarianism, the vegetarianism of Jesus' family and the vegetarianism of his disciples' was first carried out by Paul who graphically rebuked Jesus' disciples. It should be remembered that Paul was the man capable of relentlessly persecuting and killing early Christians and as the Jesus movement proved unstoppable, Paul later competed with the apostles' spiritual leadership, despite them being personally trained by Jesus to spread his spiritual vegetarian teachings.

Opposition to vegetarianism was continued by later politico-religious orthodoxy, each limiting the range of Jesus' all-embracing compassion which originally extended to all destitute, oppressed, neglected, vulnerable animals, human and non-human. Jesus was acutely aware that all of whom are sentient beings who desperately fear murder and most certainly feel pain and suffering. Importantly, even the non-flesh and blood creatures demonstrate stress, suffering and feel the pain of death. Jesus taught that all creatures are the children of the ever-concerned creative parent God.

Regarding the vegetarian roots of religions, committed followers of religion typically accept that God, the compassionate creator is omniscient, omnipotent and omnipresent. How then have they become blinded to the fact that the very soul of the God they believe in, is graphically fractured and tormented, vividly feeling every stage of suffering and pain of every individual animal's plight and murder?

Religious devotees from the most ancient times were aware of these profound insights and as such were vegetarian. The answer lies in the fact that powerful forces have been at work throughout the passage of the millennia. Commanding political and religious leaders using the full force of their authority, corrupted, distorted, edited, falsified, confused and thereby muted the vegetarian doctrines rooted in the spiritually elevated, compassionate, merciful, non-violent, non-murderous insights which lay at the heart and origin of most religions and spiritual philosophies.

Successive generations of unsuspecting future devotees seeking truth, throughout the passage of the millennia have therefore been misguided, misinformed and misdirected. They have been tirelessly fed inaccurate, edited, scriptural misrepresentations that have created and bolstered the relentless multibillion dollar animal slaughter industry! Sadly, increasingly, many religious leaders have lost touch with the earliest, original, undistorted, vegetarian, pacifist roots of their religions, which have been unremittingly secreted away and silenced throughout the centuries.

It will be shown that humankind's religions teach that all animals are children of God, each of whom should be honored and cared for as wonderful and precious. Tragically, this spiritual wisdom has been discarded, leading to humankind's responsibility for the mass suffering and annual slaughter of billions of animals and the extinction of countless species including the diminishing fecundity and well-being of the planet herself.

It is progressively being shown that incredibly the ancient vegetarian tenets of Hinduism, Judaism, Buddhism, Confucianism, that of the Greek spiritual philosophers and Christianity, are so much more spiritually advanced than many contemporary distorted versions of their teachings allow. Many millennia after these spiritual ideologies were born it is the distorted versions which are adhered to today, by people who consider themselves to be religious.

For those individuals who endorse animals being butchered in their billions simply by thoughtlessly eating them, surely they share in the responsibility for our prevalent ruthless, merciless, murderous modern day ethos. Their non-rejection of the pitilessness of the animal slaughter industry is a small step away from being oblivious to the evening news reports of the murder of fellow humans.

Likewise, there is hypocrisy associated with those individuals who, living side by side with a family pet come to love them; daily observing their pets' demonstrations of a range of emotions, intelligence, thought processes and personality. Many of these same individuals feel no empathy and kindness towards a whole host of other animals whose lives consist of nothing more than exploitation, suffering and slaughter. Eating them, they remain unmindful of the fact that these fiercely oppressed relations, like themselves are sentient, feeling, flesh and blood beings.

This serialized research intends to progressively raise awareness that every land, sea and aerial species, together with all flora and all fauna, is each amazingly made of the same building blocks of life and is therefore interrelated and interconnected! Furthermore, each vanishing species accomplishes fundamental and indispensable roles supporting the whole wheel of life on our living planetary home, our once fecund, now endangered, blue planet Earth.

Wreaking wholesale cruel havoc, agonized suffering and despair upon animals and destruction on the natural world have become a contemporary mind-set and tradition, which needs to be overturned by increasing numbers of thoughtful individuals who become spiritual warriors. Every individual who chooses to live a vegetarian life saves over the course of his/her lifetime, the lives of countless pigs, sheep, lambs, cows, calves, turkeys, chickens, ducks and geese as they are no longer needed to be slaughtered for them. Importantly, the numbers of vegetarian men, women and children across the globe is rapidly growing.

It is a sad indictment on humanity that today's brutality to animals, including dressing their tragically broken bodies up on our dinner plates has resulted in widespread chronic and fatal health issues and negative environmental problems. Indeed, we have not followed the guidance of the prophets and philosophers or heeded their warnings. Inevitably we live with their predicted consequences.

Humankind has taken the wrong path, involving merciless, murderous, destruction of animals and entire species, adversely affecting the planet and our own health. Breeding unnatural numbers of animals for human and animal food consumption, with the mass use of artificial insemination causing endless, artificially induced pregnancies, animals live out their lives on cruel rape racks. This is the pitiless, heartless norm today.

Few people are aware that many species of animals today can no longer reproduce naturally as a result of their weak, suffering bodies housing broken hearts and souls. Genetic engineering and the use of multifarious hormones, changes the animals also making them grow larger. Murder is tragic enough but driven to extinction with the end of pregnancies and birth is quite another story. The long lost vegetarian spiritual philosophy of the ancients is urgently needed to combat these modern day obscenities.

Chemicals, such as antibiotics and synthetic hormones given to animals are eventually found in the bodies of humans who eat animal flesh, causing a wide-range of negative human health consequences. All animals, human and non-human, need correct amounts of the right natural not chemical hormones to control the healthy functioning of their bodies, to facilitate unbroken sleep, reproduction, clear thinking, energy levels and a happy balanced mood. It is dangerous for any living being to have an intake of excessive and non-natural hormones.

Consuming excessive antibiotics as a result of eating animal flesh negates the effectiveness of antibiotics for humans when they are ill and in urgent need of them. The path humanity presently treads, uses endless land, for batches of sheep and cattle to glimpse before they are moved on to dark, overcrowded, noisy, filthy hell-houses, ever stronger chemical hormones, pesticides and antibiotics.

There is also an endless need for diminishing reserves of oil energy for storage, slaughter, refrigeration and transport. Most importantly, these evil human activities cause animals to suffer a living hell prior to their piece by piece brutal murder.

Any person who believes that humans have souls and finds it hard to accept that all our other sentient flesh and blood relatives have souls has most definitely been unconsciously brainwashed by the all-pervasive, dominant, materialistic, egocentric ethos in which humankind has been living for millennia. Humans were once fish, they still have the gene that creates a tail, human embryos possess tails and some humans are born with tails.

In all these aquatic and land, four- legged and two-legged incarnations the human animal along with all other animals possess souls in that they are all precious, feel pain and suffering, fear murder and all survive physical death. Did humankind not have a soul or feelings when it possessed fins, fur, tail or four legs? Humankind has callously and deliberately divorced itself from the entirety of the rest of the natural living world, of which they are a related part, in order to remain silent regarding gross animal genocide.

It is cumulatively being shown that the writers of the Hindu Upanishads, Confucius and his followers, the celebrated, Greek spiritual philosophers, the numerous Jewish prophets including Jesus, the Buddha and his devotees taught vegetarianism to honor humanity's higher nature and to honor the rights of fellow animal souls, many of whom are flesh and blood like us and demonstrate their emotions and thought processes. Many taught that the souls of all sentient beings transmigrate at death to experience new incarnations in human animal and non-human animal bodies.

All Greek institutes of learning mirrored by society far and wide were permeated by the spiritual teachings regarding animals of the wise Greek sages. Significantly, these elevated spiritual teachings regarding animals stretched far beyond the boundaries of Greece for centuries to come.

The harder a person finds it is to accept the teachings of these eminent Greeks, the more they are unwittingly consumed by western reductionist, materialist philosophy. Descartes, the first vivisectionist, claimed that the gut-wrenching howls and high pitched agonized screams of dogs nailed down on his vivisection

304

table, cut open and butchered piece by piece, shaped our materialist philosophy.

Descartes wrongly brainwashed future generations that animals' terrorized and tortured cries were just the noises of a machine. Those today who eat animal flesh unwittingly adhere to his philosophy. Descartes' philosophy represents the embodiment of materialistic attitudes, dissolving compassion, ethics and spiritual or humanitarian beliefs, shaping peoples' callous indifference to the suffering of animals, allowing them to spend lives in incarceration before being murdered in their billions every year.

This serialized volume is not simply about animals, of which we are one, it is about the human way of life and how it affects not only our health issues, our murder of each other and fellow animals, our violence, warfare and the way we think about death, but also our planetary resources. Notably, the human is biologically classified as an animal, mammal and primate, a classification long suppressed amongst humanity, deliberately and falsely separating ourselves from our fellow animals in order to treat them with cruelty and mass daily slaughter.

Surely the long line of philosophical lineages of the ancient Greek vegetarian philosophers who lived centuries before, during and after Jesus' own ministry, impacting peoples far and wide and those of Confucius, which likewise, impacted a continent and beyond, were no more compassionate or spiritually elevated than the Good Shepherd Jesus? Born in a stable surrounded by animals, his parables typically intertwined the joint suffering of animals with those of people.

Jesus' compassion was all-embracing and all-inclusive. His compassion could not be turned on and off, but encompassed all distressed, exploited, defenseless beings who were rejected and outcast by society. Notably, Jesus called himself 'the son of man,' and 'the son of the man' being the famous, well-known names applied to Pythagoras whose vegetarian followers persisted for many hundreds of years both before and after the death of Jesus.

By discarding a whole range of sentient beings and life forms, humankind show their ignorance and carelessness regarding the interrelated and interconnected relationship and destiny of all land, sea and aerial beings, sharing this planetary home together. Hence, throughout the millennia, the recurring echoes of compassion for all beings, teach us that kindness is also wisdom, inevitably fostering peace and harmony not only for our related animals but also for all races of humanity.

Throughout the ages countless remarkable men and women in unison have pleaded and continue to plead and warn, enjoining us to raise our consciousness and recognize the sacredness of all life forms, reminding us of our duty to protect all related species and our shared disastrous fate if we don't.

As we come to the close of Animal Souls Part 1 let us listen to the countless male and female voices emanating from the soul of some of the world's greatest spiritual thinkers expressing human sympathy and empathy for all animals. Their mutually shared, elevated spirituality is expressed in their all-embracing compassion for all voiceless souls, beings of the land, sea and air.

Their heartfelt pleas for universal compassion for all animals transcend global cultures and abridge the countless millennia. These relentless and astute echoes, spanning the ages and the globe, wisely reveal that a person cannot truly care for one life form such as humanity, if a person feels no compassion for other life forms, because true compassion is felt for all beings.

There is a dreadful cost to all life forms if humanity discards the wisdom of the following exhortations that bring this first installment to a close. The appeals which follow are pleas from the heart and soul for compassion and respect for animals from innumerable, famous and celebrated individuals from many different historic epochs. Yet they plead with one voice, requesting humanity demonstrate non-violence to animals.

Insights into the souls of the gentle yet strong, sympathetic yet passionate, kindhearted yet wise, far sighted souls of the world's greats, spanning all ages and religions are expressed in the small, yet graphic sample which follows. These poignant, heartbreaking pleas for humanity to elevate itself to vegetarianism, revering all life forms as precious with mutual benefits for all of creation, are pearls of wisdom given by truly great minds.

306

The truthful voices of outstanding leaders of humanity, have repeatedly been silenced and their appeals unheard by many amongst the misguided, oblivious, hard-hearted, pitiless masses. Spanning the ages and the globe, surely these kind-hearted vegetarians are not more compassionate that Jesus. Instead, like Jesus, they were/are vegetarian.

Following on from the quotations, let us continue Animal Souls' fascinating journey, uncovering the long forgotten, distorted and suppressed, authentic, original, vegetarian teachings of many global spiritual traditions including the vegetarian ministry of Jesus. This serialized volume continues its exploration, revealing the fact that many of the founders of the world's religions and spiritual philosophies sought to promote vegetarian compassion to animals thereby elevating the level of human spirituality.

Thankfully the message sent out by this serialized volume will be acted upon by all thinking, genuinely compassionate men, women and children who, as their awareness is progressively raised, will truly care about the treatment of our fellow animals.

At the outset of this conclusion, Sir Arthur Conan Doyle, the English physician, psychical researcher and author of Sherlock Holmes, speaks of compassionate vegetarianism as a spiritual transformation. Peeling back the brainwashed, indoctrinated, programmed mind-set which formerly blocked much of humanity's natural inclination for compassion, Doyle raises our awareness of our long suffering animal relatives.

In keeping with Doyles' opening insightful plea to end the murder of animals, we now conclude with a number of highly thought-provoking requests for compassion for animals, indeed, triggering each reader's own personal response. Importantly, these men and women are aware that it is imperative to show kindness and respect to all living creatures as a precondition for humanity to progress and internalize the spiritual characteristic of compassion. In doing so, we will learn to value and respect all life forms, treating all animals, human and non-human, as precious.

The vegetarian diet will feed the globe and end starvation as agricultural farming produces vast amounts more produce than pastoral farming. With compassion as a banner, wars would be universally outlawed through the bonding together of countries, creating international governments.

This is perhaps envisaged in the future utopian world expressed by the words below of H.G.Wells. In this future vegetarian world of non-violence, individuals no longer eat animal flesh and can no longer be held responsible for their involvement in and support of, the body and soul mutilation of billions of animals, perpetrated by the multimillion dollar animal slaughter industry on their behalf:

"In all the round world of Utopia, there is no meat. There used to be, but now we cannot stand the thought of slaughterhouses. We never settled the hygienic aspect of meat-eating at all. This other aspect decided us. I can still remember as a boy the rejoicings over the closing of the last slaughterhouse."

H.G.Wells

COMPASSION FOR ANIMALS REQUESTED THROUGHOUT THE AGES

1- The Buddha, (563-483 BC). From the Lankavatara sutra.

For the sake of love of purity, the Bodhisattva should refrain from eating flesh, which is born of semen, blood, etc., for fear of causing terror to living beings let the Bodhisattva, who is disciplining himself to attain compassion, refrain from eating flesh...It is not true that meat is proper food and permissible when the animal was not killed by himself, when he did not order others to kill it, when it was not specially meant for him. Again, there may be some people in the future who...being under the influence of the taste for meat will string together in various ways sophisticated arguments to defend meat eating. But...meat eating in any form, in any manner, and in any place is unconditionally and once and for all prohibited...Meat eating I have not permitted to anyone, I do not permit, I will not permit.

2-The Buddha, (563-483 BC).

All beings tremble before violence, all fear death, all love life, see yourself in others, and then whom can you hurt? What harm can you do?

3-Buddhism, Dhammapada.

Because he has pity on every living creature, therefore is a man called holy.

4-The Buddhist Mahaparinirvana.

The eating of meat extinguishes the seed of great compassion.

5-Hinduism, Upanishads.

What is religion? Compassion for all things, which have life.

6-Jainism.

Ahimsa-paramo-dharmah- Non-injury to living beings is the highest religion.

7-Yogashastra (Jain Scripture) 500 BC.

All living things love their life, desire pleasure and do not like pain; they dislike any injury to themselves; everybody is desirous of life and to every being, his life is very dear.

8-Yogashastra (Jain Scripture) 500 BC.

In happiness and suffering, in joy and grief, we should regard all creatures as we regard our own self, and should therefore refrain from inflicting upon others such injury as would appear undesirable to us if inflicted upon ourselves.

9-Ancient Chinese Proverb.

For hundreds of thousands of years the stew in the pot has brewed hatred and resentment that is difficult to stop. If you wish to know why there are disasters of armies and weapons in the world, listen to the piteous cries from the slaughterhouse at midnight.

10-Sefer Ha Chinuch, Mitzvah 596.

When a man becomes accustomed to have pity upon animals...his soul will likewise grow accustomed to be kind to human beings.

11-Plutarch 45-125AD.

Were it only to learn benevolence to humankind we should be merciful to other creatures.

12-Diogenes, (412-323 BC), Greek Philosopher.

We might as well eat the flesh of men as the flesh of other animals.

13- Ovid, (43 BC-17AD), Roman Poet.

Oh, Ox, how great are thy desserts! A being without guile, harmless, simple, willing for work! Ungrateful and unworthy of the fruits of earth, Man his own farm laborer slays and smites with the axe that toil-worn neck that has so often renewed for him the face of the hard earth; so many harvests given!

14-Ovid, (43 BC-17AD), Roman Poet.

Alas, what wickedness to swallow flesh into our own flesh, to fatten our greedy bodies by cramming in other bodies, to have one living creature fed by the death of another!

15-Seneca, (4 BC-65 AD): Famous Roman philosopher, statesman and dramatist.

If true, the Pythagorean principles as to abstaining from flesh foster innocence; if ill-founded they at least teach us frugality, and what loss have you in losing your cruelty? I merely deprive you of the food of lions and vultures. We shall recover our sound reason only if we shall separate ourselves from the herd-the very fact of the approbation of the multitude is a proof of the unsoundness of the opinion or practice. Let us ask what is best, not what is customary. Let us love temperance - let us be just - let us refrain from bloodshed.

16-Plutarch, (45-125AD): Famous Greek philosopher, historian and biographer.

I for my part do much marvel at what sort of feeling, soul or reason the first man with his mouth touched slaughter, and reached to his lips the flesh of a dead animal, and having set before people courses of ghastly corpses and ghosts, could give those parts the names of meat and victuals that but a little before lowed, cried, moved, and saw; how his sight could endure the blood of the slaughtered, flayed, and mangled bodies; how his smell could bear their scent; and how the very nastiness happened not to offend the taste while it chewed the sores of others, and participated of the sap and juices of deadly wounds.

17-Plutarch, (45-125AD).

But whence is it that a certain ravenousness and frenzy drives you in these happy days to pollute yourselves with blood, since you have such an abundance of things necessary for your subsistence? Why do you belie the earth as unable to maintain you? ...Are you not ashamed to mix tame fruits with blood and slaughter? You are indeed wont to call serpents, leopards, and lions, savage creatures; but yet yourselves are defiled with blood and come nothing behind them in cruelty. What they kill is their ordinary nourishment, but what you kill is your better fare.

18-Plutarch, (45-125AD).

For we eat not lions and wolves by way of revenge, but we let those go and catch the harmless and tame sort, such as have neither stings nor teeth to bite with, and slay them.

19-Plutarch, (45-125AD).

But if you will contend that you were born to an inclination to such food as you have now a mind to eat, do you then yourself kill what you would eat. But do it yourself, without the help of a chopping knife, mallet, or axe - as wolves, bears, and lions do, who kill and eat at once. Rend an ox with thy teeth, worry a hog with thy mouth, tear a lamb or a hare in pieces and fall on and eat it alive as they do. But if though hadst rather stay until what thou eatest is to become dead and if thou art loath to force a soul out of its body, why then dost thou against Nature eat an animate thing?

20-Plutarch, (45-125AD).

The obligations of law and equity reach only to mankind; but kindness and beneficence should be extended to the creatures of every species and these will flow from the breast of a true man, as streams that issue from the living fountain.

21-Plutarch (45-125AD).

Were it only to learn benevolence to humankind we should be merciful to other creatures.

22-Theophilus, (150 AD), Bishop of Antioch.

When man diverted from the path [of goodness] the animals followed him...If man now would rise to his original nature and would not do evil any longer, then the animals too would return to their original gentle nature.

23-St. Basil, (275 AD), Archbishop of Caesarea.

Oh God, enlarge within us the sense of fellowship with all living things, our brothers the animals to whom Thou gavest the earth as their home in common with us. We remember with shame that in the past we have exercised the high dominion of man with ruthless cruelty so that the voice of the earth, which should have gone up to Thee in song, has been a groan of travail.

24-Porphyry, (232 AD), Greek philosopher and writer of treatises. From: On Abstinence from Animal Food.

He who abstains from anything animate...will be much more careful not to injure those of his own species. For he who loves the genus will not hate any species of animals.

25-Porphyry, (232 AD).

But to deliver animals to be slaughtered and cooked and thus be filled with murder, not for the sake of nutriment and satisfying the wants of nature, but making pleasure and gluttony the end of such conduct, is transcendently iniquitous and dire.

And is it not absurd, since we see that many of our own species live from sense alone, but do not possess intellect and reason; and since we also see that many of them surpass the most terrible of wild beasts in cruelty, anger, and rapine, being murderous of their children and their parents and also being tyrants and the tools of kings.

[It is not ridiculous] to fancy that we ought to act justly towards these, but that no justice is due from us to the ox that ploughs, the dog that is fed with us, and the animals that nourish us with their milk and adorn our bodies with their wool? Is not such an opinion most irrational and absurd?

26-Jesus, (3AD-36AD), from the Essene Gospel of Peace.

And the flesh of slain beasts in his body will become his own tomb. For I tell you truly, he who kills, kills himself and whoso eats the flesh of slain beast eats the body of death.

27-John Chrysostom (400 AD).

Surely, we ought to show kindness and gentleness to animals for many reasons, and chiefly because they are of the same Source as ourselves.

28-Rabbi Nachmanides, (1184-1270).

Living creatures possess a moving soul and a certain spiritual superiority which, in this respect make them similar to those who possess intellect (people) and they have the power of affecting their welfare and their food and they flee from pain and death.

29-Chitrabhanuji.

Let us pray that our food should not be colored with animal blood and human suffering.

30-Leonardo Da Vinci, (1452-1519), Italian genius, painter, sculptor, architect, engineer and scientist. From Merijkowsky's Romance of Leonardo da Vinci.

Truly man is the king of beasts, for his brutality exceeds theirs. We live by the death of others: We are burial places!

31-Leonardo Da Vinci, (1452-1519), from his notes.

I have from an early age abjured the use of meat and the time will come when men such as I will look upon the murder of animals as they now look upon the murder of men.

32-Michel De Montaigne, (1533-1592), French essayist.

For my part I have never been able to see, without displeasure, an innocent and defenseless animal, from whom we receive no offense or harm, pursued and slaughtered.

33-St. John of the Cross, (1582).

All the creatures - not the higher creatures alone, but also the lower, according to that which each of them has received in itself from God - each one raises its voice in testimony that which God is, each one after its manner exalts God, since it has God in itself.

34-St. Catherine of Genoa.

All goodness is a participation in God and His love for His creatures. God loves irrational creatures and His love provides for them.

35-Mohandas Gandhi, (1869-1948), Hindu pacifist, nationalist leader and social reformer.

The greatness of a nation and its moral progress can be judged by the way its animals are treated.

36-Mohandas Gandhi, (1869-1948).

I do not regard flesh food as necessary for us. I hold flesh food to be unsuited to our species. We err in copying the lower animal world if we are superior to it.

37-Mohandas Gandhi, (1869-1948).

The only way to live is to let live.

38-Franz Kafka, (1883-1924), Famous Austrian-Czech writer.

(Remark made whilst sympathizing with a fish in an aquarium.)

Now I can look at you in peace; I don't eat you anymore.

39-John Harvey Kellogg, (1852-1943), American Surgeon & Founder of Battle Creek Sanatorium.

Flesh foods are not the best nourishment for human beings and were not the food of our primitive ancestors. They are secondary or secondhand products, since all food comes originally from the vegetable kingdom. There is nothing necessary or desirable for human nutrition to be found in meats or flesh foods which is not found in and derived from vegetable products.

A dead cow or sheep lying in a pasture is recognized as carrion. The same sort of carcass dressed and hung up in a butcher's stall passes as food! Careful microscopic examination may show little or no difference between the fence corner carcass and the butcher shop carcass. Both are swarming with colon germs and redolent with putrefaction.

40-Count Maurice Maeterlinck, (1862-1949).

Were the belief one day to become general that man could dispense with animal food, there would ensue not only a great economic revolution, but a moral improvement as well.

41-John Stuart Mill, (1806-1873), English philosopher and economist.

Granted that any practice causes more pain to animals than it give pleasure to man; is that practice moral or immoral? And if, exactly in proportion as human beings raise their heads out of the slough of selfishness, they do not with one voice answer "Immoral," let the morality of the principle of utility be forever condemned.

42-Henry S. Salt, (1851-1939). British philanthropist and reformer, colleague of Gandhi and George Bernard Shaw.

The cattle [transport] of present day reproduce, in an aggravated form, some of the worst horrors of the slave-ships of fifty years back…The present system of killing animals for food is a very cruel and barbarous one, and a direct outrage on what I have termed the "humanities of diet."

43-Henry S. Salt, (1851-1939).

Vegetarianism is the diet of the future, as flesh-food is the diet of the past. In that striking and common contrast, a fruit shop side by side with a butcher's, we have a most significant object lesson. There, on the one hand, are the barbarities of a savage custom - the headless carcasses, stiffened into a ghastly semblance of life, the joints and steaks and gobbets with their sickening odor the harsh grating of the bone-saw, and the dull thud of the chopper - a perpetual crying protest against the horrors of flesh-eating.

And as if this were not witness sufficient, here close alongside is a wealth of golden fruit, a sight to make a poet happy, the only food that is entirely congenial to the physical structure and the natural instincts of mankind that can entirely satisfy the highest human aspirations. Can we doubt, as we gaze at this contrast, that whatever immediate steps may need to be gradually taken, whatever difficulties to be overcome, the path of progression from the barbarities to the humanities of diet lies clear and unmistakable before us?

44-Henry S. Salt, (1851-1939).

This logic of the larder is the very negation of a true reverence for life, for it implies that the real lover of animal s is he whose larder is fullest of them:
He, prayest best, who eatest best
All things both great and small.
It is the philosophy of the wolf, the shark, the cannibal.
(From: The Humanities of Diet.)

45-Arthur Schopenhauer, (1788-1860), German Philosopher.

Since compassion for animals is so intimately associated with goodness of character, it may be confidently asserted that whoever is cruel to animals cannot be a good man.

46-Rev. Dr. Albert Schweitzer, (1875-1965), German physician and medical missionary, theologian, musician, author and Nobel Prize Winner in 1952.

Whenever any animal is forced into the service of man, the sufferings which it has to bear on that account are the concern of every one of us. No-one ought to permit, in so far as he can prevent it, pain or suffering for which he will not take the responsibility. No one ought to rest at ease in the thought that in so doing he would mix himself up in affairs which are not his business. Let no-one shirk the burden of his responsibility.

When there is so much maltreatment of animals, when the cries of thirsting creatures go up unnoticed from the railway truck, when there is so much roughness in our slaughterhouses, when in our kitchen so many animals suffer horrible deaths from unskillful hands, when animals endure unheard-of agonies from heartless men, or are delivered to the dreadful play of children, then we are all guilty and must bear the blame.

47-Rev. Dr. Albert Schweitzer, (1875-1965).

It is good to maintain and cherish life; it is evil to destroy...life.

48-Rev. Dr. Albert Schweitzer, (1875-1965).

A man is really ethical only when he obeys the constraint laid on him to help all life which he is able to succor and when he goes out of his way to avoid injuring anything living. He does not ask how far this or that life deserves sympathy as valuable in itself, or how far it is capable of feeling.

To him life as such is sacred. He shatters no ice crystal that sparkles in the sun, tears no leaf from its tree, breaks off no flower and is careful not to crush any insect as he walks. If he works by lamplight on a summer evening, he prefers to keep the window shut and to breathe stifling air rather than to see insect after insect fall on his table with singed and sinking wings.

49-Rev. Dr. Albert Schweitzer, (1875-1965).

The very fact that the animal, as a victim of research, has in his pain rendered such services to suffering, men, has itself created a new and unique relation of solidarity between him and ourselves. The result is that a fresh obligation is laid on each of us to do as much good as we possibly can to all creatures in all sorts of circumstances. When I help an insect out of his troubles all that I do is to attempt to remove some of the guilt contracted through these crimes against animals.

50-Rev. Dr. Albert Schweitzer, (1875-1965).

We are compelled by the commandment of love contained in our hearts and thought and proclaimed by Jesus, to give rein to our natural sympathy for animals. We are also compelled to help them and spare them suffering.

51-Rev. Dr. Albert Schweitzer, (1875-1965).

I must interpret the life about me as I interpret the life that is my own. My life is full of meaning to me. The life around me must be full of significance to itself. If I am to expect others to respect my life, then I must respect the other life I see, however strange it may be to mine. ...We need a boundless ethics which will include the animals also.

52-Fyodor Dostoyevsky.

Love the world with an all-embracing love. Love the animals; God has given them the rudiments of thought and joy untroubled. Do not trouble them, do not harass then, do not deprive them of their happiness, and do not work against God's intent. Man, do not pride yourself on your superiority to them, for they are without sin, and you with your greatness defile the earth.

53-Cardinal John Henry Newman.

Cruelty to animals is as if man did not love God...there is something so dreadful, so Satanic, in tormenting those who have never harmed us, and who cannot defend themselves, who are utterly in our power.

54-Annie Besant, (1847-1933), the English philosopher, humanitarian and social reformer who worked for Indian independence.

[Individuals who eat animal flesh] are responsible for all the pain that grows out of meat-eating, and which is necessitated by the use of sentient animals as food; not only the horrors of the slaughterhouse, but also the preliminary horrors of the railway traffic, of the steamboat and ship traffic; all the starvation and the thirst and the prolonged misery of fear which these unhappy creatures have to pass through for the gratification of the appetite of man...

All pain acts as a record against humanity and slackens and retards the whole of human growth..."

55-George Bernard Shaw, (1856-1950), British dramatist and critic.

Why should you call me to account for eating decently? If I battened on the scorched corpses of animals, you might well ask me why I did that.

56-George Bernard Shaw, (1856-1950).

When a man wants to murder a tiger, he calls it sport; when a tiger wants to murder him he calls it ferocity.

57-George Bernard Shaw, (1856-1950).

Animals are my friends...and I don't eat my friends. My will contains directions for my funeral, which will be followed not by mourning coaches, but by herds of oxen, sheep, swing, flocks of poultry, and a small travelling aquarium of live fish, all wearing white scarves in honor of the man who perished rather than eat his fellow creatures.

58-Robert Burns, (1759-1796), Scottish poet.
But man to whom alone is given
A ray direct from pitying
Heaven Glories in his heart humane
And creatures for his pleasure slain
(From On scaring some Waterfowl)

59-Percy Bysshe Shelley, (1792-1822), British poet.

It is only by softening and disguising dead flesh by culinary preparation that it is rendered susceptible of mastication or digestion and that the sight of its bloody juices and red horror does not excite intolerable loathing and disgust.

Let the advocate of animal food force himself to a decisive experiment on its fitness and as Plutarch recommends, tear a living lamb with his teeth and plunging his head into its vials, slake his thirst with the steaming blood; when fresh from the deed of horror let him revert to the irresistible instincts of nature that would rise in judgment against it, and say, "Nature formed me for such work as this." Then and then only, would he be consistent.

60-Dr Herbert Shelton, American naturopathic physician.

The cannibal goes out and hunts, pursues and kills another man and proceeds to cook and eat him precisely as he would any other game. There is not a single argument nor a single fact that can be offered in favor of flesh eating that cannot be offered, with equal strength, in favor of cannibalism. (From Superior Nutrition)

61-Rabindranath, (1861-1941), Hindu Poet Winner of the Nobel Prize, composer of India's National Anthem.

We manage to swallow flesh only because we do not think of the cruel and sinful thing we do. There are many crimes which are the creation of man himself, the wrongfulness of which is put down to his divergence from habit, custom, or tradition. But cruelty is not of these. It is a fundamental sin, and admits of no arguments or nice distinctions.

If only we do not allow our heart to grow callous it protects against cruelty, is always clearly heard; and yet we go on perpetrating cruelties easily, merrily, all of us - in fact, anyone who does not join in is dubbed a crank...If, after our pity is aroused, we persist in throttling our feelings simply in order to join others in preying upon life, we insult all that is good in us. I have decided to try a vegetarian diet.

62- Count Leo Tolstoy, (1828-1920), Russian novelist and social theorist.

Vegetarianism serves as a criterion by which we know that the pursuit of moral perfection on the part of man is genuine and sincere.

63-Count Leo Tolstoy, (1828-1920).

This is dreadful! ...that man suppresses in himself, unnecessarily, the highest spiritual capacity - that of sympathy and pity towards living creatures like himself - and by violating his own feelings becomes cruel. And how deeply seated in the human heart is the injunction not to take life!

64- Count Leo Tolstoy, (1828-1920).

"Thou shalt not kill' does not apply to murder of one's own kind only, but to all living beings; and this Commandment was inscribed in the human breast long before it was proclaimed from Sinai."

65-Francois Voltaire, (1694-1778), Famous French author and philosopher.

How pitiful, and what poverty of mind, [for Descartes and his followers] to have said that the animals are machines deprived of understanding and feeling...has Nature arranged all the springs of feeling in this animal to the end that he might not feel?

Has not he nerves that he may be capable of suffering? People must have renounced, it seems to me, all natural intelligence to dare to advance that animals but animated machines...

It appears to me, besides, that [such people] can never have observed with attention the character of animals, not to have distinguished among them the different Voices of need, of suffering, of joy, of pain, of love, of anger, and of all their affections.

It would be very strange that they should express so well what they could not feel...They are endowed with life as we are, because they have the same principles of life, the same feelings, the same ideas, memory, industry - as we.

66-Francois Voltaire, (1694-1778).

[Porphyry] regards other animals as our brothers, because they are endowed with life as we are, because they have the same principles of life, the same feelings, the same ideas, memory, and industry - as we. [Human] speech alone is wanting to them. If they had it should we dare to kill and eat them? Should we dare to commit these fratricides?

67-Rev. Humphrey Primatt, (1736-1779), Anglican Priest: Extract from: A Dissertation on the Duty of Mercy and the Sin of Cruelty to Brute Animals.

Pain is pain, whether it is inflicted on man or on beast; and the creature that suffers it, whether man or beast, being sensible of the misery of it whilst it lasts, suffers Evil...

68-Humphrey Primatt.

We may pretend to what religion we please, but cruelty is atheism. We may make our boast of Christianity; but cruelty is infidelity. We may trust our orthodoxy, but cruelty is the worst of heresies.

69-Ellen White, (1827-1915), Co- founder of the Seventh Day Adventists, (1827-1915).

Animals are often transported long distance and subjected to great suffering in reaching a market. Taken from the green pastures and traveling for weary miles over the hot, dusty roads, or crowded into filthy cars, feverish and exhausted, often for many hours deprived of food and water, the poor creatures are driven to their death, that human beings may feast on the carcasses.

70-Isaac Bashevis, Singer.

Early in my life I came to the conclusion that there was no basic difference between man and animals. If a man has the heart to cut the throat of a chicken or a calf, there's no reason he should not be willing to cut the throat of a man.

71-Cleveland Amory, (1917-1998), Harvard Crimson editor, TV Guide, Parade Columnist.

I consider the three most cruelly produced foods to be from lobsters, dropped alive into boiling water, veal from calves separated from their mothers and kept in crates, and pate de fois gras. (Pate de foie gras is covered in the film Mondo Kane which shows the force feeding of geese. Food is stuffed down their throats with a pole....when they want to regurgitate...a brass ring is tied around their throat...the excess food creates a stuffed liver pleasing to gourmets.) (Caviar comes from the ripping out of the ovaries of the mother sturgeon fish.)

72-Robert Louis Stevenson, (1850-1894), Scottish author of Treasure Island and Dr. Jekyll and Mr. Hyde.

We consume the carcasses of creatures of like appetites, passions and organs with our own and fill the slaughterhouses daily with screams of fear and pain.

73-Reverend William Ralph Inge, (1860-1854), Anglican priest, professor of Divinity at Oxford University, UK.

We have enslaved the rest of the animal creation and have treated our distant cousins in fur and feathers so badly that beyond doubt, if they were able to formulate a religion, they would depict the Devil in human form.

74-Reverend William Ralph Inge, (1860-1854).

Deliberate cruelty to our defenseless and beautiful little cousins is surely one of the meanest and most detestable vices of which a human being can be guilty.

75-Vaslav Nijinski, (1889-1950), Russian ballet dancer and choreographer.

I do not like eating meat because I have seen lambs and pigs killed. I saw and felt their pain. They felt their approaching deaths. I could not bear it. I cried like a child, I ran up a hill and could not breathe. I felt that I was choking. I felt the death of the lamb.

76-Gregory Dick, (Born 1932), American comedian.

Martin Luther King taught us all nonviolence. I was told to extend it to the mother and her calf.

77-Mary Tyler Moore (Born 1936), American actress.

Behind every beautiful fur, there is a story. It is a bloody, barbaric story.

78-Alice Walker (Born 1944), author of The Color Purple.

As we talked of freedom and justice one day for all, we sat down to steaks. I am eating misery, I thought, as I took the first bite. And spat it out.

79-Alice Walker (Born 1944), author of The Color Purple.

I know, in my soul, that to eat a creature who is raised to be eaten and who never has a chance to be a real being, is unhealthy. It's like…you're just eating misery. You're eating a bitter life.

80-Moby, Musician.

Intellectually, human beings and animals may be different, but it's pretty obvious that animals have a rich emotional life and that they feel joy and pain. It's easy to forget the connection between a hamburger and the cow it came from, but I forced myself to acknowledge the fact that every time I ate a hamburger, a cow had ceased to breathe and moo and walk around.

81-Drew Barrymore American Actress

The thing that has been weighing on my mind this week is that I wanted to go and save all the little live lobsters in restaurants and throw them back in the ocean. Imagine me being arrested for that? Honest chefs will confirm that lobsters like other shell fish, scream when immersed in boiling water to be boiled alive. [They feel pain as they have nervous systems.]

82-Richard Serjeant, author of the Spectrum of Pain, published in 1969.

Every particle of factual evidence supports the factual contention that the higher mammalian vertebrates experience pain sensations at least as acute as our own. To say that they feel pain less because they are lower animals is an absurdity; it can easily be shown that many of their senses are far more acute than ours - visual acuity in certain birds, hearing in most wild animals, and touch in others; these animals depend more than we do today on the sharpest possible awareness of a hostile environment.

Apart from the complexity of the cerebral cortex (which does not directly perceive pain) their nervous systems are almost identical to ours and their reaction to pain remarkably similar, though lacking (so far as we know) the philosophical and moral overtones. The emotional element is all too evident, mainly in the form of fear and anger.

83-Dr. Louis J. Camuti, (1893-1981).

Never believe that animals suffer less than humans. Pain is the same for them … [as] us: even worse, because they cannot help themselves.

84-Fruitarian Network.

Objectification reduces sensitivity. Thus cows are called beef or head of cattle pigs become pork, sheep mutton. The screams are muted… and living creatures become plastic wrapped packages.

85-Anonymous/Unknown.

I ask for the privilege of not being born…not to be born until you can assure me of a home and a master to protect me and a right to live as long as I am physically able to enjoy life…not to be born until my body is precious and men have ceased to exploit it because it is cheap and plentiful.

86-Dr Donald Coggan, Archbishop of Canterbury.

Animals, as part of God's creation, have rights which must be respected. It behoves us always to be sensitive to their needs and to the reality of their pain.

87-Reverend Carl A. Skriver.

The true God is love, goodness, and mercy - not sacrifice, cruelty, killing, and murder…We shall not kill or sacrifice other creatures for him; we shall only sacrifice ourselves for our human and animal brothers.

88-Right Reverend John Chandler White.

It is time, fully time, that all Christian people awake to the necessity of taking an active part in the fight against what I dare to call the Crime of Animal Cruelty. Everyone who loves God and animals should help bear the burden of the fight against this insidious evil.

89-Pope John Paul II.

[St Francis] looks upon creation with the eyes of one who could recognize in it the marvelous work of the hand of God. His solicitous care, not only towards men, but also towards animals is a faithful echo of the love with which God in the beginning pronounced his "fiat" which brought them into existence. We too are called to a similar attitude.

90-The author Reverend Andrew Linzey.

To stand for Christ is to stand against the evil of cruelty inflicted on those who are weak, vulnerable, unprotected, undefended, morally innocent, and in that class we must unambiguously include animals.

91-Rabbi Pinchas Peli.

We cannot treat any living thing callously, and we are responsible for what happens to other beings, human or animal, even if we do not personally come into contact with them.

92-Professor Richard H. Schwartz.

Animals are part of God's creation and people have special responsibilities to them. The Jewish tradition clearly indicates that we are forbidden to be cruel to animals and that we are to treat them with compassion.

93-Dr Robert Runcie, Archbishop of Canterbury.

In the end, a lack of regard for the life and well-being of an animal must bring with it a lowering of man's self-respect and it is integral to our Christian faith that this world is God's world and that man is a trustee and steward of God's creation who must render up an account for his stewardship.

94-James Cromwell, (born 1940), English Actor in the film Babe.

Pigs may not be as cuddly as kittens or puppies, but they suffer just as much.

95-Dr Carl Sagan and Ann Dryan; quoting from Shadows of Forgotten Ancestors, 1992.

Humans – who enslave, castrate, experiment on, and fillet other animals - have had an understandable penchant for pretending animals do not feel pain. A sharp distinction between humans and "animals" is essential if we are to bend them to our will, make them work for us, wear them, eat them – without any disquieting tinges of guilt or regret.

It is unseemly of us, who often behave so unfeelingly toward other animals, to contend that only humans can suffer. The behavior of other animals renders such pretensions specious. They are just too much like us.

96-His Holiness the XIV Dalai Lama of Tibet, (Born 1935).

In order to satisfy one human stomach, so many lives are taken away. We must promote vegetarianism, It is extremely important.

97-His Holiness the XIV Dalai Lama of Tibet, (Born 1935).

In our approach to life, be it pragmatic or otherwise, the ultimate truth that confronts us squarely and unmistakably is the desire for peace, security and happiness. Different forms of life in different aspects of existence make up the teeming denizens of this earth of ours.

And, no matter whether they belong to the higher group as human beings or to the lower group, the animals, all beings primarily seek peace, comfort and security. Life is as dear to a mute creature as it is to a man. Just as one wants happiness and fears pain, just as one wants to live and not to die, so do other creatures. Speaking at the World Vegetarian Congress, 1967.

98-His Holiness the XIV Dalai Lama of Tibet, (Born 1935).

Whenever I visit a market and see the chickens crowded together in tiny cages that give them no room to move around and spread their wings and the fish slowly drowning in the air, my heart goes out to them. People have to learn to think about animals in a different way, as sentient beings who love life and fear death. I urge everyone who can to adopt a compassionate vegetarian diet.

99-His Holiness the XIV Dalai Lama of Tibet, (Born 1935).

Life is as dear to the mute creature as it is to a man. Just as one wants happiness and fears pain, just as one wants to live and not die, so do other creatures.

100-Hadith- Teachings and Sayings of the Prophet Muhammad. (Islam).

A good deed done to an animal is as meritorious as a good deed done to a human being, while an act of cruelty to an animal is a bad as an act of cruelty to a human being.

101-Ottoman Zar-Adusht Ha'nish (Islam).

It is strange to hear people talk of Humanitarianism, who are members of societies for the prevention of cruelty to children and animals, and who claim to be ALLAH-loving men and women, but whom nevertheless, encourage by their patronage the killing of animals merely to gratify the cravings of appetite.

102-Akbarati Jetha (Islam).

There can never be peace and happiness in the world so long as we exploit other living creatures for food or otherwise.

Isaiah, Chief Seattle and Albert Schweitzer

Several millennia after the death of Isaiah, (8th century BC), the American Indian, Chief Seattle, echoed the same spiritual enlightenment as Isaiah: "This much we know. The earth does not belong to man; man belongs to the earth. This we know. All things are connected like the blood which unites one family.

Whatever befalls the earth befalls the sons of the earth. Man did not weave the web of life he is merely a strand in it. Whatever he does to the web, he does to himself."

The above sample records countless exhortations proving many spiritually enlightened thinkers became aware that we should treat all animals, human and non-human with compassion and respect.

Notably, from Isaiah in the 8th century BC to comparative contemporaries such as Chief Seattle to Albert Schweitzer, all shared in this spiritual enlightenment which spanned endless centuries and the globe.

Schweitzer implored: "Until he extends the circle of his compassion to all living things, man will not himself find peace."

The above quotations have been recorded by a wide range of sources who I wish to thank. I also extend my gratitude to the vegetarian author J.R.Hyland, writer of God's Covenant with Animals, Roshi Philip Kapleau, vegetarian author of To Cherish All Life: A Buddhist View of Animal Slaughter and Meat Eating, www.animalliberationfront.com/Saints/Authors/Quotes/ and www.kranti.org/damage/spirituality/

AN OUTLINE OF THE TIMESCALE OF EVOLUTION. (MYA=Million Years Ago)

The Cenozoic Period
Quarternary (2.6 MYA - Present Day) ~ Evolution of humans.

Tertiary (65.5 - 2.6 MYA) ~ Mammals as dominant species diversify.

The Mesozoic Period
Cretaceous (145.5-65.5 MYA) ~ Extinction of dinosaurs, First Primates, First Flowering Plants.

Jurassic (199.6 - 145.5 MYA) ~ First Birds, Dinosaurs Diversify & Dominant.

Triassic (251 - 199.6 MYA) ~ First Mammals, Mammalian Reptiles Dominant, First Dinosaurs.

The Paleozoic Period
Permian (299 - 251 MYA) ~ Major Extinctions, Reptiles Diversify, First – Mammal-like Reptiles, Amphibians Dominant.

Pennsylvanian (Carboniferous) **(318.1-299 MYA)** ~ First Reptiles, Soale Trees, Amphibians Dominant.

Mississippian (Carboniferous) **(359.2 - 318.1 MYA)** ~ Seed Ferns, Large Terrestrial Amphibians.

Devonian (416 - 359.2 MYA) ~ First Amphibians, Jawed Fish Diversify & Dominant.

Silurian (443.7 - 416 MYA) ~ First Vascular Plants.

Ordovician (488.3 - 443.7 MYA) ~ Sudden Diversification of Metazoan Families, Jawless Fish Diversify.

Cambrian (542 - 488.3 MYA) ~ First Jawless Fishes, First Chordates.

The Late Proterozoic Period
(Approx. 650 MYA & Ended 542 MYA) First Skeletal Elements, First Soft-Bodied Metazoans, First Animal Traces.

Ancient Egyptian Chronology

The Early Dynastic Period: 2950-2575 BC
Step Pyramid at Saqqara was built ~ Millions of
carefully mummified birds unearthed at Saqqara.

The Old Kingdom: 2575-2150 BC

The First Intermediate Period 2125-1975 BC
Alternatively 2160-2055 BC

The Middle Kingdom 2055 or 1975-1640 BC

The Second Intermediate Period 1630-1520 BC

The New Kingdom 1539-1075 BC

The Third Intermediate Period 1075-715 BC

The Late Period 715-332 AD
The Assyrians and Persians conquered Egypt.

The Ptolemaic Period 332-30 AD
The Greeks ruled Egypt, including Cleopatra.

The Roman Period 30 BC to 395 AD

REFERENCES

Chapter 2: Introducing the Animal Souls Research

1. Jones-Hunt, J. PhD, Moses and Jesus the Shamans, O Books, Dec. 2012, P448-449
2. Jones-Hunt, J. PhD, Moses and Jesus the Shamans, O Books, Dec. 2012, P450
3. Jones-Hunt, J. PhD, Moses and Jesus the Shamans, O Books, Dec. 2012, P450-451
4. Hyland, J.R., God's Covenant with Animals, Lantern Books,
   New York, NY, USA, 2000, P71
5. Hyland, J.R., God's Covenant with Animals, Lantern Books,
   New York, NY, USA, 2000, P71-72
6. Keith Akers, The Lost Religion of Jesus, Lantern Books, NY,
   USA, 2000, P25-26
7. The Lost Religion of Jesus by Akers, Keith, Lantern Books, NY, USA, 2000, P154-155
8. Homilies 7.4 quoted in The Lost Religion of Jesus by Akers,
   Keith, Lantern Books, NY, USA, 2000, P155
9. Homilies 7.8 as quoted in The Lost Religion of Jesus by Akers, Keith, Lantern Books, NY, USA, 2000, P155

Chapter 3: Our Single, Interrelated, Interdependent, Earth Family

1. www.brittannica.com/EBchecked/topic/197367/evolution?view-print, 2009
2. Ibid
3. Ibid
4. Bratcher, Dennis, The Date of the Exodus: the Historical Study of Scripture: www.crivoice.org/exodusdate.html
5. www.brittannica.com/EBchecked/topic/197367/evolution?view-print, 2009
6. Ibid
7. Darwin's letter of 1871 published in Darwin, Francis, ed. 1887. The Life and Letters of Charles Darwin, including an autobiographical chapter. London, John Murray. Vol. 3. P.18.
8. Oparin *A.I. (1924)* Proiskhozhdenie zhizny, Moscow (Translated by Ann Synge in Bernal (1967), The Origin of Life, Weidenfeld and Nicholson, London, P199-234
9. Bryson, Bill (2003) A Short History of Nearly Everything pp.300-302; ISBN 0-552-99704-8
10. www.brittannica.com/EBchecked/topic/197367/evolution?view-print, 2009
11. Ibid

Chapter 4: Transitional Fossils Prove Shared Common Ancestor

1. www.brittannica.com/EBchecked/topic/197367/evolution?view-print, 2009
2. Ibid
3. Ibid
4. Ibid
5. Ibid
6. Ibid

7. Ibid

8. Ibid

9. Ibid

10. Ibid

11. www.britannica.com/EBchecked/topic/228886/genetic -drift2009

12. www.brittannica.com/EBchecked/topic/197367/evoluti on?view-print, 2009

13. Ibid

14. Ibid

15. Ibid

16. www.britannica.com?EBchecked/topic/399695/mutatio n, 2009

17. www.brittannica.com/EBchecked/topic/197367/evoluti on?view-print, 2009

18. Ibid

19. Ibid

20. Ibid

21. Ibid

22. Ibid

23. Ibid

24. Ibid

25. Ibid

Chapter 5: Humankind's Most Ancient Friends: Dogs and Cats

1. Graham Harvey www.animism.org.uk
2. John Pickrell National Geographic News April 8, 2004news.nationalgeographic.com//news/2004/04/0448_0 40408_oldestpetcat.html
3. John Pickrell National Geographic News April 8, 2004 news.nationalgeographic.com//news/2004/04/0448_04040 8_oldestpetcat.html
4. John Pickrell National Geographic News April 8, 2004 news.nationalgeographic.com//news/2004/04/0448_04040 8_oldestpetcat.html
5. Ancient Egyptian Chronology: The Early Dynastic period when the step pyramid at Saqqara was built (2950-2575 BC). Millions of carefully mummified birds have been unearthed at Saqqara. The Old Kingdom dates are (2575-2150 BC), the First Intermediate Period (2125-1975 BC alternatively 2160-2055 BC). The Middle Kingdom (2055 or 1975-1640 BC). The Second Intermediate Period (1630-1520 BC). The New Kingdom (1539-1075 BC). The Third Intermediate Period (1075-715 BC). The Late Period (715-332 AD) during which, the Assyrians and Persians conquered Egypt. During the Ptolemaic Period (332-30 AD) the Greeks ruled Egypt, Cleopatra ruled during this time. The Roman Period (30 BC to 395 AD).
6. Article by James Owen for National Geographic News Sept. 15, 2004, Egyptian Animals Were Mummified the Same Way as Humans: interview with archaeologist RichardEvershed.
www.news.nationalgeographic.com/news/2004/09/0915_0 40915_petmummies.html

Chapter 6: Vegetarian Confucius and the Chinese Relationship with Animals

1. www.britannica.com/EBchecked/topic/132184/Confucius 2009
2. Ibid
3. Ibid
4. Ibid
5. Ibid
6. Ibid
7. Ibid
8. Ibid

Chapter 7: The Ancient Greek Spiritual Philosophers were Vegetarian

Poem: Animal Brothers ~ Die Tierbruder by Edgar Kupfer-Koberwitz
Wenn wir im Tier den Bruder sehen werden,
Wird viele Haerte und viel Irrtum weichen,
Und es wird heller auf der Erde warden,
Weil wir der Guete Licht vom Himmel reichen. Animal Brothers, 4th Edition, Waerland-verlagsgenossenschaft Mannheim, Federal Republic of Germany, Translated by Ruth Mossner by permission of the Waerland-Verlagsgenossenschaft EG, Mannheim.

1. www.all-creatures.org/quotes/pythagoras.html 2009
2. From the 1957 IVU Congress Souvenir book quoted on www.ivu.org/history/greece_rome/pythagoras.html
3. From the 1957 IVU Congress Souvenir book quoted on www.ivu.org/history/greece_rome/pythagoras.html
4. www.ivu.org/history/greece_rome/pythagoras.html quotes according to Ovid from The Extended Circle by Jon Wynne-Tyson
5. www.ivu.org/history/greece_rome/pythagoras.html Depicted in Ovid: The Metamorphoses translated by Mary M. Innes

6. www.ivu.org/history/greece_rome/pythagoras.html Quotes according to Ovid from The Extended Circle by Jon Wynne-Tyson

7. www.ivu.org/history/greece_rome/pythagoras.html

8. (Diels, Fragments of the pre-Socratic, Xenophanes-fragments)

9. www.biopsicocibernetica.org

10. www.all-creatures.org/quotes/magel_charles_r.html

11. www.all-creatures.org/quotes/primatt_humphrey.html

12. www.all-creatures.org/quotes/mayo_charles.html

13. www.all-creatures.org/quotes/seattle_chief.html

14. www.all-creatures.org/quotes/nietzsche_friedrich.html

15. Plato's Republic Books II & III

16. Ibid

17. Ibid

18. Plutarch: www.Encylopaedia Britannica online, 2009

19. www.all-creatures.org/quotes/plutarch.html

20. From the 1957 IVU Souvenir Book cited on www.ivu.org/greece_rome/plutarch.html

21. www.animalrightshistory.org/timeline-antiquity/plutarch.htm

22. www.vegsoc.org/news/2000/21cv/ages.html

Chapter 8: Global Beliefs in the Transmigration of the Soul

1. http://en.wikipedia.org/wiki/Metempsychosis 2009

2. www.vegsoc.org/news/2000/21cv/ages.html 2009

3. Ibid

4. Ibid

Lightning Source UK Ltd.
Milton Keynes UK
UKOW05f2252090217
294017UK00001B/7/P

9 780992 866112